NOVELL'S

ZENworks™ Administrator's Handbook

NOVELL'S

ZENworks™
Administrator's
Handbook

RON TANNER AND BRAD DAYLEY

Novell.
PRESS

Novell Press, San Jose

Novell's ZENworks™ Administrator's Handbook
Published by
Novell Press
2211 North First Street
San Jose, CA 95131

ISBN: 0-7645-4561-2

Printed in the United States of America

10 9 8 7 6 5 4

1P/SV/QY/ZZ/FC

Distributed in the United States by IDG Books Worldwide, Inc.

Distributed by CDG Books Canada Inc. for Canada; by Transworld Publishers Limited in the United Kingdom; by IDG Norge Books for Norway; by IDG Sweden Books for Sweden; by IDG Books Australia Publishing Corporation Pty. Ltd. for Australia and New Zealand; by TransQuest Publishers Pte Ltd. for Singapore, Malaysia, Thailand, Indonesia, and Hong Kong; by Gotop Information Inc. for Taiwan; by ICG Muse, Inc. for Japan; by Norma Comunicaciones S.A. for Colombia; by Intersoft for South Africa; by Le Monde en Tique for France; by International Thomson Publishing for Germany, Austria and Switzerland; by Distribuidora Cuspide for Argentina; by LR International for Brazil; by Galileo Libros for Chile; by Ediciones ZETA S.C.R. Ltda. for Peru; by WS Computer Publishing Corporation, Inc., for the Philippines; by Contemporanea de Ediciones for Venezuela; by Express Computer Distributors for the Caribbean and West Indies; by Micronesia Media Distributor, Inc. for Micronesia; by Grupo Editorial Norma S.A. for Guatemala; by Chips Computadoras S.A. de C.V. for Mexico; by Editorial Norma de Panama S.A. for Panama; by American Bookshops for Finland. Authorized Sales Agent: Anthony Rudkin Associates for the Middle East and North Africa.

For general information on IDG Books Worldwide's books in the U.S., please call our Consumer Customer Service department at 800-762-2974. For reseller information, including discounts and premium sales, please call our Reseller Customer Service department at 800-434-3422.

For information on where to purchase IDG Books Worldwide's books outside the U.S., please contact our International Sales department at 317-596-5530 or fax 317-596-5692.

For consumer information on foreign language translations, please contact our Customer Service department at 800-434-3422, fax 317-596-5692, or e-mail rights@idgbooks.com.

For information on licensing foreign or domestic rights, please phone +1-650-655-3109.

For sales inquiries and special prices for bulk quantities, please contact our Sales department at 650-655-3200 or write to IDG Books Worldwide, 919 E. Hillsdale Blvd., Suite 400, Foster City, CA 94404.

For information on using IDG Books Worldwide's books in the classroom or for ordering examination copies, please contact our Educational Sales department at 800-434-2086 or fax 317-596-5499.

For press review copies, author interviews, or other publicity information, please contact our Public Relations department at 650-655-3000 or fax 650-655-3299.

For authorization to photocopy items for corporate, personal, or educational use, please contact Novell, Inc., Copyright Permission, 1555 North Technology Way, Mail Stop ORM-C-311, Orem, UT 84097-2395; or fax 801-228-7077.

For general information on Novell Press books in the U.S., including information on discounts and premiums, contact IDG Books Worldwide at 800-434-3422 or 650-655-3200. For information on where to purchase Novell Press books outside the U.S., contact IDG Books International at 650-655-3021 or fax 650-655-3295.

Library of Congress Cataloging-in-Publication Data

Tanner,Ron.

Novell's ZENworks administrator's handbook / Ron Tanner and Brad Dayley.

    p.   cm.

    ISBN 0-7645-4561-2 (alk. paper)1

    1. Graphical user interfaces (Computer systems) 2. Z.E.N.works. I.Dayley, Brad. II Title. III. Title: Novell's Z.E.N.works administrator's handbook IV. Title: ZENworks administrator's handbook V. Title: Z.E.N.works administrator's handbook

    QA76.9.U83 T36 1999

    005.4'38—dc21   99-22684

                                      CIP

John Kilcullen, *CEO, IDG Books Worldwide, Inc.*
Steven Berkowitz, *President, IDG Books Worldwide, Inc.*
Richard Swadley, *Senior Vice President & Publisher, Technology*
The IDG Books Worldwide logo is a registered trademark or trademark under exclusive license to IDG Books Worldwide, Inc. from International Data Group, Inc. in the United States and/or other countries.

Marcy Shanti, *Publisher, Novell Press, Novell, Inc.*
Novell Press and the Novell Press logo are trademarks of Novell, Inc.

Welcome to Novell Press

Novell Press, the world's leading provider of networking books, is the premier source for the most timely and useful information in the networking industry. Novell Press books cover fundamental networking issues as they emerge — from today's Novell and third-party products to the concepts and strategies that will guide the industry's future. The result is a broad spectrum of titles for the benefit of those involved in networking at any level: end user, department administrator, developer, systems manager, or network architect.

Novell Press books are written by experts with the full participation of Novell's technical, managerial, and marketing staff. The books are exhaustively reviewed by Novell's own technicians and are published only on the basis of final released software, never on prereleased versions.

Novell Press at IDG Books Worldwide is an exciting partnership between two companies at the forefront of the knowledge and communications revolution. The Press is implementing an ambitious publishing program to develop new networking titles centered on the current versions of NetWare, GroupWise, BorderManager, ManageWise, and networking integration products.

Novell Press books are translated into several languages and sold throughout the world.

Marcy Shanti
Publisher
Novell Press, Novell, Inc.

Novell Press

Publisher
Marcy Shanti

IDG Books Worldwide

Acquisitions Editor Jim Sumser	**Copy Editor** Larisa North
Development Editor Kurt Stephan	**Production** Publication Services, Inc.
Technical Editor Tim Crabb	**Proofreading and Indexing** Publication Services, Inc.

About the Authors

Ron Tanner is a networking professional who has been with Novell since 1993. He currently is the director of engineering for the Management Products Group. Prior to Novell, Ron worked at AT&T Bell Laboratories developing advanced networking systems. Ron has been the lead engineering manager for the ZENworks project since its inception.

Brad Dayley is a software engineer on Novell's Critical Problem Resolution team. He has eight years of experience installing, troubleshooting, and coding Novell's products. He co-developed an advanced debugging course used to train Novell's support engineers and customers, and is the coauthor of *Novell's Guide to Resolving Critical Server Issues*.

I dedicate this book to TT, MRT, KT, JNT, and my Peach Queen. LYA.

— Ron Tanner

For D, A, & F!

— Brad Dayley

Foreword

Over the last decade, companies have become increasingly dependent on network technology for running critical aspects of their businesses. This, along with a dynamic business climate and the explosion of the Internet, has created an insatiable demand for the adoption of new and more complex network services. This rapid adoption of technology has brought with it many different and more difficult issues for IT staffs, as they struggle to manage these increasingly complex networks, while at the same time attempting to reduce the total cost of ownership.

One of the most costly IT functions is managing the large numbers of networked desktops deployed in today's corporate environment. The capability to support these systems and the software on them is critical to the success of any company. Desktop management solutions must recognize these needs and be flexible enough to provide the ease of traditional centralized management in today's complex distributed environments. ZENworks leverages the power of directory services to provide a distributed desktop management solution that allows administrators to more easily manage desktops and their applications.

Since its initial release in 1998, ZENworks continues to grow in popularity. *Novell's ZENworks Administrator's Handbook* is the first book concentrating exclusively on the deployment and use of ZENworks. The authors' in-depth knowledge of the internals of both ZENworks and NDS provides insight on how to get optimal use out of this product. A complete reference, this book is set up to guide you through the installation, setup, troubleshooting, and use of ZENworks. In this book, you will get detailed feature descriptions, including a look at some features planned for the future. A book to be used and reused, *Novell's ZENworks Administrator's Handbook* will serve as the definitive reference for those deploying or considering the deployment of ZENworks.

Peter J. Morowski
Vice President, Management Products Group
Novell, Inc.

Preface

The computer industry has made incredible progress with information sharing since the introduction of local area networks (LANs) in the 1980s. These advancements have produced services and tools that increase the productivity of users while decreasing their workload. Companies have come to rely on networks for virtually all aspects of business, such as accounting, payroll, mail, communications, advertising, banking — the list goes on. All this comes at the price of maintenance, however. In return for having a high-speed network to increase employee and company productivity, each business must also incur an often enormous support cost. Novell recognizes this and provides a solution: Zero Effort Networks, or ZENworks.

ZENworks is the first directory services-based desktop management tool that reduces the cost of owning networked PCs and makes using networks easier. ZENworks leverages the functionality of NDS to make Windows-based desktops easier to use and manage without sacrificing power or flexibility. It allows network administrators to leverage NDS to ensure that users can focus on their business, not their PCs. With automated application delivery and repair, desktops customized for users' needs, and easy problem resolution, ZENworks enables users to take advantage of all the power of the PC without high administrative cost.

Novell's ZENworks Administrator's Handbook is your guide to leveraging ZENworks to distribute applications, manage users, and maintain desktop PCs. This book provides steps to set up and use the advanced features of ZENworks to cut your administrative efforts and costs, while making the network environment much more friendly to users.

Who Should Read This Book?

This book is for anyone responsible for setting up or maintaining a Novell network. If you are a network administrator, support technician, CNE, or consultant, this book will give you the edge you need to streamline application distribution and manage users and desktops much more efficiently. You will save valuable time by using the advanced features of ZENworks to automate time-consuming tasks such as application distribution and workstation management.

How This Book Is Organized

This book is organized into the following chapters to guide you through installing ZENworks, setting up ZENworks in NDS, and then leveraging the advanced features of ZENworks to reduce your network management costs.

Chapter 1: Introduction to ZENworks

Chapter 1 provides a high-level overview of the ZENworks system and its components. Additionally, it discusses the different packages of ZENworks that are available.

Chapter 2: Installing ZENworks

This chapter discusses the prerequisites and design considerations of installing ZENworks. It also takes you through the installation of the server and client pieces of ZENworks, helping you avoid any pitfalls that could result in later problems.

Chapter 3: Setting Up ZENworks in Your Tree

Chapter 3 identifies the steps that must be taken following the install to get your ZENworks system up and functioning. In order to get the full effects of ZENworks, you must deliver the proper agents to the workstations in your system and import workstations into your tree, enabling you to manage all your desktops centrally from your NDS tree.

Chapter 4: Creating Application Packages Using snAppShot

This chapter discusses the snAppShot utility and how to use it to create an application object template for later distribution. It discusses why and when you should use snAppShot, and describes how snAppShot creates the application object template. It also discusses how to use snAppShot's advanced features, including preferences, special macros, and partial installation detection.

Chapter 5: Creating and Using Application Objects

After you have gained an understanding of application object templates, Chapter 5 covers using the template to create application objects and setting them up for distribution. This chapter will also familiarize you with how to set up properties to customize your application objects, as well as customize how and when they are distributed to users.

Chapter 6: Setting Up User Policies

ZENworks provides several policies that describe how the system should deal with users. Chapter 6 discusses the various policies associated with users of the tree, how to set them up, and the value they can provide to your system.

Chapter 7: Setting Up a Computer Policy Package

Chapter 7 identifies the various computer policies available in the ZENworks system. These policies affect the behavior, security, and desktop of all the workstations in your network. This chapter tells you how to set up these policies and make them effective.

Chapter 8: Creating a Container Policy Package

Additional policies available for ZENworks help describe how the ZENworks system can be most effective in your tree and network. Chapter 8 discusses these policies and how they affect the behavior of the agents that are working to get your settings to your desktops.

Chapter 9: Maintaining a Workstation

Chapter 9 identifies the other programs and systems that accompany the ZENworks product that help identify and fix problems with desktops in the network. These tools include Remote Control and Remote Diagnostics. Additionally, this chapter identifies the inventory system available in ZENworks and how it scans each desktop for hardware and software inventory.

Chapter 10: Using ZENworks Software Metering

Chapter 10 discusses how to use the ZENworks software metering features to give your organization the capability to manage software licenses and track software usage with ZENworks application management and Novell's Licensing Services (NLS). This chapter discusses how to use the NLS manager to create a licensed or metered certificate, and then shows how to assign users to licenses.

Chapter 11: Using ZENworks Check 2000 to Resolve Y2K Issues

The purpose of this chapter is to introduce you to the Check 2000 components that are included with ZENworks, and to show how to use them to scan workstation and server hardware, software, and data for year 2000 issues. Chapter 11 then discusses how administrators can use ZENworks to repair problems by pushing fixes out to all clients on the network.

Chapter 12: Advanced Features of ZENworks

Chapter 12 discusses some of the features that are being considered for future releases of ZENworks, including full application multi-tiered distribution.

Chapter 13: Troubleshooting ZENworks

ZENworks is an extremely powerful tool that will save network administrators precious time. Because of the complexity of network environments, however, problems can occur that prevent ZENworks from doing its job. Chapter 13 covers how to troubleshoot and diagnose problems in the following areas: desktop management, distributed applications, policy packages, and NetWare errors.

Appendix A: Understanding Changes to NDS Objects

Appendix A discusses the powerful administration and management system ZENworks adds to NDS by extending existing objects and creating new ones. This appendix discusses how these additions to the NDS schema give administrators considerably more flexibility and control over applications, workstations, and users. Appendix A also covers the most important changes made to NDS by ZENworks, including the container object, the user object, and the New Workstation Object.

Appendix B: Using snAppShot to Create Application Object Packages

Appendix B expands on the coverage in Chapter 4 by providing a detailed example of using the snAppShot utility to create an application object package for distribution to other workstations. Finally, Appendix B gives a detailed review of the application object template created. The purpose of this appendix is to give you practical experience and knowledge of application object templates.

Acknowledgments

Our sincere gratitude goes out to the following persons, without whom this book could not have come into being:

To Jim Sumser, thanks for helping to keep this book alive through all the struggles of getting it kicked off the ground.

To Kurt Stephan, thanks for your patience through the rewrites and updates.

To Marcy Shanti, thanks for making sure we were saying the right things.

To all members of the ZENworks team, who put a lot of significant effort into creating the product — especially through the typical struggles of a first release of any product. You all did a great job. We're looking forward to many updates to make the product even better.

To all those at Novell who helped with coaching and explaining about publishing and details of the product; with apologies to any whose names we have forgotten, we would like to specifically express gratitude to Kevin Prior, Matthew Lewis, Matt Brooks, and Dave Romanek.

To our technical editor Tim Crabb, our profound thanks for putting ZENworks into production and helping root out our errors by sharing your experience with us. This is a significantly better book thanks to your efforts.

Contents at a Glance

Contents

Introduction to ZENworks

This guide will help you through some potential rough spots when you deliver ZENworks to your system. It also explains a little about how ZENworks functions and affects your Novell network. This particular chapter focuses on introducing you to the purpose and advantages of using ZENworks in your network by discussing three questions regarding ZENworks. These questions are:

- ▶ What is the purpose of ZENworks?
- ▶ What packages of ZENworks are available?
- ▶ What are the benefits of using ZENworks?

What Is the Purpose of ZENworks?

ZENworks is a desktop management system introduced by Novell. *ZENworks* stands for Zero Effort Networks, and is named to reflect the zero effort required for end users, and the minimum effort necessary for the administrator, to manage the desktops in their systems. By reducing the effort necessary to manage desktops, the goal is to reduce the total cost of ownership (TCO) of dealing with desktops in the network.

ZENworks initially focuses on three areas of desktop management and maintenance, which are discussed in the following sections.

Application Management

The ZENworks area of *Application Management* is designed to easily deploy applications from the network to individual desktops. These applications can be automatically installed on the workstation, or can just have an icon applied to a desktop that references a software executable or installation bundle on a server in the network. All the applications that are deployed to the desktop allow the administrator to control when they are deployed, how they are applied, and which desktops get certain applications.

ZENworks also enables you to customize the settings for each individual user by referencing values in Novell Directory Services (NDS) and embedding them in the registry keys and files for the particular applications. Then, when that application is deployed to the desktop, these values are customized for the particular user. In addition to customization, the Application Management portion of ZENworks includes the capability to help you equalize the usage on the network through its load-balancing features, and attempts to make the application always available with its fault-tolerance features.

With the integration of NDS, ZENworks Application Management ensures that the applications follow users to whichever desktop they use in the network, keeping their connection to the network always functioning in a familiar way.

ZENworks Application Management provides a wide range of features that enable you to distribute applications and assign applications to users, making the management of applications for desktops and your users on the desktop simple and consistent.

Application Management features of ZENworks are currently provided for the following platforms: Windows 3.1, Windows 95, Windows 98, and Windows NT.

Desktop Management

Desktop Management refers to the administrator's capability to effect direct changes on the desktop and manage the registry, Novell clients, printers, and even ZAW and ZAK policies of the Windows operating systems. With the advantages of the Novell Directory Services, you can make a change to a configuration object that affects the client, for example, and then have it applied to all or a portion of the workstations in your entire organization. Because of the inheritance rules of NDS and the introduction of workstation objects into the tree, these configuration objects can be applied to many users and workstations in the tree through associations with objects, groups, or containers.

Microsoft introduced to its Windows environments the products ZAW (Zero-Administration Workstation) and ZAK (Zero-Administration Kit) as a first step to allow administrators to manage the workstation. These products resulted in registry settings that could be stored in a .pol file and then be accessed by each workstation as it attaches to the server. These registry settings would then be applied to the workstation, resulting in the interface the administrator wants for the users. ZENworks has taken the ZAW and ZAK features of Windows to the next level by providing these registry manipulations (resulting in desktop changes) and placing them into the NDS tree. Rather than having to create a .pol file and then have that deployed across the network servers, you can administer the same features in NDS. Once the ZAW and ZAK features have been administered into the NDS system, that "policy" can then be applied to any workstation in the system or follow any user as he or she moves from desktop to desktop, regardless of which server the user is working with in the tree. Novell, through ZENworks, has truly introduced fault-tolerance and manageability to these policies introduced by Microsoft.

ZENworks also allows the administrator to create a configuration object for the Novell client. This way, all workstations that are associated with this configuration object will use the configurations specified to manage the client. One customer was told by Novell that in order to fix their problem, they needed to change only one line in the net.cfg file of the client. The customer was not too happy because the company had over 10,000 clients of that type, and determined that with their current staff it would take them years to make that change. Now, with ZENworks, one administrator can make the change in one client configuration policy object; the change is forwarded and made to clients of all associated workstations, and then becomes effective the next time the users log into the system. This one change could be done in a matter of minutes, instead of years.

In addition, the Desktop Management feature of ZENworks includes a hardware inventory of the desktop. An inventory "sweet spot" is stored in the workstation object that is associated with the physical workstation device. This inventory can be useful to you, the administrator, for understanding the capabilities of the workstation as you manage and maintain the desktop. ZENworks also provides a complete hardware and software scanning capability that is stored in a separate database. There is a link between the workstation objects and the database, allowing you easy access to the scanned information. Reports are also included in ZENworks, to provide you with useful, tabular information of what is stored in the scanned database.

Included with the Desktop Management features of ZENworks are enhanced versions of the original Workstation Manager 1.0 (WSM) features, including dynamic NT account management. Enhanced versions of the account management give even greater control to the administrator for having automatic accounts created on NT for users logging into the system. When these users log into NDS, a local account is automatically created and customized for each particular user. When they log out, this account can either remain or be removed from the local NT system.

Through the Desktop Management features of ZENworks, Novell provides the capability to manage all aspects of the desktop, including access to basic features of Windows as well as the automatic deployment of printers. And, like many ZENworks features, these capabilities will follow users as they move across the organization from one workstation to another — and that includes your printer drivers and printers!

Desktop Management features of ZENworks are currently provided for the following platforms: Windows 95, Windows 98, and Windows NT.

Remote Management

The *Remote Management* feature of ZENworks includes the capability to discover information about a workstation and to do some remote diagnostics and repairs on that workstation. As mentioned earlier, ZENworks introduces into the tree a new object representing the workstation. This workstation object is associated with the physical desktop, and is a repository for information about the specific desktop. You can then use this information in determining how to most effectively maintain and repair that desktop.

In addition to the introduction of the workstation object, the Remote Management feature of ZENworks provides you with the capability of NDS Authenticated Remote Control and a minimal Help Request System. The NDS Authenticated Remote Control feature prevents anyone without rights to remote control a particular workstation from being able to remote control the system. This way, both administrators and end users are assured that only authorized personnel can remote control their desktops. The Help Request System allows end users to send mail to help desk personnel who have been identified and administered in NDS for resolving problems on the workstation. The e-mail that is sent includes information about the error, the user who is currently on the system, and the workstation object NDS directory name, thus enabling you to go quickly to the workstation object. By accessing the object quickly, you can then discover the type of desktop involved and the hardware inventory of the system, and from the object you can automatically remote control the desktop (if the user has appropriate rights) and make any repairs necessary on the desktop. This should considerably reduce the travel time to a desktop, and therefore reduce the cost involved in maintaining these systems.

To help with the diagnostics and repair of the workstations, Remote Management of ZENworks includes remote diagnostics, chat, and file transfer capabilities. All of these also require proper rights in the NDS tree in order to perform the tasks.

Remote Management features of ZENworks are currently provided for the following platforms: Windows 3.1, Windows 95, Windows 98, and Windows NT.

What Packages of ZENworks Are Available?

The following sections discuss the features included in each ZENworks package. ZENworks is currently available in three packages:

- ZENworks
- ZENworks Starter Pack
- ZENworks and ManageWise Bundle

Because ZENworks only requires access to a file system and the existence of Novell Directory Services, it will work on an NT server with the use of Novell's NDS for NT product. This allows the benefits of ZENworks to be available not only to NetWare customers, but to NT customers as well.

ZENworks

This package of ZENworks includes all the features of the product and the latest Novell clients. It is sold as a separate package, and is available through standard Novell, Inc. channels. This package is not intended to be included with any other offering (except for the ManageWise bundle discussed in a later section). This ZENworks product includes all the features of Application Management, Desktop Management, and Remote Management. As additional features are added to the product-line, they will always be included in this package.

ZENworks Starter Pack

This packaging of the ZENworks system is free to all Novell, Inc. customers and is available with most Novell products including NetWare 5. The ZENworks Starter Pack is also available from the Novell Web site (www.novell.com) and is free for downloading.

The ZENworks Starter Pack includes all the features of the Application Management and Desktop Management features of ZENworks 1.0 and the latest clients. It does not include any of the Remote Management features, including the following: NDS Authenticated Remote Control, Help Request System, Remote Management tools (chat, file transfer, and diagnostics), and Desktop hardware and software inventory. These features are included only in the full ZENworks product offering.

ZENworks and ManageWise Bundle

The full-featured ZENworks product is also available with a ManageWise bundle.

Administrators who are familiar with ManageWise may recall that a desktop management system is currently offered in the ManageWise product line. There is an obvious overlap between ZENworks and ManageWise desktop management features, particularly in the remote control and inventory features.

In the first release of ZENworks, there was an incompatibility with the remote control; since that first release, however, ZENworks and ManageWise remote control capabilities have become compatible. To maintain the security of the remote control features of ZENworks, the ManageWise console requires that you log into NDS with the appropriate level of rights in order to remote control a ZENworks agent. Additionally, before a ManageWise console can control a ZENworks agent, the hardware and software scanning features of ManageWise must be executed. The scanner picks up the fact that the workstation has a ZENworks agent, and records this fact in the database. Therefore, when the remote control session is started, it checks in the database to see which system it needs to remote control the agent.

NOTE ManageWise and ZENworks remote controls are compatible. The ManageWise software scanner must have executed and recorded the information in the database before you can remote control a ZENworks agent.

What Are the Benefits of Using ZENworks?

There are significant benefits of using the ZENworks product in your NetWare and NT environments. The greatest benefit comes from the effective leveraging of existing information that is currently in your directory, and combining this with the new components and tree extensions provided in ZENworks. By building these relationships in the directory between users and their desktops, enormous management potential is uncovered and is easily available to the administrator. Using the NDS tree and its hierarchical nature enables you to manage all the desktops in your tree from one place in the tree, or delegate to local administrators and containers in subtrees.

ZENworks also is an easy extension of the current administration system. All the administration requirements for ZENworks may be administered via snap-ins that are provided and that plug directly into the NetWare Administration utility. Additionally, ZENworks uses the familiar rights associated with your tree to govern the accessibility of the features to each user in your system.

The cost of managing the desktops in your network is the largest cost involved in having a network. Some analysts estimate the cost of maintaining desktops to be 78% of all network costs. ZENworks will help reduce this cost, and specifically, will make your life easier by allowing you to manage most of the end users' desktop needs from your own office. From your office you can deploy applications to any user in the tree, deliver printers and printer drivers, create NT workstation accounts, and configure Novell clients on any set or on all desktops across the network. You can also designate specific policies that will be applied to each user's desktop or a group of desktops, that can lock down a system or just customize a background screen. Without leaving your office you can receive help requests from the user, look at the hardware and operating system information of the desktop, and even remote control and repair the problems. One of the greatest costs of maintaining a workstation involves traveling from one desktop to the next. With ZENworks, most of that effort is minimized.

CHAPTER 2

Installing ZENworks

One of the biggest keys to using software tools effectively is to install them properly. Properly installing a software product enables you to get started faster and avoid problems later. This chapter focuses on helping you get set up to install ZENworks and its components.

We have broken the installation of ZENworks into the following main sections, which will help you prepare and install the product quickly and correctly:

- ▶ Prerequisites Steps for Installing ZENworks
- ▶ Installing Server Components
- ▶ Installing Client Components
- ▶ Installing Documentation

Steps for Installing ZENworks

The first step when installing ZENworks is to make sure your hardware and software are correctly set up. Before installing ZENworks, spend some time making sure the following criteria have been satisfied and that your environment is ready for the install.

Required Hardware

Prior to installing ZENworks, ensure that your systems meet the minimum hardware requirements. The next few sections cover the hardware requirements for installing ZENworks.

Server Hardware

You will initially install the ZENworks components to a server or servers on your network. You must make sure those servers meet the following criteria for installation:

- ▶ 32MB of available server memory
- ▶ 125MB of disk space on install volume
- ▶ 24MB of disk space on SYS volume

Client Hardware

During the ZENworks install, you will install files to one or more clients. You should ensure that those clients meet the minimum hardware requirements. The client hardware requirements will differ according to which supported operating system you are using.

Windows NT   When installing ZENworks on a Windows NT client, you should ensure that the following minimum hardware requirements are met:

- *486/33 processor* — Although this is the absolute minimum, we recommend at least a Pentium processor when using ZENworks on a Windows NT client machine.

- *24MB of RAM* — Once again, this is the absolute minimum to run the Windows NT operating system and the ZENworks client utilities. If you choose to run other applications at the same time, we recommend that additional memory be added to the client to compensate for the memory those applications use.

- *24MB of disk space (full install)* — The minimum install only takes 4MB of disk space; however, we recommend being prepared by having enough disk space to do a full install.

TIP   One of the hardest things to deal with when installing software is running out of disk space. When this happens, the install is usually stopped in the middle and you are left with a partially installed product. You must then free up disk space and re-complete the entire install. You should watch for this especially when installing on the C: drive. Windows usually has a swap file on the C: drive, and other applications such as Netscape create their caches to the C: drive as well; also, Windows will often spool print jobs to a file on the C: drive. For these reasons, the C: drive can fill up quickly and unexpectedly, so you should make sure that the disk space is available immediately before installing ZENworks.

Windows 98   When installing ZENworks on a Windows 98 client, ensure that the following minimum hardware requirements are met:

- *486/33 processor* — Although this is the absolute minimum, we recommend at least a Pentium processor when using ZENworks on a Windows 98 client machine.

- *16MB of RAM* — Once again, this is the absolute minimum to run the Windows 98 operating system and the ZENworks client utilities. If you choose to run other applications at the same time, we recommend that additional memory be added to the client to compensate for the memory those applications take up.

▶ *24MB of disk space (full install)* — The minimum install only takes 4MB of disk space; however, we recommend being prepared by having enough disk space to do a full install.

Windows 95 When installing ZENworks on a Windows 95 client, you should ensure that the following minimum hardware requirements are met:

▶ *486/33 processor* — Although this is the absolute minimum, we recommend at least a Pentium processor when using ZENworks on a Windows 95 client machine.

▶ *16MB of RAM* — Once again, this is the absolute minimum to run the Windows 95 operating system and the ZENworks client utilities. If you choose to run other applications at the same time, we recommend that additional memory be added to the client to compensate for the memory those applications take up.

▶ *24MB of disk space (full install)* — The minimum install only takes 4MB of disk space; however, we recommend being prepared by having enough disk space to do a full install.

Windows 3.1 When installing ZENworks on a Windows 3.1 client, you should ensure that the following minimum hardware requirements are met:

▶ *486/33 processor* — ZENworks will run fine with a 486/33 processor in a Windows 3.1 client machine.

▶ *16MB of RAM* — This is plenty of RAM to run the ZENworks utilities on a Windows 3.1 client. However, if you choose to run other applications at the same time, we recommend that additional memory be added to the client to compensate for the memory those applications take up.

▶ *24MB of disk space (full install)* — The minimum install only takes 4MB of disk space; however, we recommend being prepared by having enough disk space to do a full install.

Required Software

Prior to installing ZENworks, you should also make sure your systems meet the minimum software requirements. The next few sections cover the minimum software requirements to install ZENworks.

Network Software

You will initially install the ZENworks components to a NetWare server or servers on your network. You must ensure that your network meets the following criteria for installation

NetWare 4.1 Server   To install ZENworks, you must have at least one available NetWare 4.1 or later server that meets the aforementioned hardware requirements. ZENworks will install to a NetWare 4.11 or NetWare 5 server equally well. During the installation process, ZENworks installs additional utilities and the client installs to the server(s) you choose.

> Make sure you have applied the latest support pack for the operating system you are using.
>
> **NOTE**

NDS Connection   You must also have NDS installed on your NetWare server and an NDS connection to the server you wish to install ZENworks to. We recommend that you use the latest DS.NLM available from http://support.novell.com. The new versions include fixes that solve many DS problems.

Application Server   ZENworks requires that an application server be available on the network as well. This can be a NetWare or Windows NT server. Users must have access to the server(s) because files they must use will be stored there.

Client Software

During the ZENworks install, you will install files to one or more clients. Prior to installing ZENworks, you should ensure that those clients meet the following minimum software requirements:

- ► Windows NT, Windows 98, Windows 95, or Windows 3.1 Client
- ► Client32
- ► NDS Connection

Windows NT, Windows 98, Windows 95, or Windows 3.1 Client   The ZENworks client will install to a Windows NT, Windows 98, Windows 95, or Windows 3.1 workstation. It does not currently support UNIX or Macintosh clients.

Client32   The latest Client32 NetWare must be installed on the windows workstation. ZENworks will have the option to set up a client install to make this happen. Later in this book, we discuss how to update the clients automatically.

NDS Connection   The client you will install ZENworks to must have an authenticated NDS connection to a server on which ZENworks is installed.

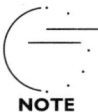

> The ZENworks install must use an authenticated NDS connection to install components. Even though a mapped drive using bindery emulation may give an administrator file access to the SYS: volume, the ZENworks install will not complete without an NDS authentication.
>
> **NOTE**

Installing Server Components

Once you have verified the hardware and software prerequisites for the server(s) and network you plan to install ZENworks to, you can begin the procedure to install the ZENworks server components as outlined in this section.

Login to Tree as Admin
The first step in installation of the ZENworks server components is to log in to your NetWare tree as Admin, or as a user with supervisor rights to the NetWare servers and NDS containers where you wish to install ZENworks.

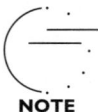

> You must be logged in from a Windows 95, Windows 98, or Windows NT workstation. You will be unable to install ZENworks from a DOS or Windows 3.1 client.
>
> **NOTE**

Launch Install from CD
Once you are logged in as Admin or an Admin equivalent, you are ready to launch the ZENworks install. The ZENworks installation CD-ROM is supplied with an auto-run feature, which means that it is automatically launched when you insert the CD-ROM into your client. You can also launch the install by double-clicking the Winsetup file located in the root folder/directory of the CD, as shown in Figure 2.1.

FIGURE 2.1
Root folder of the ZENworks CD-ROM

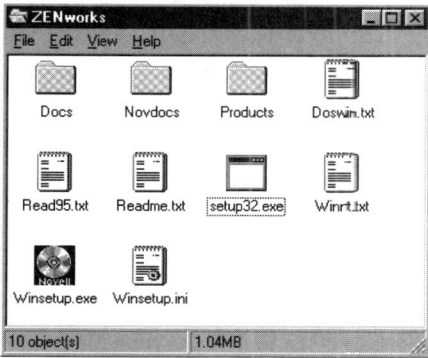

Select Which Language to Install

Once you have launched the install, a screen similar to the one shown in Figure 2.2 will appear. From this screen, you must select the language of ZENworks to install.

FIGURE 2.2
Language screen for ZENworks install

Currently, the only language supported is English; however, there are plans to include other languages with later releases.

NOTE

Select Server Install

Once you have selected the language, you are given the option of selecting the server install or one of the following client installs:

- ► Windows 95/98 Client
- ► Windows NT Client
- ► Windows 3.x Client

You should select the ZENworks option. A new menu appears, as shown in Figure 2.3, giving you the option of installing the ZENworks server components, software metering, documentation, and third-party products. From this screen, select Install ZENworks. This begins installing the server components.

F I G U R E   2 . 3   *Options screen for ZENworks install*

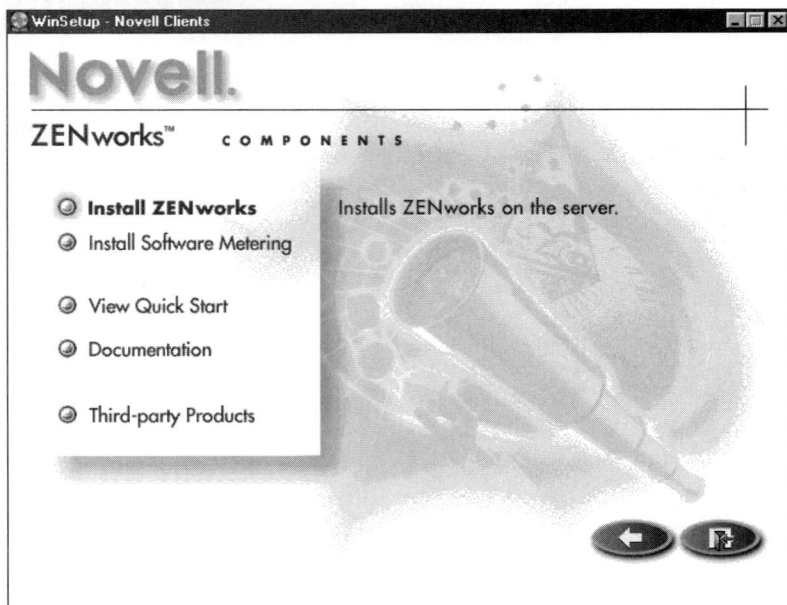

WinSetup - Novell Clients

Novell.

ZENworks™   C O M P O N E N T S

◯ **Install ZENworks**   Installs ZENworks on the server.
◯ Install Software Metering

◯ View Quick Start
◯ Documentation

◯ Third-party Products

Before continuing past this screen, you should do two things:

1. Make sure that no other Windows applications are running on your client. This can cause problems, later on in the install, which require restarting the install.

2. Make sure that none of the files in SYS:\PUBLIC or its subdirectories are in use. This can cause problems for both the ZENworks install and the applications using those files.

Select Installation Type

After you select the Install ZENworks option, you need to click Next and then accept the license agreement. Once you've done this, a menu appears enabling you to choose which type of install to perform, as shown in Figure 2.4.

FIGURE 2.4 *Setup Type menu in ZENworks install*

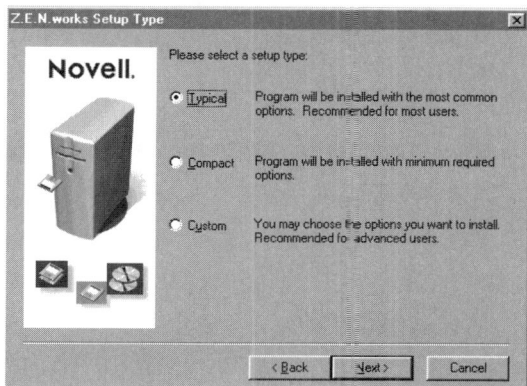

From the ZENworks Setup Type menu, you have the option of selecting one of the following installation options, depending on your needs.

Typical

The *Typical* installation puts in place all the ZENworks server-side components, including NWAdmin. It also stores a copy of the Novell Clients for Windows 95 and Windows NT on the network. This is the easiest and fastest way to install ZENworks on your servers.

Compact

The Compact option installs the ZENworks application along with the minimum required options. You should only select this option if you are extremely low on disk space.

Custom

The Custom option enables you to specify which ZENworks components to install. If you know for sure which components you need, you can use this option to select from the following products, as shown in Figure 2.5:

- ► *Application Management* — This is the software distribution piece. (NetWare Application Launcher (NAL))
- ► *Workstation Maintenance* — This is the workstation manager piece.
- ► *Desktop Management* — Provides remote control features.
- ► *NWAdmin32* — Required for all installs.
- ► *ConsoleOne* — Java components for ConsoleOne utility on the server.
- ► *Copy Clients to Network* — Enables you to install client setups to network for easier updates later.

FIGURE 2.5 *Options in custom setup menu in ZENworks install*

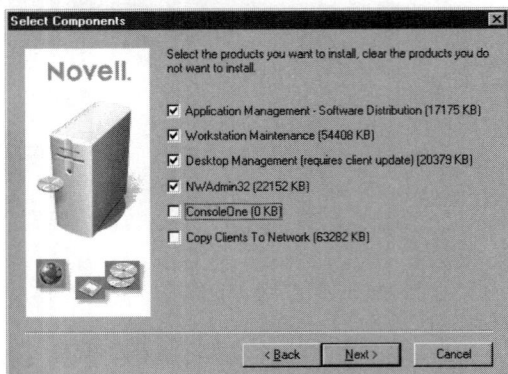

Once you have selected the products you wish to install and clicked Next, you have the option of choosing which parts to install, as shown in Figure 2.6. You can select from the following available options by checking the box next to:

- ► Files
- ► Schema Extensions

- ▸ Application Objects
- ▸ Workstation Registry Entries

Component parts menu in ZENworks install

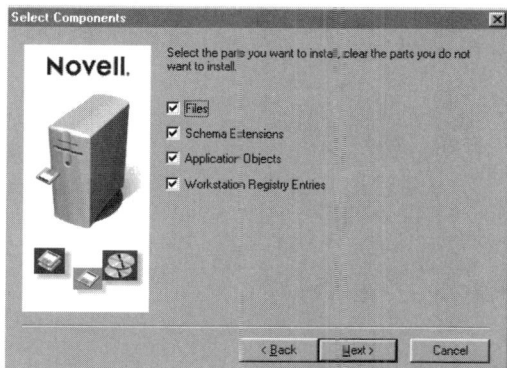

Select Server(s) on Which to Install

Once you have selected the installation type and options, you are given a list of servers in your tree to install ZENworks to, as shown in Figure 2.7. You can select any of these servers by checking the box to the left of the server name. Select the servers you wish to install ZENworks to, and click Next to continue.

Server list menu in ZENworks install

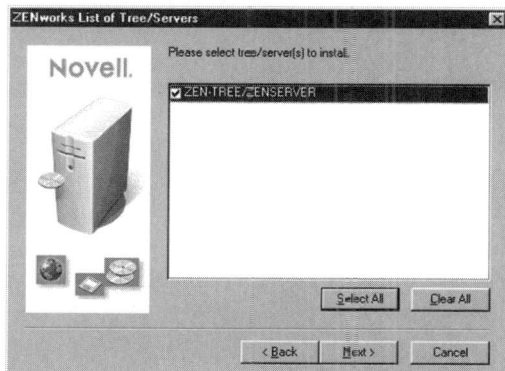

NOTE

> Before you proceed, make sure you have verified the server hardware and software prerequisites for installing ZENworks on all the servers you check in this menu.

Once you have selected the servers and the language, the ZENworks install performs the following tasks.

Check File System

The ZENworks install checks for available disk space on the servers you requested to install to. If there is insufficient disk space, you are given the option to proceed. The ZENworks install will install some files that already exist on the server. The older files will be overwritten. Therefore, there may be enough disk space to install ZENworks even if the available space shown is less than what's needed.

Check Schema

The ZENworks install will also check the DS schema for problems before updating it.

Check DS Objects

The ZENworks install will also check the DS objects for problems before updating them.

Copy Files

When the file system, schema, and DS objects are checked and any problems are resolved, the ZENworks install copies the files to each server selected in the previous menu in sequential order. A status screen lets you know which server is being installed and the percentage of progress to completion. Once the file copying is done, click the Finish button, and the ZENworks server component install is complete.

Create Workstation Inventory

Once the files have been copied, ZENworks creates a workstation inventory database on the server. When this is done, you are given the option to set the context to grant rights to workstation objects. This is necessary for workstations to write a workstation entry to their container. It is not necessary to set the context during install; however, you will need to set it later using the Prepare Workstation Registration option in NWAdmin or WSRights.EXE utility.

> To create the workstation inventory database, TCP/IP must be set up on the target server.
>
> **NOTE**

Log Problems

All problems with the file system, schema, or DS objects will be reported in a log file and displayed on the screen. You will be able to review the log file and correct any errors before continuing.

> We highly recommend that you carefully review the log file for all errors and review the readme file (available from the same screen). Any errors will be much easier to correct at this point than later.
>
> **NOTE**

Installing Client Components

Once you have properly installed the ZENworks server components, you need to install the ZENworks client components to be able to take advantage of ZENworks. Setting up the ZENworks client components means installing the new NetWare client on all workstations managed by ZENworks and used to manage ZENworks.

Automatic Client Upgrade

Often, the best way to update the NetWare clients on all workstations is through an automatic client upgrade. The Automatic Client Upgrade (ACU) provides a way to upgrade client workstations to the latest NetWare client software. This upgrade will occur as users log in.

To setup the ACU process, perform the following five tasks:

1. Create an ACU folder on the NetWare server.
2. Copy the Novell Client files into the folder.
3. Grant users rights to the new folder.
4. Update the appropriate .CFG, .INI and/or unattended file for each platform-specific client.
5. Modify the login script to allow for the upgrade when users log in.

Manual Client Upgrade

Another method to update NetWare clients on workstations is to request that users install from the network. The server install of ZENworks allows you to install the client setup to the network, enabling users to install from the network at their convenience.

This can be helpful for users, because they are not forced into an upgrade they are not ready for; however, it is often a much more difficult process to control and support.

Setting Up the NWAdmin Icon on a Workstation

Once you have updated the NetWare clients, you need set up at least one machine to use as a ZENworks administrator. This means having one workstation that can access NWAdmin to administer ZENworks objects.

The best way to have access to NWAdmin32 is to set up an icon to it on the desktop of the workstation you will use to administer ZENworks. This is accomplished through the following task, illustrated in Figure 2.8:

1. Click the right mouse button on the desktop and select New ⇨ Shortcut.

2. In the Command Line window, type the location of your NWAdmin application, depending on your workstation and public mapping. For example: Z:\PUBLIC\WIN95\NWADMN95.EXE.

3. Select Finish in the window that pops up.

> **NOTE**
> You can create a shortcut to NWAdmin by navigating to the directory though Explorer or by double-clicking folders; however, the PUBLIC directories on NetWare servers contain a large number of files. This means that the directory scan to refresh the folder or Explorer window in those directories can take an inordinate amount of time. The preceding method is much faster and recommended.

Shortcut creation window

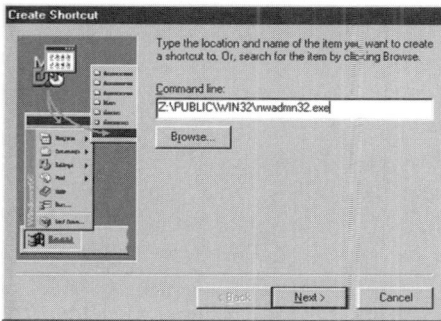

Once you have set up a shortcut to NWAdmin, you can launch it to administer ZENworks by double-clicking the icon, as shown in Figure 2.9.

NWAdmin icon on desktop

NWAdmin
icon

There are both benefits and problems with the different versions of NWAdmin. The following sections cover any enhancements and difficulties you may experience.

NWAdmin32

Using ZENworks NetWare Administrator 32, ZENworks supports NetWare Administrator 95 and NetWare Administrator NT. To take full advantage of the new features included in ZENworks, however, you should use NetWare Administrator 32 (the version of NetWare Administrator that ships with ZENworks). The following sections discuss some issues to be aware of when using NWAdmin32 with ZENworks.

Using NetWare Administrator 32 with NetWare 5 Client   Creating the Workstation Manager Client Configuration (WMCC) in NetWare Administrator 32 requires that the latest NetWare 5 Client for Windows 95 or Windows NT be installed on the workstation used to create the policy. The snap-in depends on being able to access the GUI Login Active-X controls in order to properly configure the WMCC policy for login settings.

User Profiles Snap-in   In the User profiles snap-in in NetWare Administrator 32, when you choose desktop preferences/display options/ and browse to a filename for either the screen saver or wallpaper, the snap-in converts your local drive mappings to a UNC mapping. Therefore, when you type in a path, make sure the mapping you enter corresponds to the right UNC path on the local machine making the changes, not to the user's workstation. The program uses the current workstation mappings for the conversion.

Policy Objects May Show Up in NWAdmin32   If you run NetWare Administrator 95 or NetWare Administrator NT, save settings, and run NetWare Administrator 32, you will see all the Policy objects in the browser window.

To hide the policy objects in NWAdmin32, you can close all browser windows and open new browser windows, or you can remove the registry key for NWAdmin: HKEY_CURRENT_USER\Software\NetWare\Parameters\NetWare

Administrator. You can also hide Policy objects in NWAdmin95, NWAdminNT, and NWAdmin32 if you use the View-Sort and Include dialog to remove individual policies from the current browser window and save your settings.

NWAdmin95 and NWAdminNT

To take full advantage of the new features included in ZENworks, we highly recommend that you use NetWare Administrator 32 (the version of NetWare Administrator that ships with ZENworks). The following sections cover some issues to be aware of when using NWAdmin95 and NWAdminNT with ZENworks:

DMPOLICY.DLL is Required If you use NetWare Administrator 95 and NT, ZENworks requires that the DMPOLICY.DLL snap-in is the first ZENworks snap-in loaded by NetWare Administrator 95 or NetWare Administrator NT (this does not apply if you are using NetWare Administrator 32). In some instances, NetWare Administrator 95 and NetWare Administrator NT do not read these DLLs out of the registry in order. In these scenarios, the DMPOLICY.DLL snap-in will detect the problem and display a warning message recommending that you fix the problem.

When DMPOLICY.DLL is not the first ZENworks DLL loaded, NetWare Administrator 95 and NetWare Administrator NT may have problems, such as not being able to delete, move, or rename Workstation objects, and certain Policy objects appearing in the Create Object dialog but not being able to be created there.

Authenticating to a New NDS Tree When Using NWAdmin95 and NWAdminNT When running on the ZENworks client, NetWare Administrator 95 and NT may be unable to launch the NetWare Login dialog when you try browsing to a tree to which you are not currently authenticated. However, you can task-switch to Windows Explorer, browse to the Network Neighborhood, and authenticate to the new tree without shutting down NWAdminNT or NWAdmin95. When you return to NWAdminNT or NWAdmin95, you should be able to browse to the new tree. This problem will not occur with NWAdmin32.

Installing Documentation

Once you have a client set up to administer ZENworks, you should install the documentation and have it ready to use as a reference on the workstation you plan to use to administer ZENworks before you begin setting things up.

The documentation is installed from the same install as the ZENworks server components. Once the install has been launched, select the language you wish to install, the same way you did to install the server components. When you have selected the language, you can perform the following options.

Select Workstation Type

This time, however, you will select your workstation type from the main installation screen in ZENworks, as shown in Figure 2.10. Select the type of workstation from which you are running the install.

F I G U R E   2 . 1 0   *Main menu in ZENworks install*

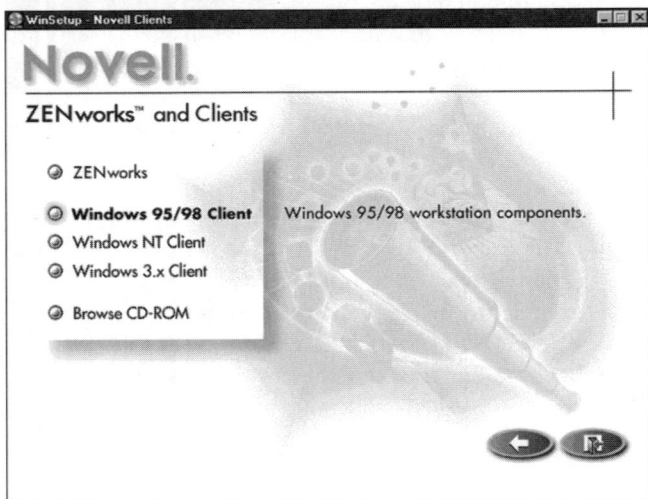

A new menu will appear, as shown in Figure 2.11. From this menu, select Documentation. This brings up the documentation in your Web browser.

FIGURE 2.11
Workstation menu in ZENworks install

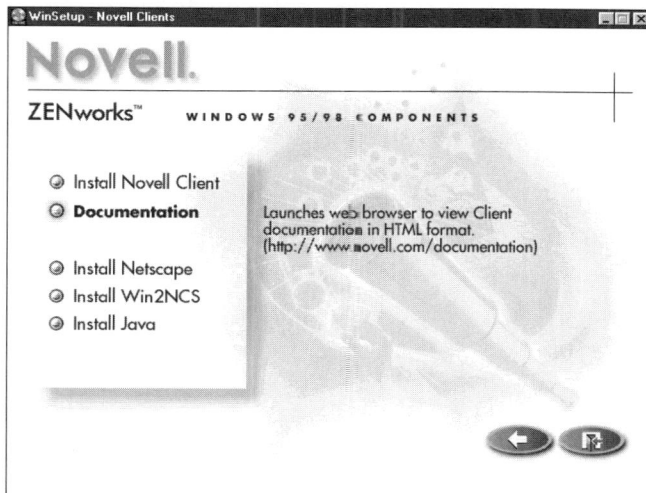

The only way currently available to view documentation in ZENworks 2.0 is from the Web, or from the help files installed during the server install. If you do not have a supported browser, Netscape can be installed from the same menu shown in Figure 2.11.

CHAPTER 3

Setting up ZENworks in Your Tree

This chapter provides a quick overview of the ZENworks system and a high-level view of the changes that will occur within your tree. Make sure you understand this system and how it will impact your current Novell Directory Services installations. Other chapters will get into the details of installation and feature execution.

General ZENworks Architecture

Novell ZENworks requires some changes to your tree structure in addition to extensions to the Novell Administrator (NWAdmin). Additionally, a new client needs to be placed on the workstation with the addition of some agents. This section details the changes that need to occur for you to implement ZENworks into your tree.

Objects in NDS and Impact on the Tree

When you install ZENworks into your tree, not only does it copy the executable files necessary to run the software, it also extends the schema in your tree. The schema extension in your tree introduces several new objects and attributes to your system. Each object is discussed in detail in future chapters.

- *Policy Package Object.* The Policy Package Object is created to hold policies that affect behavior of the agents and programs associated with ZENworks. The ZENworks system looks for these policies when dealing with both users and workstations. A Policy Package Object can be created for each of the supported workstation systems (Windows 3.1, Windows 95/98, Windows NT) and each of the user types (Windows 3.1 User, Windows 95/98 User, Windows NT User), along with miscellaneous collections of policies in a Container Policy.

- *Workstation Object.* This object is created when you import workstations into your tree. This object holds information about the workstation, such as its network addresses and inventory information.

- *Workstation Group Object.* This object is a new group object that enables you to group a set of workstations together. Once the workstations are identified in the group object, you can apply rights and associations to the group just as you do with user groups today.

▶ *Cookie Attribute on Container Object.* This attribute is used in the process of registering the workstation to the tree. The first time a user logs in to a workstation, the agents register information into the container of the user object. This registration information is placed in this attribute. Additionally, when you import the workstation, this attribute is modified with the DN of the created workstation. The next time someone logs in to the workstation (after your import) the workstation discovers its DN by looking into this attribute, where it originally registered.

▶ *Associated Workstations on User Object.* This simply keeps track of the workstations that a user registered with NDS by being the first user to log into the tree through that workstation.

The introduction of most of these objects to the tree is of minimal impact. The only object you need to consider is the workstation object. Individually, this object will only introduce approximately 4KB of information. However, the culmination of all workstation objects in your environment needs to be managed carefully, and you must use good design techniques in the placement of your partitions to make your tree most efficient. Included with the ZENworks CD from Novell is a document in the Docs directory called ZENDSGN.HTM that offers some guidelines for tree design.

Administration Through Novell Administrator

When you install ZENworks, additional snap-ins are delivered to the Novell Administrator. The latest version of the Novell Administrator, NWAdmin32, is introduced to your system, and the snap-ins for ZENworks are placed in NWAdmin32's directory structure. Because Novell realizes that you may not want to convert immediately to the new NWAdmin32, ZENworks also places these snap-ins into the appropriate directories to work with NWAdmin95 and NWAdminNT.

The NWAdmin32 program has had enhancements made to it that allow ZENworks administration to be less cluttered. When using the other version of the Novell Administrator, you see additional objects in the tree that you don't see with NWAdmin32. This is because support objects are administered through the policy package and not as individual objects.

The administration of ZENworks follows the familiar method of administering Novell Directories. ZENworks leverages all the features of the Directory including inheritance, rights, and standard associations.

Novell Client

ZENworks required some enhancements to the Novell client, and consequently the new client is included in the ZENworks package. Future clients delivered from Novell will continue to have support for ZENworks regardless of which bundled system is shipped. These enhancements include the addition of agents that are specific to ZENworks and hook into specific events that occur on the workstation, such as user login, user logout, screen saver activation, and so on. These hooks allow ZENworks agents to be notified when these events occur so they can begin doing their work.

When you install ZENworks into your network, you have the option of copying the clients to the servers. If you do this, your end-users can then have their login scripts modified to include calls to the client's ACU (Automatic Client Update) system, which will check its client to see if it is as new as the one on the server. If changes have been made to the client on the server and it is newer than the client on the workstation (resulting in the need to have the workstation), then the new client is automatically installed on the workstation.

Novell Workstation Agents

For convenience, several ZENworks agents that are necessary to interact with the Remote Control and Software Distributions system have been included with the client that is now being delivered from Novell. In particular, these items are Novell Workstation Manager, ZENworks Remote Control, and the Novell Application Launcher service. Currently, the Novell Workstation Manager and Novell Application Launcher services can only be installed with the clients. The Remote Control facilities, in addition to being included with the clients, are also delivered as application objects in the tree when ZENworks is installed. Once delivered as application objects, this service can then be installed independently on any workstation by associating the application object with the user object in the tree, and having the user run the ZENworks Application Launcher.

Policy Packages and Policies

To help in the administration of all of the features and policies of ZENworks, the policies are conveniently grouped into policy packages. These policy packages are logical grouping of policies that are valuable for a user or device. There are policy packages for Windows 3.1 users, Windows 95/98 users and Windows NT users. There are also policy packages for Windows 3.1 workstations, Windows 95/98 workstations and Windows NT workstations.

Policies that are appropriate for each package are included in each policy package, and are effective only for the devices and users that are associated with that package. Although some policies are the same in a Windows 95 workstation package and a Windows NT workstation package, the actual policies are kept independent. In other words, individual policies are not shared between policy packages.

Policy packages may be associated to the various appropriate objects. For example, user policy packages may be associated with a single user, a group of users, or a container. Workstation policy packages may be associated with a single workstation, a group of workstations, or a container. A single policy package may also be associated with several users, groups, and containers.

Because the system looks for policies by searching up the tree from the user or workstation object (depending on the application), there is a desire to keep this search from proceeding too far up the tree. Therefore, ZENworks included a search policy found in the Container policy package. This policy limits the number of levels and the search order that all ZENworks systems use to discover and apply policies.

ZENworks Policy and Policy Package Wizards

To assist you in constructing policies, ZENworks has included two wizards in the product. The two wizards are the ZENworks Policy Wizard and the Policy Package Wizard.

ZENworks Policy Wizard

The ZENworks Policy Wizard is activated from within NWAdmin by selecting the Tools ⇨ ZENworks Policy Wizard menu choice. This wizard is used to construct the proper policy packages and policies when you know what policy you want but you need some help knowing what packages to make.

When the Policy Wizard is launched, a screen similar to the one in Figure 3.1 appears, enabling you to create and modify all the policies in the system.

The main window in the ZENworks Policy Wizard utility

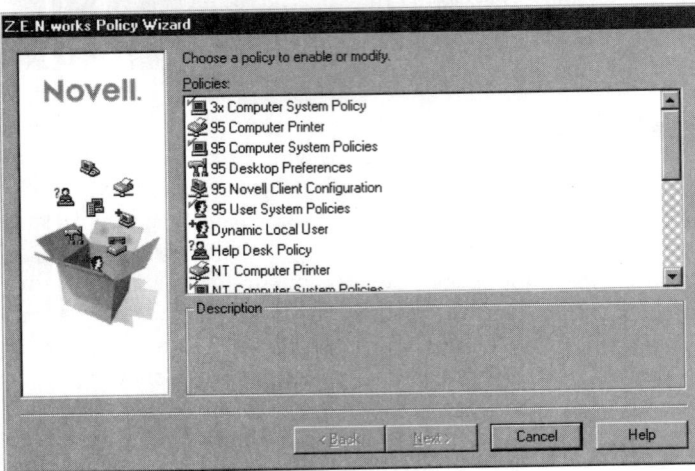

Z.E.N.works Policy Wizard

Novell.

Choose a policy to enable or modify.

Policies:

- 3x Computer System Policy
- 95 Computer Printer
- 95 Computer System Policies
- 95 Desktop Preferences
- 95 Novell Client Configuration
- 95 User System Policies
- Dynamic Local User
- Help Desk Policy
- NT Computer Printer
- NT Computer System Policies

Description

< Back   Next >   Cancel   Help

The best way to understand how to use the Policy Wizard is to take a look at a the following examples.

Example of Enabling an NT Novell Client Configuration Policy

For the first example, we will enable an NT Novell Client Configuration policy.

The first step is to select NT Novell Client Configuration from the main screen in the Policy Wizard and click the Next button.

When the policy type is selected, you have the option to use an existing package, or you can create a new one, as shown in Figure 3.2. If the Use an existing policy package option is selected, a dialog box appears, enabling you to specify a context for the policy package object or navigate to it, as shown in Figure 3.3. If the Create the policy package option is selected, you are given the option to specify a name and select the context it will be created in, as shown in Figure 3.4.

FIGURE 3.2 *The Create new policy package option*

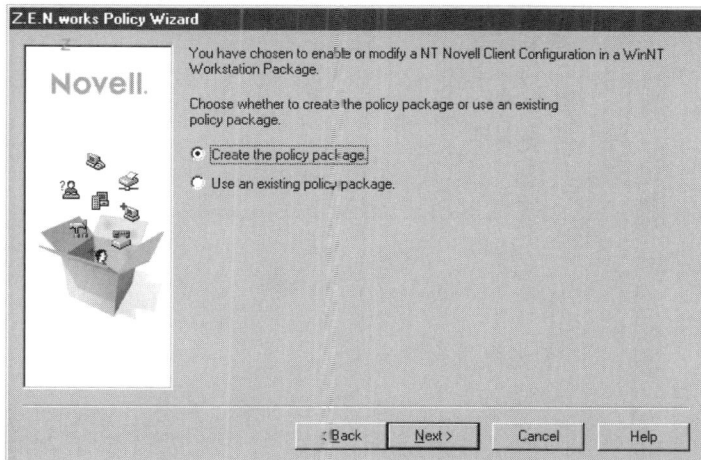

Z.E.N.works Policy Wizard

You have chosen to enable or modify a NT Novell Client Configuration in a WinNT Workstation Package.

Choose whether to create the policy package or use an existing policy package.

- Create the policy package.
- Use an existing policy package.

< Back | Next > | Cancel | Help

FIGURE 3.3 *The Use existing policy package option in the Policy Wizard utility*

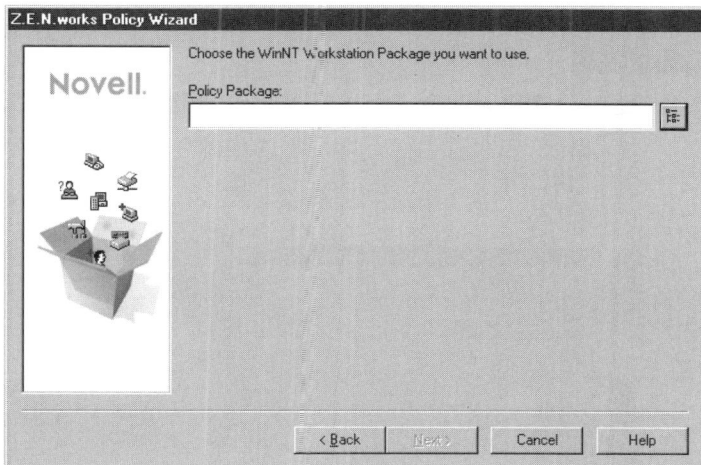

Z.E.N.works Policy Wizard

Choose the WinNT Workstation Package you want to use.

Policy Package:

< Back | Next > | Cancel | Help

► · ◄

FIGURE 3.4 The Use existing policy package option enables you to specify the creation context

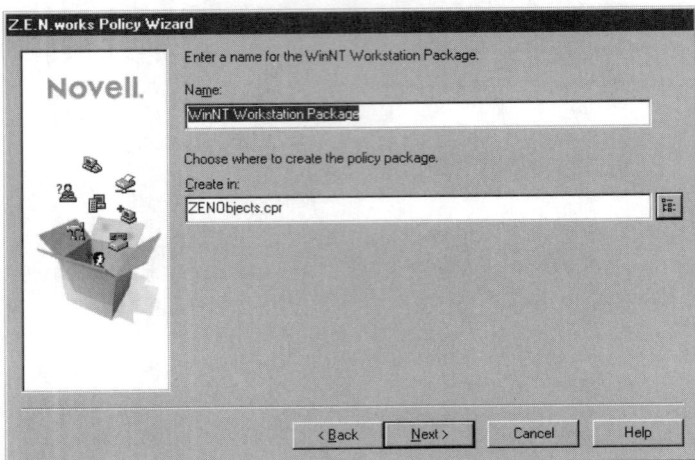

When the policy package has been established, a new screen similar to the one in Figure 3.5 is displayed. From this screen, you can view and select policies you wish to be enabled, as well as edit properties of those policy objects.

► · ◄

FIGURE 3.5 The policy settings window

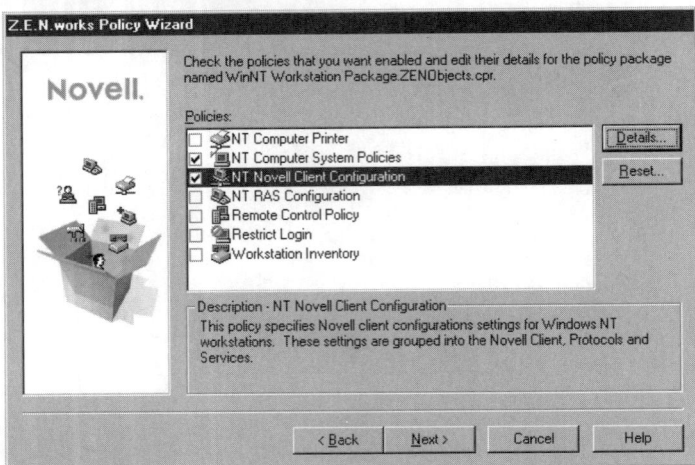

To edit the properties of a policy from this window, highlight it and click the Details button shown in Figure 3.5. This brings up the normal screens associated with the policy and enables you to modify the attributes of the policy.

Example of Enabling a Restrict Login Policy

Now that an NT Novell Client Configuration policy and a WinNT Workstation Package exists, let's look at an example of enabling a Restrict Login Policy for that package.

The first step is to select the Restrict Login policy from the main window in the Policy Wizard. A new window appears, similar to the one in Figure 3.6. From this window, select WinNT Workstation Package and the Restrict Login policy, and then click Next.

At this point, you may wonder why you see a different screen than in the first example. This is because the Restrict Login policy is a valid policy for either the Windows 95/98 Workstation Package or the Windows NT Workstation Package, whereas the NT Novell Client Configuration Policy in the first example is only valid for the Windows NT Workstation Package. Consequently, this screen is skipped in the first example and displayed in this case.

F I G U R E   3 . 6   *The Restrict Login policy*

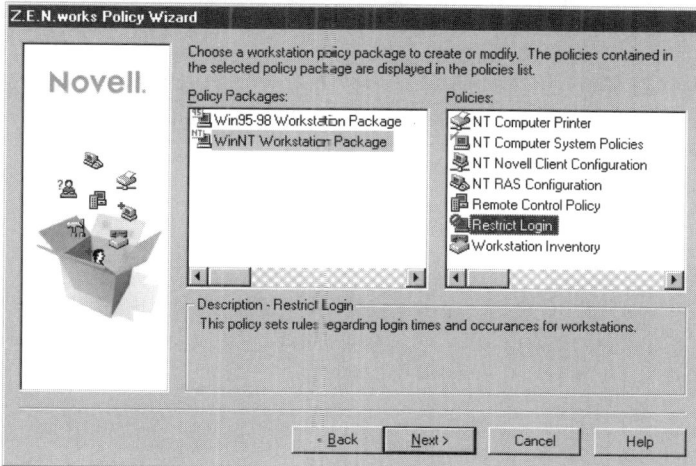

Next you would select Use existing policy package and find the policy created in the previous example. A new window appears with the Restrict Login policy already selected, as shown in Figure 3.7.

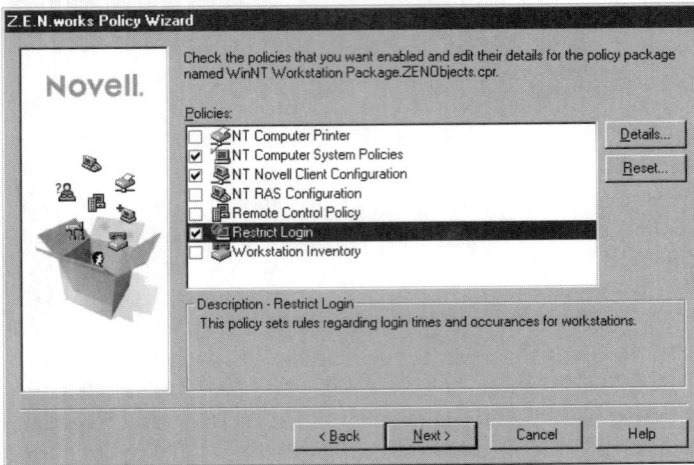

To set up the login restrictions for this WinNT Workstation package, click the Details button and make the necessary changes in the specific policy.

Policy Package Wizard

The Policy Package Wizard is activated when you create a policy package from the Create menú choice. The first screen, shown in Figure 3.8, presents you with the list of all available policy packages and the list of policies that are contained in each policy package.

Select a policy package, and click Next. The dialog box that appears asks you to enter the name of the policy package and the container where the package should reside. This screen is similar to Figure 3.4.

After selecting the name and container, you are presented with the set of policies that are available with this policy package. You can then select each policy you want to activate and adjust the values for each by highlighting the policy and pressing the Details button. This screen is similar to Figure 3.5.

The next screen of the wizard enables you to select the containers, users, or groups that should be associated with the policy. The association will activate this policy for those users or workstations. Figure 3.9 is a sample of this screen. The wizard places a default value of the current container to be associated with the policy package. You can add and remove associations through this screen. When you've finished, press the Next button to move on to a summary screen.

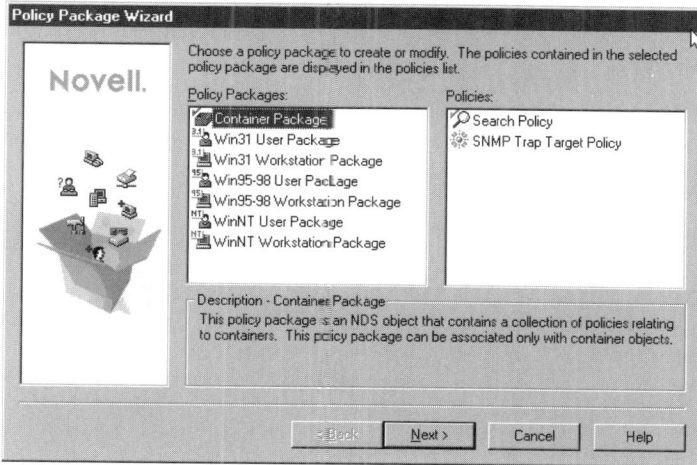

FIGURE 3.8 *Initial screen from the Policy Package Wizard*

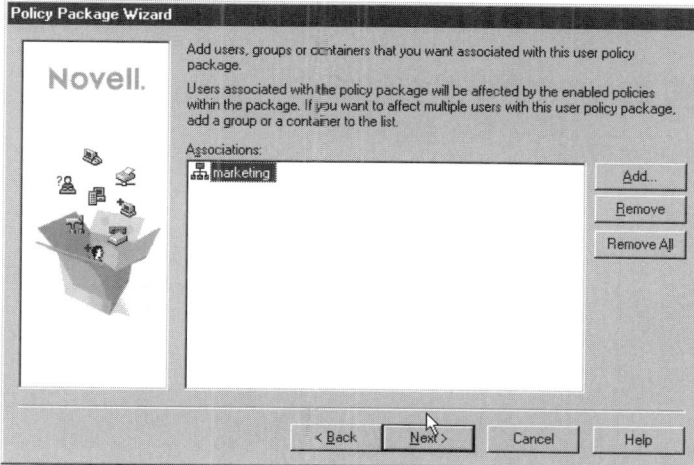

FIGURE 3.9 *Associations screen*

The summary screen displays a description of what the wizard will be doing. This description reiterates the package type to be created, the name of the package, the container holding the package, the enabled policies in the package, and the associated objects. When you press the Finish button on this screen, the policy package is created and the associations are made.

Setting Up Workstations in the Tree

Before you can start managing the workstation, you must create workstation objects and associate them with physical workstations. This step is not necessary if you do not want to manage the physical device, but instead want to manage only the desktop. For example, if you only want to deliver applications to the workstation and apply Microsoft policies to the desktop when a user is logged in to the workstation, then associating a user policy to the particular user accomplishes all this. However, should you want to manage the physical inventory and perform remote control functions, in addition to managing the workstation accounts, then you must first have the workstation object.

You must perform the following steps to place a functioning Import Policy in your tree:

1. Create a policy package.

2. Turn on the Import Policy in the policy package.

3. Associate the policy package with a user container.

4. Allow login cycles to register the workstation to the tree.

5. Import the workstations into the tree. (This creates the workstation object.)

6. Associate other policies to the workstation objects to effect management.

Creating a Policy Package

Before you can start working with ZENworks workstation features, you must first create a policy package to hold the policies associated with users and workstations. To get the ball rolling, you must first create a user policy package. To create a user policy package, follow these steps:

1. Start NWAdmin32.

2. Select a container to hold the policy package object.

3. Select the Create menu choice and create a policy package object.

4. In the Policy Package Wizard, select a user policy package for the type of package, and name the object. Follow the wizard along and associate the policy package with the container that has the user objects for which you would like to have these policies in effect. Remember that these policies will be effective in subcontainers as well, so you can associate the policy package high enough in the tree to affect as many users as desired.

Creating a Workstation Import Policy

Now that you have created a user policy package and associated it with a container that holds the users you want to affect, you can create a workstation import policy. To create the Workstation Import Policy, follow these steps:

1. Start NWAdmin32.

2. Browse to the container that has the user policy package you want to administer.

3. Select the user policy package and request details on the object.

4. Select the workstation import policy from the list of policies available. When you select and activate the import policy, the checkbox to the side is checked.

5. Perform details of the workstation import policy if desired.

6. Select OK and close out the dialog boxes.

When you've created a workstation import policy, the workstations that are registered with their cookie to the tree can have workstation objects associated with their physical devices.

In Step 5, you had the option of modifying the details of the import policy. Let's discuss briefly some of these options. If you decide to take the default import policy, then workstations, when created, will be located in the same container as the user object and will be named by the concatenation of the user login name and the MAC address of the network card. The user object that is associated with the workstation and is used in its naming is the first user to log in to the network on that physical workstation. By going into the details of the import policy, you can change the policy to identify under which container you want the workstation object to reside (this can be absolute or relative to the user container) and select options on how to name the workstation object. The import process uses the information in the cookie to generate the name of the workstation object and the initial data that is placed in the object.

Associations of Policy Packages

The ZENworks system will always start with the relevant user or workstation object, depending on the feature being executed. Once the user or workstation object is located, then the system will "walk the tree" until it locates the first policy package it can find. Generally, when a package is found, the configuration set in that policy is applied to the system, and the ZENworks feature activates. Some features, such as the Microsoft Windows desktop policies, are an accumulation of several ZAW/ZAK policies to which the user may be associated. These policies require that the search proceed to the root of the tree.

"Walking" to the root of the tree for policy packages can be time-consuming, especially if the tree spans across a WAN link. Therefore, ZENworks introduced the Search Policy, contained in the Container Policy Package. This Search Policy limits the levels of containers that all processes search to find their policies.

Novell Workstation Registration

Once an import policy has been created and associated with user objects, either by direct association or by association to the user's container, the workstations that have registered their cookie with the tree may now be imported.

The first person to log in to the tree from the workstation (once the ZENworks-enabled Novell Client has been installed on the workstation) will initialize the ZENworks agents on the workstation. The first thing these agents do is to register the workstation with the tree of the user. A workstation is only registered once, in one tree.

The registration of the workstation results in information being placed on the workstation and in the immediate container of the user object. This information includes the name of the user that is logged in when this cookie was created, the computer name, the MAC/IPX address of the workstation, the IP address, the workstation DNS name, the type of CPU, the operating system on the workstation, and the preferred server. This cookie is placed in the container and is then used later by the import process. The workstation remembers where it placed this cookie and goes back there to look for its workstation object when it is finally created. Each of these fields may or may not have values in the registration, based on the environment of your system.

Some administrators set up a workstation and validate that it can successfully connect to the network before allowing the end user to use the workstation. In this case, all the workstations would then be associated with the administrator rather than the end user of the workstation. Therefore, ZENworks includes the tool unreg.exe in the SYS:\PUBLIC directory; this tool, when run on a workstation, will essentially reset the workstation registration back to being unregistered. After the administrator runs this tool, the administrator can then give the workstation to the end user; then, when the end user logs in to the network, his or her user object will be associated with the workstation. This technique can also be used for having a workstation reregister. If you delete the workstation object in the tree and then run unreg.exe, the workstation will then redo the process of registration the next time a user logs in to the network.

Importing Workstations

Once the registration of the workstation has occurred and this cookie has been placed in the tree, and a workstation import policy has been created, you can import these cookies and create workstation objects from this information. This process will also automatically notify the workstation that an object has been created for it, and will allow it to know the name of its object. You import workstations by following these steps:

1. Start NWAdmin32.

2. Browse to the container where you want to start importing workstations.

3. Import Workstations by doing either of the following:

   a. Launch Tools ⇨ Import Workstations. This brings up a set of dialog boxes to walk you through importing the workstations whose registration cookies are found in the current container and all subcontainers.

   b. Activate details on the container object and select the Workstation Registration tab. From there, you can select individual cookies and import the workstations from that page.

   c. Run the WSIMPORT.EXE utility found in the SYS:\public\winnt directory. This utility is a separate Windows utility that imports workstations into the tree. The tool can be scheduled through the ZENworks scheduling facilities should you want your workstation to automatically import workstations. You can also use WSIMPORT to remove cookies and old workstation objects from the tree. Obviously, you must be the administrator in order to have these operations succeed. The WSIMPORT.EXE utility has the following command-line options: wsimport [context | /T treename | /S [-] | /H | /C | /R days | /?].

The WSIMPORT.EXE command-line options are:

▶ context — This is the context in the tree where you wish the wsimport to begin its work. Remember, if the context has a space in it, you need to enclose the context in double quotes. If no context is specified, then the current context of the workstation user is used.

▸ /T treename — This enables you to specify the tree you wish wsimport to work on. It is assumed that the context specified or defaulted is in the tree; if not, an error will occur.

▸ /S [-] — This tells wsimport to include subcontainers in its work. The default is for it to walk the tree into subcontainers. With the /S- option, you can turn off the subcontainers, and wsimport will only do its work in the context specified.

▸ /H — This option runs wsimport in hidden mode with no user interface or dialog boxes.

▸ /C — This option requests that all the registration cookies in the containers be removed.

▸ /R #days — This option removes all the workstation objects that are older than *#days* from the current date. The workstation object has a registration page indicating the last time a workstation has touched the workstation object (it happens at each login). If this date is older than *#days* specified from today's date, then the object will be removed from the tree.

▸ /? — This is a brief command-line help dialog.

Here are a couple of examples to help out. The next line will import all workstations from the marketing.xyz context and below in the company tree. Remember, it will use the import policy that is associated with the marketing.xyz or above containers.

```
wsimport marketing.xyz /T company /S
```

The next example will remove all workstations that have not been accessed in the last 60 days from the xyz container of the company tree.

```
wsimport xyz /T company /R 60
```

When you import workstations, the workstation object is created, and the cookie left by the workstation is updated to reflect the name of the workstation object that was made for that entry. The next time any user logs in to the network from that workstation, the agents will look up their cookie in the tree and will now discover that they have an associated workstation object. This workstation object name is then saved on the physical workstation, so that now the agents know the object in the tree that represents this workstation.

Until this registration process is completed (1. Workstation places cookie in tree; 2. Administration imports the workstation; 3. The user logs into the NDS tree again), the workstation physical device does not have a complete association with the tree and the workstation object. Without this association, the features that require rights or access to attributes on the workstation object will not function properly. This includes most of the remote management functionality and the hardware and software scanning features.

Creating Other Policies

When you have your users associated with their appropriate policy packages, you can then create other policies in that package and have them affect the user's environment. This also is true with workstation objects and their associated policy packages.

Remote Management Rights

A majority of the remote management features are available to users and administrators via rights in the NDS tree on the objects that represent the target device. For example, in order to remote control a target workstation, you must have rights in the target workstation object in order to perform the remote control function.

You must grant individuals rights in the tree to allow them to perform remote management functions on workstations and user desktops. The following objects in the tree may be granted remote management rights: user, group, organizational role, organization, organization unit, country, locality, [Root], [Public]. There are two methods that you can use to set up these rights. The following subsections discuss these methods.

Remote Operators Page

There is a Remote Operators page associated with each workstation object. Figure 3.10 displays this page.

FIGURE 3.10   *Remote Operators page in a workstation object*

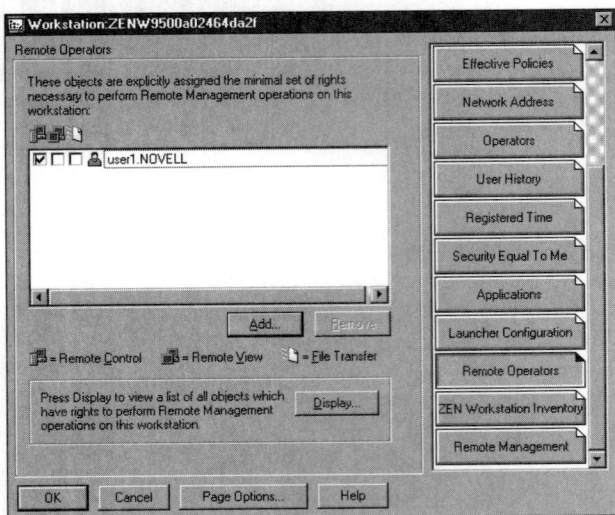

From within this page, you may add either users or groups to the list of operators. With each addition, you can check which of the remote management utilities this addition has rights to perform. The three choices available are Remote Control, Remote View, and File Transfer. By checking the box underneath the icon associated with each of these functions, you grant that user or group the rights to perform those functions on this particular workstation.

Remote Operators Wizard

Another method of granting users or groups access to the remote management functions is through the Remote Operators Wizard. Figure 3.11 displays the initial page of the wizard.

The wizard walks you through selecting the workstation object or containers and then identifying the remote management operations. Following these selections, you must identify the users, groups, or containers to which you want to grant these rights. Once this is specified, the wizard looks up all the workstation objects in the tree below the specified container, and sets the appropriate rights for each of the users, groups, or containers.

FIGURE 3.11 ZEN*orks Remote Operators Wizard

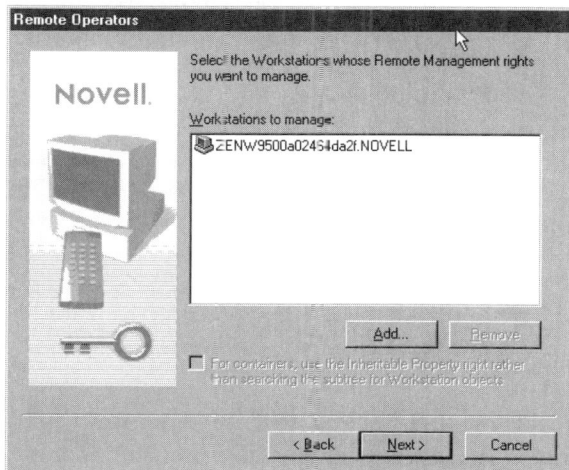

Reporting

ZENworks has introduced some reporting capabilities to Novell management utilities. As information is stored in the database for hardware and software scanning and for the SNMP trap information that is a result of application distribution, it is important to be able to retrieve this information and review reports. Currently, you cannot retrieve any reports from ZENworks unless you have installed the database. Also, if you want application reports you must have an SNMP trap target policy that sends the SNMP information to the database, and you must have run the workstation inventory in order to get inventory information out of the database.

Currently, ZENworks reporting relies on an ODBC driver to the embedded ZENworks database. Before you can perform any reporting functions against the database, you must first properly install the ODBC drivers on your administrator workstation. This is best accomplished by launching the application object that was installed with ZENworks for the ODBC driver. The name of this application object is ZENworks Reporting – ODBC. Just associate this application object with your login and run the NAL program. When the application appears on the desktop or in the NAL window, double-click it to install the ODBC drivers.

With ODBC drivers, you are required to specify the database to which your queries will be directed. When ZENworks is installed and creates the ODBC driver application object, it places in the object the location of the database that you installed during the install process. If you have multiple databases, then you should have multiple ODBC objects and you will need to launch each one prior to running reports against the desired database.

Once you have installed the ODBC driver, you can launch NWAdmin32 and select reporting from the Tools menu. This launches the reporting dialog box that enables you to select the report you wish to generate. The "canned" reports are categorized into two types — Application Management and Inventory — and are found under the File menu of the reporting tool. The Application Management canned reports display data on application deployment to the desktop, and Inventory reports have information on the hardware and software scan results for each workstation. You can generate any of the following reports:

- ▶ Inventory:
  - General Workstation — This gives the list of hardware installed, networking information, and the operating system installed on one or more workstation.

  - Asset Management — This displays a list of the bios information, processor, and operating system on one or more workstations.

  - Hardware — This is a list of the memory information, video, processor, and hard disks installed on one or more workstations.

  - Workstation Based Software — This provides a list of the workstation-specific software installed on one or more workstations, grouped by workstation. The list of software is generated from the software list identified in the policy.

  - Product Based Software — This provides a list of the product software installed on one or more workstations, grouped by workstation. The list of software is generated from the software list identified in the policy.

  - Driver Information — This gives a list of the drivers that are installed on one or more workstations.

  - Networking Information — This provides a list of networking details on one or more workstations.

► Application Management:

- Application Distribution Successes by Workstation — This provides a list of the successful application distributions that have occurred that were distributed by the ZENworks Application Launcher, grouped by workstation.

- Application Distribution Failures by Workstation — A list of the failed application distributions that have occurred that were distributed by the ZENworks Application Launcher, grouped by workstation.

- Application Distribution Successes by Application — This displays a list of successful application distributions that have occurred through the ZENworks Application Launcher, grouped by application.

- Application Distribution Failures by Application — This displays a list of failed application distributions that have occurred through the ZENworks Application Launcher, grouped by application.

- Application Distribution Successes by User — This displays a list of successful application distributions that have occurred through the ZENworks Application Launcher, grouped by user.

- Application Distribution Failures by User — This displays a list of failed application distributions that have occurred through the ZENworks Application Launcher, grouped by user.

- Application Launch Successes by Workstation — This gives a list of the successful application launches that have occurred, via the ZENworks Application Launcher, grouped by workstation.

- Application Launch Failures by Workstation — This gives a list of the failed application launches that have occurred, via the ZENworks application launcher, grouped by workstation.

- Application Launch Successes by Application — This gives a list of the successful application launches that have occurred, via the ZENworks Application Launcher, grouped by application.

- Application Launch Failures by Application — This gives a list of the failed application launches that have occurred, via the ZENworks application launcher, grouped by application.

- Application Launch Successes by User — This gives a list of the successful application launches that have occurred, via the ZENworks Application Launcher, grouped by user.

- Application Launch Failures by User — This gives a list of the failed application launches that have occurred, via the ZENworks application launcher, grouped by user.

Once a report is generated, you can either view it online, in the utility that pops up after generating the report, or send it to a printer.

CHAPTER 4

Creating Application
Packages Using snAppShot

One of the most useful tools provided in the ZENworks products is the snAppShot utility. The snAppShot utility will save you an extensive amount of time when installing and updating applications on client workstations. It enables you to create a template during a single install that can be used to easily distribute applications and upgrades to several workstations on your network.

This chapter familiarizes you with the snAppShot utility and shows you how to use it to create application packages. To do this, we will first discuss the following topics:

- ▶ What Is snAppShot?
- ▶ When Should You Use snAppShot?
- ▶ How snAppShot Works
- ▶ Advanced Features of snAppShot
- ▶ Limitations of snAppShot
- ▶ Using snAppShot

Once we have covered these topics, we will take you through an extensive example of how to use snAppShot to package a common network application.

What Is snAppShot?

The first step in using the snAppShot utility is to understand is what it is. The snAppShot utility is an application used to create "before" and "after" images of a model workstation when installing or upgrading an application to it. In effect, snAppShot takes a picture of the workstation before an application is installed or upgraded to it, and another picture after the application has been fully installed or upgraded.

Once snAppShot has both pictures, it is then able to discern the differences between the two pictures. It saves the differences and can use them later to upgrade or install applications to other workstations on the network.

When Should You Use snAppShot?

Now that you understand what snAppShot is, you need to know when to use it. By default, snAppShot is generally used to package an application to distribute to other users based on NDS and the Application properties.

However, since snAppShot will capture changes made to a workstation during install, there are many situations where you can use it to save time. This section describes how snAppShot is useful in three situations.

Complex Installations or Upgrades

Using snAppShot to aid in complex installations or upgrades can keep you from wasting time repeating the same steps. By using snAppShot, you can simply perform the complex installation or upgrade once, record the differences, and then apply those differences to the other workstations.

An example of snAppShot's usefulness in a complex upgrade would be when you're installing and configuring a printer driver on a Windows 95 client. To do this, you must follow these steps:

1. Enter the network path to the printer or browse the network to find the appropriate queue.

2. Use the Windows 95 CD-ROM or the path to the CAB files that have the necessary files to install the printer driver.

3. Configure the printer for the desktop.

4. Make the appropriate configuration changes also for the printer.

The above procedure is tolerable if it is for one or two workstations, but if one hundred or more workstations need the printer set up, the task becomes monumental.

Using snAppShot on one Windows 95 machine to "package" a printer installation enables you to create an application object template that you can use to create an application object.

Once the application object is created for the printer installation, other Windows 95 clients can now install the printer with drivers without having to use CAB files or the Windows 95 CD-ROM, or make the configuration changes!

The same concept also holds true with Windows NT Workstations, but you need to be administrator equivalent for this to work (unless the NAL NT Service is installed).

Numerous Installations or Upgrades

Using snAppShot to aid in installations that must be done on numerous workstations can also save you a lot of time. Often, application upgrades or installations are very simple to perform and only take a short time, on one workstation. However, that time is multiplied by the number of clients you have on your network. Many companies have thousands of clients, and installing an application that takes only a few minutes on one client takes days to complete on all network clients.

Using snAppShot, you can configure the upgrade or install to be automatically performed throughout the network. Instead of running the install or upgrade on one workstation after another, you simply perform it once on the model workstation and use snAppShot to record the differences. Once recorded, the changes can be made to several other workstations easily and efficiently.

Using snAppShot to record the changes during the update, and then packaging it into an application object, enables you to have the upgrade performed automatically as the users log in to the network. This will save a lot of time and effort when upgrading a large number of users. It will also guarantee that every client has been upgraded.

To Verify Changes Made During an Install or Upgrade

Another situation where snAppShot is useful is when you verify or view the changes made by an application install or upgrade. Although snAppShot was not designed for this purpose, it works well because it captures the changes made during the install.

There may have been instances when you've installed an application that has caused other applications to have difficulties. Using snAppShot enables you to detect what the application install did to your client, and allows you to correct it without uninstalling or reinstalling an application.

A good example of where snAppShot can help with reviewing an application install is when installing a new application that updates shared DLLs in the SYSTEM directory for Windows 95. The application replaces a working DLL with a newer DLL that has bugs.

Once the new DLL is installed, the new application works fine, but a previously installed application fails to load properly. Normally you would have two options: either reinstall the application that is failing to unload, or uninstall the new application and hope that its uninstall mechanism backed up the old DLLs before copying over them.

Using snAppShot, however, enables you to see which DLLs were replaced by the new application install, and you can simply replace them from a backup or CD-ROM.

How snAppShot Works

Now that you know what snAppShot is and what it is for, you need to understand how it works. This section discusses how snAppShot is able to analyze and store the changes made by an installation or upgrade.

Files Created by snAppShot

When snAppShot is used to determine the changes made by an installation or upgrade, many files are created to store information. These files are used later when the installation or upgrade needs to be performed again. They contain all the information needed to update other clients without having to run the installation program or upgrade again.

The following sections describe the file types created by snAppShot when recording the changes during an installation or upgrade.

.AXT Files

AXT stands for Application Object Text Template, meaning that the .AXT file is written in human-readable text format. Therefore, you can open it in a text editor and edit the contents.

> **NOTE**
> The .AXT file takes longer to import into an Application object than an .AOT file, and it is prone to inaccuracies if certain .AXT file format standards are not followed.

An .AXT file is a collection of information about what happened on a workstation when an application was installed to it. You can also think of it as a "change log" that contains the differences between the pre- and post-application installation states of a workstation. snAppShot discovers these differences and records them in the .AXT file, as shown in Figure 4.1.

You use the .AXT file when creating and setting up Application objects using Application Launcher for large-scale distribution. The .AXT file delivers the information about the application to the new Application object.

.AOT Files

.AOT stands for Application Object Template. The .AOT file is written in binary format and cannot be edited in a text editor.

> **NOTE**
> AOT files import faster into an Application object and can be more accurate than their text-based counterpart, the .AXT file.

An .AOT file is a collection of information about what happened on a workstation when an application was installed to it. You can also think of it as a "change log" that contains the differences between the pre- and post-application installation states of a workstation. snAppShot discovers these differences and records them in the .AOT file.

► . . . . ◄

FIGURE 4.1 *Sample excerpt from a snAppShot .AXT file*

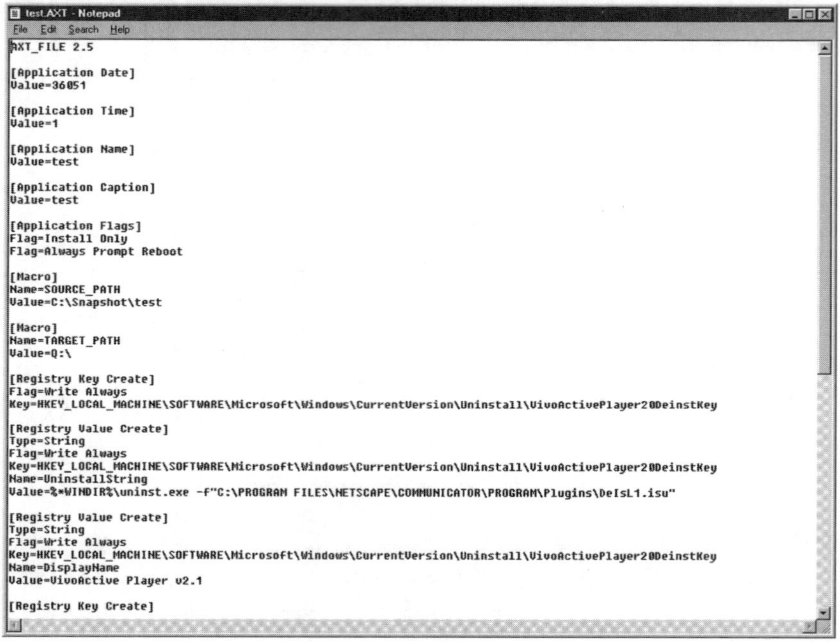

```
test.AXT - Notepad                                              _ □ ×
File  Edit  Search  Help
AXT_FILE 2.5

[Application Date]
Value=36051

[Application Time]
Value=1

[Application Name]
Value=test

[Application Caption]
Value=test

[Application Flags]
Flag=Install Only
Flag=Always Prompt Reboot

[Macro]
Name=SOURCE_PATH
Value=C:\Snapshot\test

[Macro]
Name=TARGET_PATH
Value=Q:\

[Registry Key Create]
Flag=Write Always
Key=HKEY_LOCAL_MACHINE\SOFTWARE\Microsoft\Windows\CurrentVersion\Uninstall\VivoActivePlayer20DeinstKey

[Registry Value Create]
Type=String
Flag=Write Always
Key=HKEY_LOCAL_MACHINE\SOFTWARE\Microsoft\Windows\CurrentVersion\Uninstall\VivoActivePlayer20DeinstKey
Name=UninstallString
Value=%*WINDIR%\uninst.exe -f"C:\PROGRAM FILES\NETSCAPE\COMMUNICATOR\PROGRAM\Plugins\DeIsL1.isu"

[Registry Value Create]
Type=String
Flag=Write Always
Key=HKEY_LOCAL_MACHINE\SOFTWARE\Microsoft\Windows\CurrentVersion\Uninstall\VivoActivePlayer20DeinstKey
Name=DisplayName
Value=VivoActive Player v2.1

[Registry Key Create]
```

You use the .AOT file when creating and setting up Application objects using Application Launcher for large-scale distribution. The .AOT file delivers the information about the application to the new Application object.

.FIL Files

One .FIL file represents one application file that was installed to a workstation. There can be hundreds of files installed to a workstation during an application's installation or upgrade, therefore there can also be hundreds of .FIL files representing that application.

Think of .FIL files as the Application object's copy of the originally installed application files.

For convenience later when you create Application objects, we recommend that you store .FIL files in the same place as the .AOT file. If you place these files in a network location, it will be easier to access them as you build and distribute the Application object.

A list of the .FIL files that need to be copied to run an application is kept in the .AOT file. This list can be viewed from the Application Files property page in the Application object in NWAdmin.

FILEDEF.TXT

The FILEDEF.TXT file is a "legend" that compares originally named installed files with the newly named .FIL files. snAppShot copies the FILEDEF.TXT file to the same directory where the .FIL files are created. Use it to compare .FIL files, which you may not know the meaning of, to the originally installed files. A sampling from the FILEDEF.TXT file is shown in Figure 4.2.

FIGURE 4.2 *Sample excerpt from a snAppShot FILEDEF.TXT file*

```
filedef.txt - Notepad
File  Edit  Search  Help
1.fil=C:\Program Files\Netscape\Communicator\Program\Plugins\Np32dsw\RAXTRA.X32
2.fil=C:\Real\Player\graphic.gif
3.fil=C:\Real\Player\notes.htm
4.fil=C:\Real\Player\playrlic.txt
5.fil=C:\Real\Player\readme.htm
6.fil=C:\Real\Player\realplay.exe
7.fil=C:\Real\Player\start.ram
8.fil=C:\Real\Player\thankyou.rm
9.fil=C:\Real\Player\thankyou.swf
10.fil=C:\Real\Player\bookmark.sav
11.fil=C:\Program Files\Netscape\Communicator\Program\DynFonts\fonts.cat
12.fil=C:\Program Files\Netscape\Communicator\Program\Plugins\Npra32.dll
13.fil=C:\Program Files\Netscape\Communicator\Program\Plugins\RAClass.zip
14.fil=C:\Program Files\Netscape\Users\me\abook.nab
15.fil=C:\Program Files\Netscape\Users\me\bookmark.htm
16.fil=C:\Program Files\Netscape\Users\me\Cache\fat.db
17.fil=C:\Program Files\Netscape\Users\me\Cache\M01N7UP0.GIF
18.fil=C:\Program Files\Netscape\Users\me\Cache\M04L9HUS.GIF
19.fil=C:\Program Files\Netscape\Users\me\Cache\M08UNN9U.GIF
20.fil=C:\Program Files\Netscape\Users\me\Cache\M09BIDQA.GIF
21.fil=C:\Program Files\Netscape\Users\me\Cache\M0JABCRN.GIF
22.fil=C:\Program Files\Netscape\Users\me\Cache\M0L23U4I.GIF
23.fil=C:\Program Files\Netscape\Users\me\Cache\M0T9TCI4.JPG
24.fil=C:\Program Files\Netscape\Users\me\Cache\M140MJPC.GIF
25.fil=C:\Program Files\Netscape\Users\me\Cache\M15U96GF.GIF
26.fil=C:\Program Files\Netscape\Users\me\Cache\M1AGPPI9.GIF
27.fil=C:\Program Files\Netscape\Users\me\Cache\M1KB2R25.GIF
28.fil=C:\Program Files\Netscape\Users\me\Cache\M1MT69AJ.GIF
```

Information Saved by snAppShot

snAppShot is able to determine what changes have been made during an installation or upgrade, by saving information before and after and then determining the differences. Installations and upgrades can change many different files and settings on a workstation, so snAppShot saves many different types of information about the configuration of the workstation.

The following sections describe things that snAppShot stores before and after an installation or upgrade, and then uses to determine changes to the workstation.

Files and Folders

First, snAppShot saves a list of all files that were added or modified during the installation or upgrade. It also saves a copy of the file named as a .FIL file to be used in later installations or upgrades.

.INI Files

snAppShot also saves any changes to application or system .INI files, so that those files can be modified when the application object is used later. Following are some of the files that snAppShot monitors for changes:

- WIN.INI — This file contains information about the Windows workstation setup, such as desktop settings, file types, and so on.
- SYSTEM.INI — This file contains information about device and driver settings for the Windows workstation.
- PROTOCOL.INI — This file contains information about the network settings for the Windows network protocols.

System Configuration Text Files

snAppShot will record any changes to system configuration text files as well. That way, any changes to drivers being loaded, paths being set, or environment variables being added or changed will be recorded and can be applied to other systems when the application object is used to install or upgrade the workstation.

The following are the two files that snAppShot monitors for system configuration changes:

- AUTOEXEC.BAT
- CONFIG.SYS

Windows Shortcuts

Any changes to Windows shortcuts are also recorded by snAppShot. Therefore, if an application installation or upgrade adds a new shortcut to the desktop or Start menu, or modifies the path in an existing shortcut, those changes will be applied to other systems as well, when the application object is applied to them.

Registry

snAppShot is also able to record any changes made to a Windows workstation's registry by an installation or upgrade. This is extremely important later on, because even if you copy all files installed by an installation or upgrade and make the appropriate changes to configuration files, the application will often fail to run because registry settings have not been made.

Using snAppShot fixes that problem by saving the changes to the registry, and then applying them when the application object is used to install or upgrade the application on a new workstation.

Advanced Features of snAppShot

Although snAppShot is a relatively easy program to run, there are some advanced features that make it an extremely powerful tool. This section discusses advanced features included in the snAppShot utility.

Using snAppShot Preferences

If you think of snAppShot as a camera, and of the .AOT file as the output "picture," then you can think of snAppShot preferences as the adjustments you make to a camera (aperture settings, film speed, focus) before you take the picture.

snAppShot preferences let you control what snAppShot "sees" when it discovers the changes made to a workstation as a result of installing an application. In other words, during an installation or upgrade, you can specify or control information recorded about the items described in the following sections.

Files/Folders

Using snAppShot preferences, you can include or exclude particular changes to particular folders and files from being recorded. This enables you to protect certain directories you do not wish to be disturbed on other workstations when the application object is used on them to install or upgrade an application.

Windows Shortcuts

Using snAppShot preferences, you can exclude particular Windows shortcut files from being recorded. This enables you to protect certain application shortcuts from being created or altered on other workstations when the application object is used on them to install or upgrade an application.

.INI Files

Using snAppShot preferences, you can exclude particular application .INI files from being recorded. This enables you to protect application .INI files from being created or altered on other workstations when the application object is used on them to install or upgrade an application.

System Configuration Files

Using snAppShot preferences, you can define which system configuration file changes will be recorded. This enables you to indicate which system configuration changes should be recorded and created or altered on other workstations when the application object is used on them to install or upgrade an application.

Registry Entries

Using snAppShot preferences, you can also include or exclude changes from particular portions of the Windows registry from being recorded. This enables you to protect certain areas of the Windows registry that you do not wish to be altered on other workstations when the application object is used on them to install or upgrade an application.

Special Macros

Special macros are built-in machine- and user-specific values that the snAppShot utility can use to control how application object templates are created. These special macros, read from the registry, allow for the customization of application objects in snAppShot. This customization enables you to distribute the same application to several machines that may have Windows installed or configured differently.

The following is a list of some common macros:

- ▸ WinDir — Directory containing the windows OS; typically C:\Windows or C:\WINNT

- ▸ WinSysDir — Directory containing the windows system files (DLLs)

- ▸ TempDir — Windows temporary directory; typically C:\Windows\temp

- ▸ Favorites — File system directory that serves as a common repository for the user's favorite items

- ▸ Fonts — Virtual folder containing system fonts

- ▸ Personal — File system directory that serves as a common repository for personal documents

NOTE The online help that appears when you click the Help button on the application object macros property page, in NWAdmin, gives a detailed list and explanations of the macros available to snAppShot.

When snAppShot starts, it asks the client library for a list of the special macros. This list, combined with the user macros (created in the Custom mode), make up the complete list of macros, which are then ordered from the longest value to the shortest.

When snAppShot is running, it records the differences between the preinstallation scan and the second scan. It then creates an entry in the .AOT file, during which snAppShot calls the routine that searches and replaces data with the macro's name. Later, when the application launcher is used to distribute the object, it gets the macro values from the .AOT file.

The application launcher receives the values and names for these special macros by looking in the registry under the key:

```
HKEY_CURRENT_USER
+Software
+Microsoft
+Windows
+CurrentVersion
+Explorer
+Shell Folders
```

The application launcher client creates a special macro using the name and value.

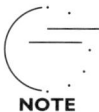

NOTE If the value does not exist, then the special macro is returned and the data value is set to blank.

Let's say that a special macro is defined for a directory containing temporary files. The entry in the Windows registry would appear as:

```
HKEY_CURRENT_USER
+Software
+Microsoft
+Windows
```

```
+CurrentVersion

+Explorer

+Shell Folders

TempDir=C:\DATA\TEMP
```

This registry entry would correspond to the special macro:

```
%*TempDir%
```

Therefore, when snAppShot adds the creation information for the registry entry in the .AOT or .AXT file, it writes an entry similar to the following:

```
[Registry Value Create]

Type=String

Flag=Write Always

Key=HKEY_CURRENT_USER\Software\Microsoft\Windows\Current
Version\Explorer\SHell

Folders

Name=TempDir

Value=%*TempDir%
```

When the application launcher tries to distribute the settings, it sees the special macro value, and in an attempt to set this registry key, tries to read the value from this exact registry key.

If the registry value was set before the application is distributed, this works beautifully; however, if the value is not set until the application is distributed, then the application launcher will try to use data from the same registry entry it is trying to create.

This problem can be remedied in two ways:

1. The first way to resolve this problem is to set the registry value before the user clicks the icon (perhaps using ZENworks workstation policies, discussed later in this book). Then, when the application launcher client reads the data for these special macros, it reads the correct value and knows how to replace the special macro correctly.

2. The second and better (though more difficult) solution is to manually edit the .AXT file created for the application object template. Instead of using the macro you are trying to create, add in an additional entry with a different macro name but the same value.

Partial Install Detection

If your application needs to reboot the workstation to finish the installation, snAppShot recognizes this and picks up where it left off before the reboot. All snAppShot data is stored in a hidden directory on the C: drive. Furthermore, snAppShot is automatically run after the machine is restarted. When snAppShot restarts, it will detect a partial installation; a window will pop up, and you will be allowed to continue with the previous installation.

Limitations of snAppShot

Now that you know how snAppShot works, and understand some of its advanced features, you need to know its limitations. snAppShot is a very powerful tool; however, it cannot be used for the tasks described in the following sections.

Capture Install Logic

snAppShot is unable to capture the "logic" of an installation involving choices based on existing hardware, software, or other settings. For example, if the application's Setup program installs a particular video driver or modem setting file to a workstation, these settings may not be valid when transferred to another workstation.

Guarantee Impact on All Workstations

Although snAppShot can be used to install or upgrade applications on all workstations, it cannot guarantee the impact that the application install or upgrade will have on all workstations.

Image Entire Workstation

snAppShot is designed to record changes made by a single application install; therefore, it cannot image an entire workstation for disaster recovery purposes. When snAppShot discovers a workstation, it only saves certain information about the files, such as the date, time, and size of the files. It does not save a copy of all the files on the workstation.

Using snAppShot

Once you are familiar with when and why to use the snAppShot utility and some of its advanced features, you are ready to begin using it to create application objects. When you start snAppShot, you will see a screen similar to the one in Figure 4.3.

F I G U R E   4.3   *Main menu in the snAppShot utility, which enables the user to select which discovery mode to use*

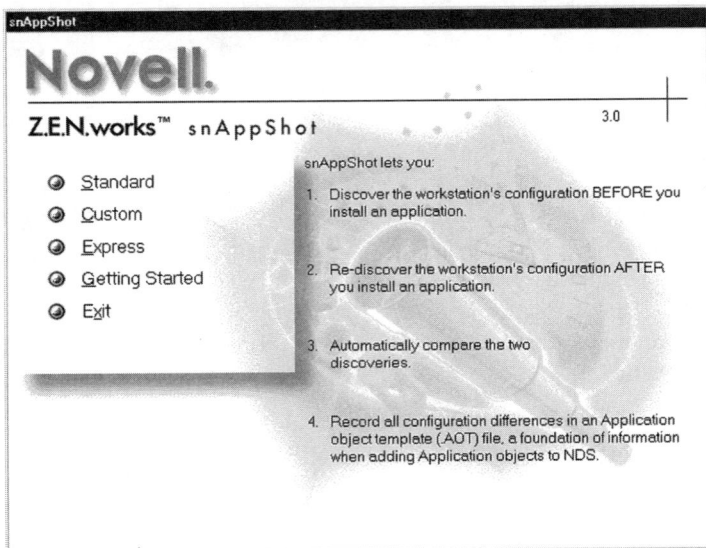

This is the startup screen for snAppShot, which enables you to select one of the following four options, depending on your needs and whether you have already have a preference file ready.

Standard

You should use the Standard Mode in snAppShot to discover the application installation changes on a workstation using default settings. If you have never run snAppShot before and are unfamiliar with the available settings, this is the best option. It will require little intervention.

To use the Standard Mode simply select it and perform the following operations to create the needed files

Name the Application Object Icon Title

Once you select the Standard Mode installation from the main screen in snAppShot, a window similar to the one shown in Figure 4.4 is displayed. From this screen, you need to input the name that the application object will have in the NDS tree, and a title for the icon that represents the application object.

NOTE

We recommend that you choose names for the object and its icon that are descriptive enough to distinguish which application it is, and often which version. This will save confusion and time later on.

FIGURE 4.4 *Naming the application object and the application's icon*

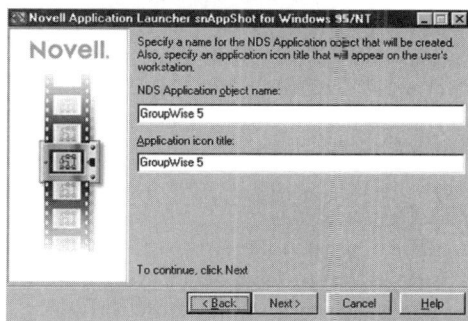

Specify the Network Location of the Application Source (.FIL) Files

Once you have set the name for the application object and the title for its icon in the Standard Mode install, a screen similar to the one in Figure 4.5 enables you to set the network location to store the application source files (.FIL).

When setting this location, you should remember the following:

1. Make sure you select a location that all users who must use the application object will have access to.

2. Make sure there is enough disk space in the network location that you set to store the entire application.

F I G U R E 4.5

snAppShot window that enables the user to specify the location to store the application source files

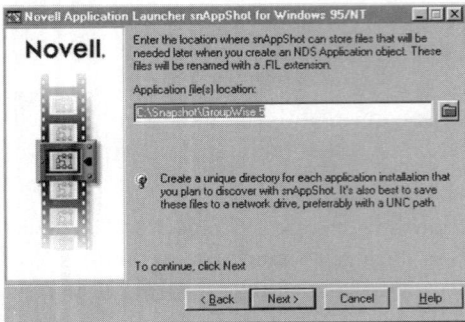

Specify the Network Location of the Application Template (.AOT and .AXT) Files

Once you have specified a network location for the .FIL files, snAppShot enables you to set a network location for the application template (.AOT and .AXT files). Set the network location either by entering it into the text window, or by clicking the folder button and navigating to the appropriate directory.

Specify the Drives That Will Be Discovered

Once you have selected the network location in which to store the application object support files, you are given the option to select which disk drive to scan on the workstation to determine changes, as shown in Figure 4.6.

You can add drives to the list by clicking the Add button and selecting the drives you wish to scan. Conversely, you can remove drives from the list by selecting the drive and then clicking the Remove button.

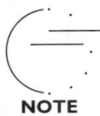

NOTE

You will be able to select network drives as well; however, you can only do this if they are mapped. This enables you to install applications to a larger network drive if needed, and still discover the changes.

F I G U R E   4 . 6 *Specifying which disk drives, network and local, will be scanned during discovery*

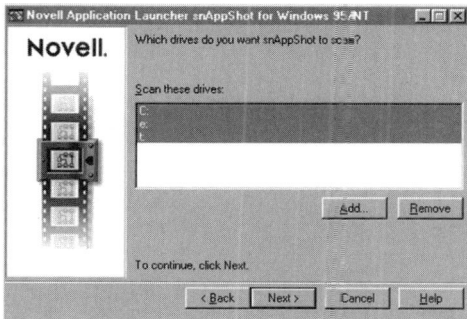

> **NOTE**
> Make sure you select all drives that the application install or upgrade will affect. If you do not select a drive and the application install or upgrade adds, removes, or modifies files on that drive, the changes will not be discovered.

Read the Pre-discovery Summary to Check Settings

Once you have added all the drives you wish to the list of drives to be scanned, click Next and a summary of the preferences is displayed in the next window, as shown in Figure 4.7. The information displayed includes:

- ► Application Object Name
- ► Application Icon Title
- ► Template Filename
- ► Application Files Directory
- ► Snapshots Working Drive
- ► Scan Options
- ► Disks to Scan
- ► Directories to Exclude
- ► Files to Exclude
- ► System Text Files to Scan

snAppShot window that allows review of the summary of the current preference setting before starting the first discovery

NOTE

Click Save Settings to save the snAppShot preferences you have defined thus far to a file. Later, during a similar snAppShot session, you can choose the preferences you save now to accelerate the process.

Run the First snAppShot Discovery

The first snAppShot discovery is run when you click Next from the preference summary window. A screen will show the status of the discovery and a count of the following items that have been discovered:

- Folders and files
- Windows shortcuts
- .INI files
- System configuration files
- Registry entries

Run Application's Installation or Upgrade

Once the first snAppShot discovery is completed, a Run Application Install button is available. When you select the Run Application Install button, a file pop-up menu appears, and you can navigate to the application install executable and execute it.

Once the application install is complete, you can continue on with the discovery process of the snAppShot application.

> Write down where the installation program installs the application's executable file. This will be useful later on when you're creating and distributing the application object.
>
> **NOTE**

Enter the Path to the Application's Executable

Once you have completed the application install, snAppShot gives you the option to specify a path to the application's executable on this workstation. You can enter the location of the installed application files on this workstation in the text field.

Of course, if you do not want snAppShot to set a target distribution location, then leave this field blank and continue.

Run the Second snAppShot Discovery

Once you are finished setting the path to the applications executable, click the Next button, and snAppShot will run the second discover. Once again, you will be able to monitor the status of the discovery by noting the count of the following items:

- Folders and files
- Windows shortcuts
- .INI files
- System configuration files
- Registry entries

Once the discovery is finished, snAppShot will begin generating an object template. This is where the actual differences between the two discoveries are discerned and the template files are created.

> Depending on the number of folders, files, and registry entries on your workstation, the second discovery process can take a considerable amount of time. However, both the discovery and the template generation screens have status counters to let you know how far along they are.
>
> **NOTE**

Read the Completion Summary

Once the second snAppShot discovery is completed and the template files are generated, a completion summary of what took place is displayed in the window shown in Figure 4.8. The completion summary contains information about the application template creation, including:

► The location of the new application object template (.AOT)

► The location of the new .FIL files

► The location of the textual version of the application object template (.AXT)

► Listing of the steps to take to create the application object

► Statistical totals from the second discovery

► Statistical totals from entries added to the application object template (.AOT)

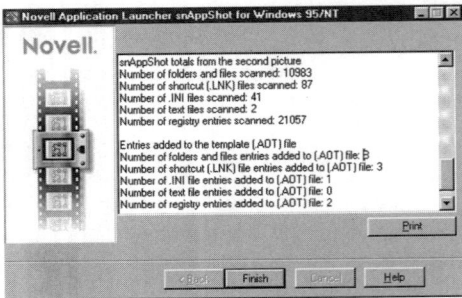

F I G U R E   4 . 8   *snAppShot window that enables the user to review the summary of the application object template generation*

> You have the option from this window to print out the summary. We recommend doing so, and keeping the summary as a record to aid in troubleshooting future problems if they occur.
>
> **NOTE**

Custom

You should use the Custom Mode in snAppShot to set specific options when discovering the application installation or upgrade changes on a workstation. Custom Mode is much like Standard Mode, only it gives you the added opportunity to specify the drives, files, folders, Registry hives, and shortcuts you want to include or exclude in the discovery process. You can save these settings in a preferences file for later use, in case you need to run snAppShot for a similarly configured application.

Only in Custom Mode are you able to see and use all of snAppShot's features. To use the Custom Mode simply select it and perform the following operations to create the needed files:

1. Choose the snAppShot preferences file.

2. Name the application object and icon title.

3. Specify the network location of the application source (.FIL) files.

4. Specify the network location of the application template (.AOT and .AXT) files.

5. Specify which parts of the workstation to include or exclude.

6. Specify the drives that will be discovered.

7. Read the pre-discovery summary.

8. Run the first snAppShot discovery.

9. Run the application's installation or upgrade.

10. Specify how to handle the creation of files, folders, .INI file entries, and registry settings.

11. Enter the path to the application's executable file.

12. Define macros for distribution automation.

13. Run the second snAppShot discovery.

14. Read the completion summary.

Choose the snAppShot Preferences File

The first window that comes up after you select the custom mode in snAppShot enables you to choose snAppShot preferences. From this window, you have the option of either using a previously saved preference file or using the snAppShot default settings.

If you have previously created and saved a preference file in a previous custom mode, you can navigate to that file or enter the path to it in the text field, as shown in Figure 4.9.

Name the Application Object and Icon Title

Once you select the preference file option in express mode in snAppShot, a window is displayed. From this screen, you need to input the name that the application object will have in the NDS tree and a title for the icon that represents the application object.

► · · · · · · · · · · · · · · · · · ◄

FIGURE 4.9 *Specifying a pre-created preference file or using the default settings*

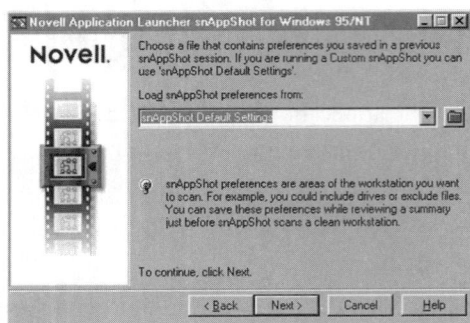

Specify the Network Location of the Application Source (.FIL) Files

Once you have set the name for the application object and title for its icon in the Standard Mode install, a screen enables you to set the network location to store the application source files (.FIL).

When setting this location, you should remember the following:

1. Make sure you select a location that all users who must use the application object will have access to.

2. Make sure there is enough disk space in the network location that you set to store the entire application.

Specify the Network Location of the Application Template (.AOT and .AXT) Files

Once you have specified a network location for the .FIL files, snAppShot enables you to set a network location for the application template (.AOT and .AXT files). Set the network location either by entering it into the text window, or by clicking the folder button and navigating to the appropriate directory.

> If files already exist with the same object name, you are given the option of whether or not to overwrite the older ones.

NOTE

Specify Which Parts of the Workstation to Include or Exclude

Once you have selected the network location in which to store the application object support files, you are given the option to select which of the following parts of the workstation you wish to include or exclude, as shown in Figure 4.10.

► . . . . ◄

F I G U R E   4 . 1 0 *Specifying which parts of the workstation to include or exclude*

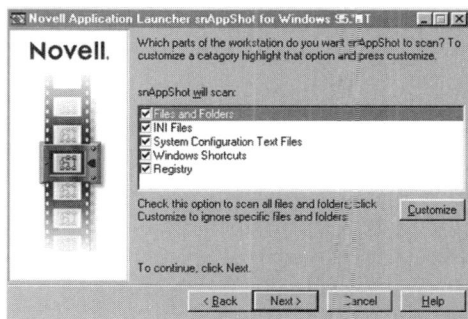

Files and Folders   From the workstation scan customization menu in snAppShot, you can modify which files and folders you wish to include or exclude. Simply select the Files and Folders option and click the Customize button. A window similar to the one in Figure 4.11 pops up, and you can select which files and folders to ignore.

► . . . . ◄

F I G U R E   4 . 1 1 *Specifying which files and folders will be created in the application object template*

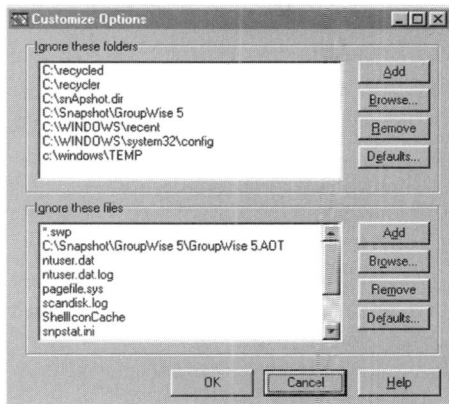

Wild Cards are completely valid here. Therefore, if you wish to exclude all .DAT files, you could specify *.DAT in the list of files to ignore.

.INI Files   From the workstation scan customization menu in snAppShot, you can modify which .INI files to exclude. Simply select the .INI Files option and click the Customize button. A window pops up and you can select which .INI files to ignore.

System Configuration Text Files   From the workstation scan customization menu in snAppShot, you can modify which system configuration text files you wish to include in the scan. Simply select the System Configuration Text Files option and click the Customize button. A window similar to the one in Figure 4.12 pops up and you can select which system configuration text files you wish to include.

F I G U R E   4 . 1 2   *snAppShot window that enables the user to specify which system configuration files will be created in the application object template*

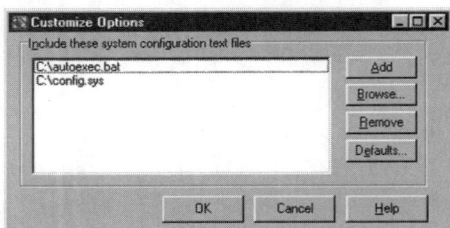

Windows Shortcuts   From the workstation scan customization menu in snAppShot, you can modify which Windows shortcuts to exclude. Simply select the Windows Shortcuts option and click the Customize button. A window pops up and you can select which Windows shortcuts to ignore.

Registry   From the workstation scan customization menu in snAppShot, you can modify which registry hives you wish to include or exclude. Simply select the Registry option and click the Customize button. A window similar to the one in Figure 4.13 pops up and you can select and deselect from a list of hives to include.

Indicating which Windows registry hives will be created in the application object template

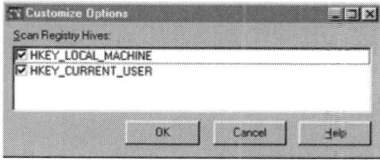

Specify the Drives That Will Be Discovered

Once you have specified which parts of the workstation to include or exclude, you are given the option to select which disk drive to scan on the workstation to determine changes.

You can add drives to the list by clicking the Add button and selecting the drives you wish to scan. Conversely, you can remove drives from the list by selecting the drive and then clicking the Remove button.

NOTE You will be able to select network drives as well, but only if they are mapped. This allows you to install applications to a larger network drive if needed, and still discover the changes.

Read the Pre-discovery Summary

Once you have all the drives you wish to select added to the list of drives to be scanned, click Next, and a summary of the preferences is displayed in the next window. The information displayed includes:

▶ Application object name

▶ Application icon title

▶ Template filename

▶ Application files directory

▶ Snapshots working drive

▶ Scan options

▶ Disks to scan

▶ Directories to exclude

▶ Files to exclude

▶ System text files to scan

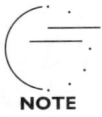

> **NOTE**
> Click Save Settings to save the snAppShot preferences you have defined thus far to a file. Later, during a similar snAppShot session, you can choose the preferences you save now to accelerate the process.

Run the First snAppShot Discovery

The first snAppShot discover is run when you click Next from the preference summary window. A screen shows the status of the discovery and a count of the following items that have been discovered:

- ▶ Folders and files
- ▶ Windows shortcuts
- ▶ .INI files
- ▶ System configuration files
- ▶ Registry entries

Run the Application's Installation or Upgrade

Once the first snAppShot discovery is completed, a Run Application Install button is available. When you select the Run Application Install button, a file pop-up menu appears, and you can navigate to the application install executable and execute it.

Once the application install is complete, you can continue on with the discovery process of the snAppShot application.

> **NOTE**
> Write down where the installation program installs the application's executable file. It will be useful later on when you create and distribute the application object.

Specify How to Handle the Creation of Files, Folders, .INI File Entries, and Registry Settings

Once the application's installation or upgrade is complete, snAppShot lets you specify how to handle the creation of entries for the application object. From the screen shown in Figure 4.14, you can set the addition criteria for the following entries.

Specifying how snAppShot will handle the creation of file, folder, .INI file, and registry entries in the application object template

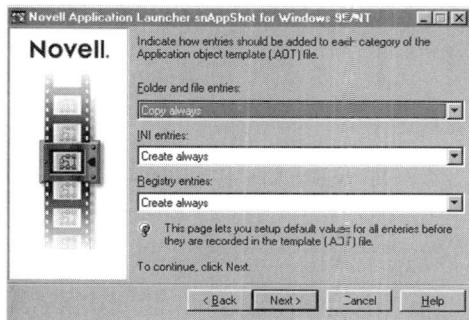

Folder and File Entries From the application object entry addition window in snAppShot, you can configure whether or not files and folders will be added to the application object by clicking the down arrow under the Folder and file entries option and selecting one of the following addition criteria, as shown in Figure 4.15:

- ► Copy always
- ► Copy if exists
- ► Copy if does not exist
- ► Copy if newer
- ► Copy if newer and exists
- ► Request confirmation
- ► Copy if newer version

.INI Files From the application object entry addition window in snAppShot, you can configure whether or not .INI files will be added to the application object by clicking the down arrow under the .INI entries option and selecting one of the following addition criteria, as shown in Figure 4.16:

- ► Create always
- ► Create if does not exist
- ► Create if exists
- ► Create or add to existing section

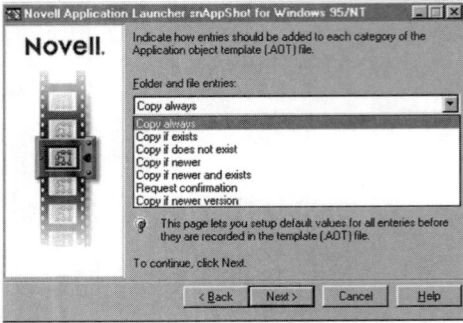

FIGURE 4.15 *snAppShot window that enables the user to specify how snAppShot will handle the creation of file and folder entries in the application object template*

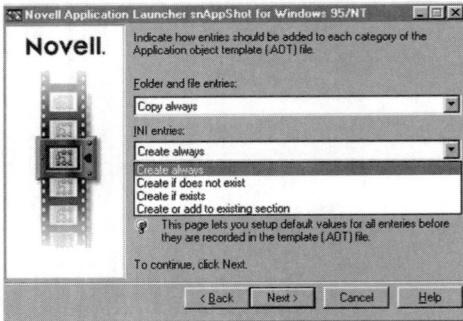

FIGURE 4.16 *Indicating how snAppShot will handle the creation of .INI file entries in the application object template*

Registry Entries From the application object entry addition window in snAppShot, you can configure whether or not registry entries will be added to the application object by clicking the down arrow under the registry entries option and selecting one of the following addition criteria, as shown in Figure 4.17:

- ► Create always
- ► Create if does not exist
- ► Create if exists

FIGURE 4.17   snAppShot window that enables the user to specify how
snAppShot will handle the creation of registry entries in the
application object template

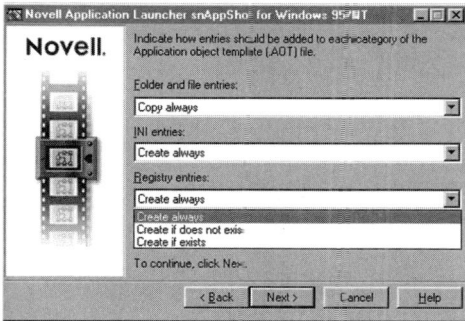

Enter the Path to the Application's Executable File

Once you have defined the addition criteria for entries into the application object, snAppShot gives you the option to specify a path to the application's executable on this workstation. You can enter the location of the installed application files on this workstation in the text field.

Of course, if you do not want snAppShot to set a target distribution location, then leave this field blank and continue.

Define Macros for Distribution Automation

Once you've finished setting the path to the applications executable, click the Next button, and you are given the option to define macros to control the distribution of application objects. A screen similar to the one shown in Figure 4.18 enables you to add, edit, or remove macros to control automation of application distribution.

When you click the Add button in the macro definition window, you are given the option to specify a variable name and a string that it will be replaced with in the template data, as shown in Figure 4.19.

F I G U R E   4.18 *snAppShot window that enables the user to add, edit, and remove macros to be used in the application object template*

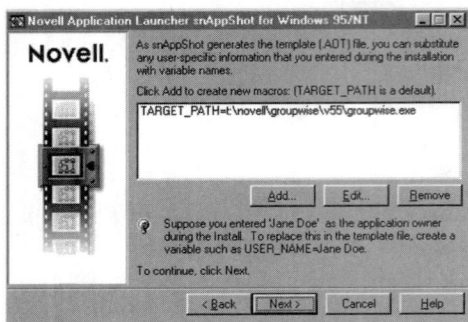

F I G U R E   4.19 *Specifying a variable name and string in macros*

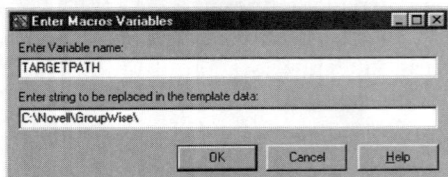

Run the Second snAppShot Discovery

When you've finished defining macros to automate application object distribution, click Next, and snAppShot will run the second discover. Once again, you can monitor the status of the discovery by noting the count of the following items:

- ► Folders and files
- ► Windows shortcuts
- ► .INI files
- ► System configuration files
- ► Registry entries

Once the discovery is finished, snAppShot begins generating an object template. This is where the actual differences between the two discoveries are discerned and the template files created.

Read the Completion Summary

Once the second snAppShot discovery is completed and the template files generated, a completion summary of what took place is displayed. The completion summary contains information about the application template creation, including:

- The location of the new application object template (.AOT)

- The location of the new .FIL files

- The location of the textual version of the application object template (.AXT)

- Listing of the steps to take to create the application object

- Statistical totals from the second discovery

- Statistical totals from entries added to the application object template (.AOT)

Express

You should use Express Mode when you've already saved a snAppShot preferences file from a previous discovery process. By choosing this file, you can skip over most of the Standard or Custom Mode settings, which enables you to discover a new application installation much more quickly and in Standard or Custom Mode.

To use the Express Mode, simply select it and perform the following operations to create the needed files.

Choose the snAppShot Preferences File from a Previous snAppShot Session

The first window that comes up after you select the Express Mode in snAppShot is the Choose snAppShot Preferences window. From this window, you have the option of using a previously saved preference file.

If you have previously created and saved a preference file in a previous custom mode, you can navigate to that file or enter the path to it into the text. If you have not previously created and saved a preference file, you must do so before selecting the Express Mode.

Read Summary Page to Verify snAppShot Discovery Settings

Once you have selected a preference file from a previous application package, click Next, and a summary of the preferences is displayed in the next window. The information displayed includes:

- ► Application object name
- ► Application icon title
- ► Template filename
- ► Application files directory
- ► Snapshots working drive
- ► Scan options
- ► Disks to scan
- ► Directories to exclude
- ► Files to exclude
- ► System text files to scan

Run the First snAppShot Discovery

The first snAppShot discovery is run when you click Next from the preference summary window. A screen shows the status of the discovery and a count of the following items that have been discovered:

- ► Folders and files
- ► Windows shortcuts
- ► INI files
- ► System configuration files
- ► Registry entries

Run Application's Installation Program

When the first snAppShot discovery is completed, a Run Application Install button will be available. When you select the Run Application Install button, a file pop-up menu appears, and you can navigate to the application install executable and execute it.

Run the Second snAppShot Discovery

When the application install or upgrade is finished, click Next, and snAppShot runs the second discovery. Once again, you can monitor the status of the discovery by noting the count statistics of the following:

- Folders and files
- Windows shortcuts
- .INI files
- System configuration files
- Registry entries

Once the discovery is finished, snAppShot will begin generating an object. This is where the actual differences between the two discoveries are discerned and the template files created.

Read the Completion Summary

When the second snAppShot discovery is completed and the template files are generated, a completion summary of what took place is displayed. The completion summary contains information about the application template creation, including:

- The location of the new application object template (.AOT)
- The location of the new .FIL files
- The location of the textual version of the application object template (.AOT)
- Listing of the steps to take to create the application object
- Statistical totals from the second discovery
- Statistical totals from entries added to the application object template (.AOT)

Super Express (Command Line) Mode

You should use the Super Express (Command Line) Mode to discover changes to a workstation in the fastest possible way. The Super Express Mode of snAppShot enables you to run snAppShot from a command prompt, which allows you to discover changes to a workstation faster than the other available modes.

To use this mode of snAppShot, which you do exclusively from the command line, you must use a preference file from a previous snAppShot session. To use the Super Express Mode, simply select it and perform the operations in the following sections to create the needed files.

Change to the Directory Where snAppShot Is Located

The first step for using the Super Express (Command Line) Mode in snAppShot is to enter DOS and change to the directory where the snAppShot utility is located.

Enter the snAppShot Command

Once you are in the directory of the snapshot utility, enter the following command from the DOS prompt:

```
snapshot /u:<filename>
```

where `<filename>` is the name of a snAppShot preferences file that you defined and saved earlier when running snAppShot in Custom or Express Mode.

Specify Whether To Overwrite a Previous snAppShot Discovery

Once you have executed the snapshot command from the DOS session, a window appears and gives you the option to overwrite the existing application object template, as shown in Figure 4.20. You must select Yes to continue.

F I G U R E   4 . 2 0   *snAppShot window that enables the user to overwrite the previous snAppShot discovery when using the Super Express Mode*

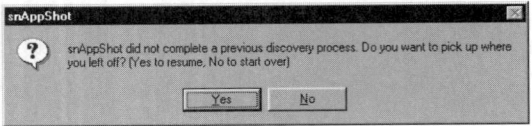

When you select Yes, the application object template creation continues the same as in the regular Express Mode, by displaying the pre-discovery summary screen, followed by the first discovery.

CHAPTER 5

Creating and Using Application Objects

Now that you have an understanding from Chapter 4 of how to create an application object template, we need to discuss how to use that template to create an actual application object and distribute it to users. This chapter covers the following main points to consider in the process of application object creation and distribution:

▶ Creating the application object

▶ Setting properties for the application object

▶ Setting up application distribution

▶ Distributing the application

Creating the Application Object

The fist step in using ZENworks to distribute applications to users is creating an application object. The application object is an actual object in the NDS tree. ZENworks uses this object to distribute the application to users based on the properties with which the object is created. This section guides you through creating an application object using the following three methods: with an .AOT or .AXT file, without an .AOT or .AXT file, and by simply duplicating an existing application object.

> **NOTE**
> Because it greatly simplifies the setup, distribution, and management of applications on users' workstations, we highly recommend starting with an .AOT or .AXT file, or duplicating an existing application object. You can create .AOT and .AXT files using snAppShot, which is a component of Application Launcher.

With an .AOT or .AXT File

Creating an application object with a .AOT or .AXT file is usually done to create more complex application objects — that is, objects that make changes to registry settings, .INI files, text configuration files, and so on.

An example of when to use an .AOT or .AXT file would be the Netscape Communicator application object template we created in Chapter 4. Installing Netscape caused several changes to be made to the registry, and modified existing .INI files. Therefore, it is better to use a template to create the Netscape Communicator object.

To use an .AOT or .AXT template file to create an application object, perform the following steps:

1. Open NWAdmin32. Browse the NDS tree and right-click the container in which you wish to install the application object. Then select Create.

2. From the Create menu, select Application. This launches the Create Application Object Wizard.

3. From the Create Application Object Wizard, select Create an Application object with an .AOT/.AXT file, and then select Next (see Figure 5.1).

FIGURE 5.1 *The Create Application Object Wizard showing the creation options*

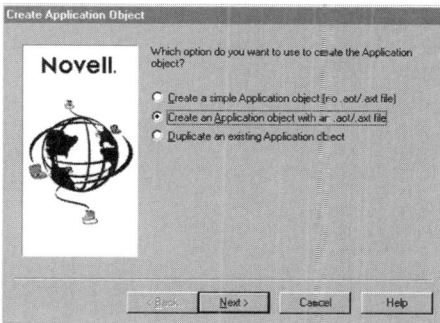

4. Browse for the .AOT or .AXT file, select it, and then click Open. A window appears, displaying the path to the .AOT or .AXT file. From this window, click Next.

5. Type the object name of the Application object in the Object Name text box.

6. Check (and change, if necessary) the target and source directories of the Application object as shown in Figure 5.2, and then click Next.

7. Review the information about the Application object (click the Back button to make any changes).

FIGURE 5.2   *The target and source directories*

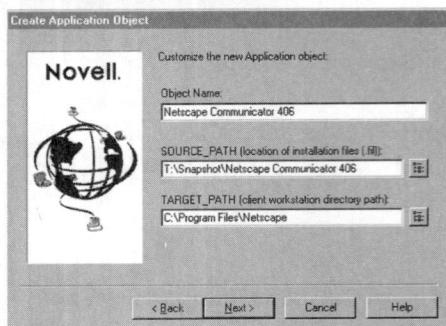

8. You have the option to select Display Details After Creation to access the property pages of this Application object. This is recommended to ensure that the application object was correctly created.

9. You also have the option to select Create Another Application Object After This One if you want to create another after finishing with the current one.

10. Once you have made your selections from this window, click Finish and the application object is created.

Without an .AOT or .AXT File

Creating an application object without an .AOT or .AXT file is usually done to create simple Application objects that do not make any changes to registry settings, such as .INI files, text configuration files, and so on.

A good example of when to create an application object without an .AOT or .AXT file is creating an Application object for a corporate calendar program. Many corporations have small, home-grown calendar applications that contain information specific to their business. These programs rarely modify the registry or change system .INI files, and therefore are great candidates for this option.

To use an .AOT or .AXT template file to create an application object, perform the following steps:

1. Open NWAdmin32.Browse the NDS tree and right-click the container in which you wish to install the application object. Then select Create.

2. From the Create menu, select Application. This launches the Create Application Object Wizard.

3. From the Create Application Object Wizard, choose Create a simple Application Object (no .AOT/.AXT file), and then choose Next.

4. From this window, type the name of the application object in the Object Name dialog box.

5. Use the Browse button to specify the location of the executable in the path to executable text box.

6. You have the option to select Display Details After Creation to access the property pages of this Application object. This is recommended to ensure that the Application object was correctly created.

7. You can also select Create Another Application Object After This One if you want to create another after finishing with the current one.

8. Once you have made your selections from this window, click Finish and the application object is created.

Duplicating an Existing Application Object

You should use the Duplicate an existing Application object option when the object you wish to create has already been created, but you wish to create another to allow for different properties and distribution options.

A good example of when to use the Duplicate an existing Application object option would be if you are setting up application fault tolerance and need several nearly identical Application objects. The quickest way to accomplish this is to create the primary Application object, and then create as many duplicate Application objects as needed. You can then adjust each duplicate Application object as necessary — for example, specify different application source (.FIL) locations for each.

To use the duplicate of an existing Application object method to create an Application object, follow these steps:

1. Open NWAdmin32. Browse the NDS tree and right-click the container in which you wish to install the application object. Then select Create.

2. From the Create menu, select Application. This launches the Create Application Object Wizard.

3. From the Create Application Object Wizard, choose Duplicate an existing Application object, and then click Next.

4. From this window, browse the NDS tree and identify the reference Application object by its Distinguished Name. Once the reference application is selected, click Next.

5. Specify a custom source path (where the .FIL files are stored) and target path (where the files are copied during a distribution, usually a workstation's C: drive).

6. Review the new, duplicated Application object's summary and click Back to make changes.

7. You have the option to select Display Details After Creation to access the property pages of this Application object. This is recommended to ensure that the Application object was correctly created.

8. You can also select Create Another Application Object After This One if you want to create another after finishing with the current one.

9. Once you have made your selections from this window, click Finish and the application object is created.

Setting Properties for the Application Object

Once you have created the Application object, you need to set the Application object's properties to define how it will behave. This section covers using NWAdmin32 to set up the application object's executable and define the distribution properties for the application object, and then covers some of the more advanced (optional) settings available for the application object.

Setting Up the Application Object Executable

The first step in setting up the application object in NWAdmin32 is to access the Identification property page to control the application icon that the user sees at the workstation. To do this, follow these steps:

1. Right-click the Application object and click Details.

2. Click the Identification button.

3. Change the Identification properties as needed, as shown in Figure 5.3, and then click OK.

. . . . ◄

F I G U R E   5.3 *The application property page in NWAdmin*

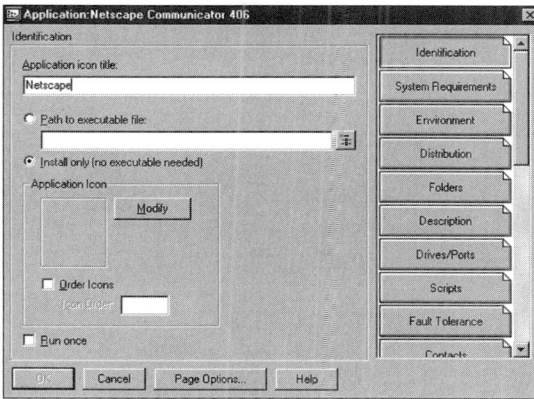

From the Application object's Identification property page, you should perform the functions in the following sections.

Name Application Icon Title

First, set the name of the application in the Application icon title box. The application icon title, which is mandatory, can be different from the Application object name (the name that NDS uses to identify the application) and may contain periods and other special characters. You can also use the Description property page for longer descriptions of the application.

Set Path to Executable File

Next, set the path in the Path to executable file text box to the executable that is to be run when an Application object icon is double-clicked in Application Launcher or Application Explorer. Use the Browse button to browse the file directory structure to find the executable you want. UNC pathnames are permitted. For example:

- ► `server\volume:path`
- ► `\\server\volume\path`
- ► `volume_object_name:path`
- ► `directory_map_object_name:path`
- ► `driveletter:\path`

NOTE

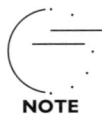

If you don't want to run an application (for example, this Application object's purpose might be to simply update some files on the workstation), use the Install Only option and do not specify a path.

Install Only (No Executable Needed)

If you just want users to install an application but not run it, you should check the Install Only option. An example of this would be if the Application object's purpose is to simply update some files on the workstation. When you select the Install Only option, the software is installed but not run.

Specify Application Icon

Next, you should use the Application Icon option to assign an icon for the Application object. The icon you choose appears in Application Launcher or Application Explorer, depending on what you have specified on the Applications property page. If you do not specify an icon, a default Application Launcher icon is used.

TIP

If icon titles do not appear in their entirety, you may need to increase your icon spacing. Do this using Windows. After you have adjusted the icon spacing in Windows, exit Application Launcher or Application Explorer and restart for the changes to take effect. You can also use the Description property page for longer descriptions of the application.

Order Application Icons and Force Run Sequence

From this window, you also have the options to set the order icons and set the force run sequence. These options perform two very useful functions. First, they organize the icons in Application Launcher and Application Explorer. Second, they dictate the order in which Application objects that are set to force run will run.

To set ordering, enter a numeric value into the Icon Order text box. All Application objects you wish to order must have a numeric value. The value of zero gives the icon the highest priority and thus the highest prominence in the list. The maximum value is 999. If you do not order Application objects, they will be ordered alphabetically (the default order).

For example, suppose you have ten icons (applications A, B, C, D, E, F, G, H, I, and J) that you want to organize in Application Launcher. You specify an order number of 0 for application G, 1 for application F, 2 for application E, and 3 for application D. You specify an order number of 4 for applications C, B, H, and I. You do not order the remaining applications, A and J.

The result is that the first four applications will be ordered with G being the first in the list, followed by F, E, and D. After that, applications C, B, H, and I will be gathered together and arranged alphabetically. The last two icons, A and J, come at the end of the list and will be arranged alphabetically (the default order).

If users (who have been associated with these Application objects) run Application Launcher, they will see a list of icons according to this order. If these applications have all been set to force run, they will run in this order as soon as Application Launcher has loaded itself into the memory.

> **NOTE** Ordered and force run applications will run in sequential order without waiting for the last force run application to terminate.

Run Applications Once

The final option you have from the object Identification properties window is to set the Run once option. This will run the application once and then remove the icon from the workstation.

You should select this option when an Application object's purpose is to install software to a workstation. It can be confusing and annoying to users if an install icon remains in the Application Launcher window or in Application Explorer after the software has already been installed

> **NOTE** If you selected Run once and also specified a version stamp for this application, the application runs once until the next time you change the version stamp, whereupon the application runs once more. This latter method is useful for upgrading applications.

Setting Up Application Distribution Options

Once you have set up the application object's executable, the second step in setting up the Application object in NWAdmin32 is to access the Distribution property page to control the distribution of the application:

1. Right-click the Application object and click Details.

2. Click the Distribution button, and a screen similar to the one in Figure 5.4 is displayed.

▶ • ◀

F I G U R E 5 . 4 *The Distribution property page*

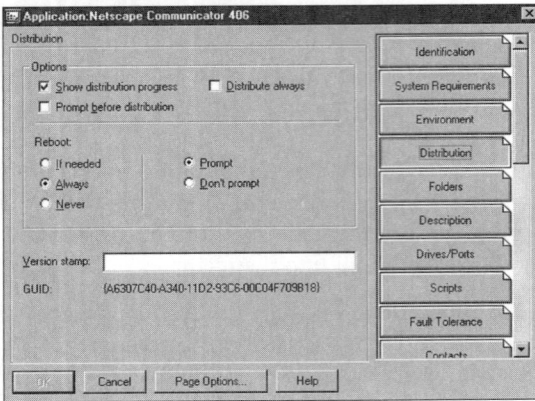

From the application object's Distribution property page, you should perform the functions covered in the following sections.

Show Distribution Progress to Users

First, use the Show distribution progress option to determine whether or not an easy-to-read progress bar is displayed to users the first time they distribute an application to their workstations.

> **TIP** Turn off this option if you are distributing only a small change to the application, such as a registry modification. Turn it on if you are distributing a large application and want to give the user a general idea of how long to expect the distribution to take. This option is on by default.

Prompt User Before Distribution

Next, use the Prompt before distribution option to display a message to users after they have clicked an Application Launcher-distributed application for the first time. This message asks them to confirm if they want to distribute the application to their workstation. This option is turned off by default.

> **TIP** To better inform users, the text that you write in the Application object's Description property page appears in this distribution confirmation dialog box. For example, you may write a note to the user such as "This is an essential application for your workstation

that will take approximately ten minutes to distribute. Please answer Yes to distribute it now."

Distribute Always

Use the Distribute always option to force a distribution of the entire Application object every time the user runs the application or the application is set for a force run on the workstation (see the user or container object's Applications property page). This option is useful to ensure that all application settings are updated every time the application runs.

You can also update settings on a case-by-case basis. For example, if you want to always distribute a particular registry key and value, you can set the Distribute always option on the Registry Settings property page for that particular key and value. The Distribute Always option on the Distribution property page overrides the Distribute always option on the Registry Settings, .INI Settings, Application Files, Icons/Shortcuts, and Text Files property pages.

Prompt User for Reboot

Next, use the options in the Reboot group box to control how a workstation reboot should occur according to the following options:

▶ If Needed — The If needed option (the default setting) will only prompt for reboot if Application Launcher or Application Explorer needs to make changes that cannot occur while Windows is running (such as replacing open DLLs).

▶ Always — The Always option prompts the user to reboot every time a distribution takes place.

▶ Never — The Never option does not prompt the user to reboot. In this case, the changes take effect the next time the workstation reboots.

Use Version Stamp to Trigger Redistribution

Use the Version stamp option to trigger a redistribution of the application. A version stamp is simply a text string representing the version of the application that is used to the customize the Application object's GUID. In fact, any change you make to the version stamp is like changing the GUID.

NOTE

The version stamp may or may not have anything to do with the actual version of the software. It is a tool to help you upgrade applications. It helps you control the version of the Application Launcher-delivered application.

If the Run once option on the Identification property page is checked, and you change the version stamp, the Run once option causes the application to run again once. This is useful when upgrading application software to a new or different version.

For example, suppose you purchased new application software and want to update an Application object. By changing the version stamp number and selecting the Run once option, the application runs once after installation even though a previous version may have already run once.

View Application's GUID (Globally Unique Identification)

Finally, you have the option to view the application's GUID, which is stamped in the workstation's registry when ZENworks distributes an application to a workstation. The GUID is a randomly generated number for tracking, such as: {5A0511440-77C5-11D1-A663-00A024264C3E}. This is the GUID for one Application object.

> **TIP**
> Use GUIDs to track and troubleshoot distributed applications. For example, if you want to ensure that a particular application has been distributed to a workstation, you can compare the GUID as recorded in the Application object's Distribution property page with the GUID that is currently stamped in the workstation's registry.

You can find Application object GUIDs in the Windows registry by browsing to the following location:

```
HKEY_LOCAL_MACHINE
    SOFTWARE
        NetWare
        NAL
            1.0
                Distribute
                    <treename>
```

Click the GUID to see the Application object's Distinguished Name (DN) among the registry values. Note that GUIDs can be stamped on a per-user and per-workstation basis. You can make several application objects use the same GUID by using the Synchronize Distributed GUIDs option on the Tools ⇨ Application Launcher Tools menu. This is useful if you are distributing a suite of applications. You can also "regenerate" or "re-randomize" the GUIDs for those same applications.

Changing (Optional) Application Object Settings

Once you have set up the application object executable and defined distribution, you have the option of defining several advanced application object settings. This section discusses the advanced settings available, including: Grant File Rights, Set System Requirements, Schedule Availability, Set Description for Users, Set Termination Behavior, Modify Application Files, Modify Icons and Shortcuts, Modify .INI Settings, Modify Registry Setting, and Modify Text Files.

Grant File Rights

The first advanced option available for application objects is the capability to use the File Rights property page to grant rights to files, directories, and volumes. This is used when this Application object is associated with a User object or with a Group, Organizational Unit, Organization, or Country object with which the user is already associated.

To grant file rights to users when an application object is associated with them, use the following procedure:

1. Right-click the Application object.

2. Click the File Rights button.

3. Click Add and specify the volume or directory to which users will need access when they run the Application object.

4. Highlight the volume or directory and specify Supervisor, Read, Write, Create, Erase, Modify, File Scan, and Access Control rights as necessary, then click OK.

5. Click OK, and then associate this Application object with a User, Group, Organizational Unit, Organization, or Country object to grant the rights.

Set System Requirements

The next advanced option available for application objects is the capability to use the System Requirements property page as a filter to display application icons only on workstations that meet certain criteria that you specify. You can use filters such as the specific version of an operating system, the amount of RAM, or free disk space. If workstations do not meet the criteria you specify, the icons do not appear on that workstation.

For example, suppose you want a word processing application icon to appear only on Windows 95 workstations that have at least 32MB of RAM, a Pentium processor, and 500MB of free disk space on the C: drive. Using the following options on the System Requirements property page, you can filter the workstations that will see and run the application object icon from the system requirements screen shown in Figure 5.5.

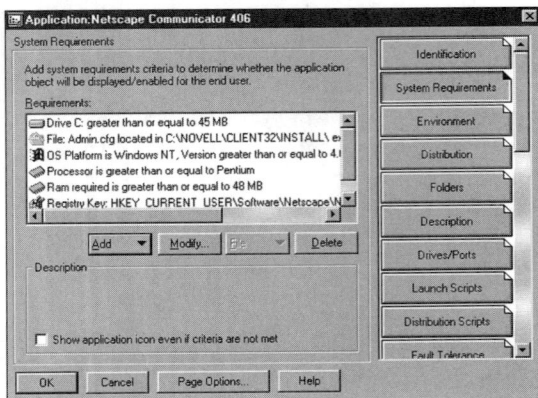

F I G U R E   5.5   *The system requirements property page for Application objects*

Display Applications on a Particular Operating System   The system requirements tab for application objects enables you to filter applications based on the operating system installed on the client. To filter workstations by operating system, click the Add button from the system requirements screen and then select Operating System from the pop-up menu. A screen similar to the one in Figure 5.6 appears. From this screen, first select the desired Windows platform. Next, you have the option of specifying a specific version of the operating system by specifying a version number as well as one of the following logical requirements:

- ► Less than
- ► Less than or equal to
- ► Equal to
- ► Greater than or equal to
- ► Greater than

The operating system requirements box from the system requirements property page for Application objects

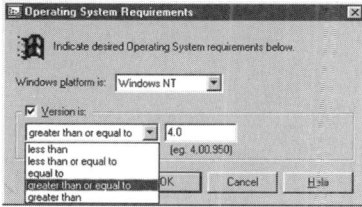

An example of when to use the operating system option would be if you create an application object for an application that will run only on Windows NT 4.0 or later workstations. You can specify that specific criteria by selecting Windows NT, clicking the Version is box, and then typing 4.0 in the version text box. Then select the greater than or equal to option.

Memory   The system requirements tab for Application objects enables you to filter applications based on the amount of memory installed on the client. To filter workstations by memory installed, click the Add button from the system requirements screen and then select Memory from the pop-up menu. A screen similar to the one in Figure 5.7 appears. From this screen, first type in the MB of RAM needed to install and run the application. Next, you have the option of specifying one of the following logical requirements:

- ▶ Less than
- ▶ Less than or equal to
- ▶ Equal to
- ▶ Greater than or equal to
- ▶ Greater than

An example of when to use this option would be if the application requires 8MB of RAM — then you enter 8 in this text box. The application object will not appear on workstations that do not have at least 8MB of RAM.

F I G U R E   5.7 *The Memory Requirements box from the system requirements property page for application*

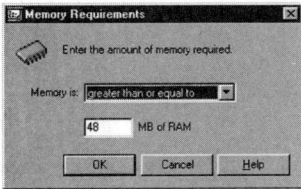

> *This field is valid only for Windows 95 and Windows NT workstations (Windows 3.x is ignored). Use it by entering the minimum amount of total installed RAM that the workstation must have in order to see and run this application.*
>
> **NOTE**

Processor   The system requirements tab for application objects enables you to filter applications based on the speed of the processor installed on the client. To filter workstations by processor, click the Add button from the system requirements screen and then select Processor from the pop-up menu. A screen similar to the one in Figure 5.8 appears. From this screen, first select the minimum processor needed to install and run the application from the following list:

- ▶ 386
- ▶ 486
- ▶ Pentium
- ▶ Pentium Pro
- ▶ Pentium II
- ▶ Pentium III

Next, you have the option of specifying one of the following logical requirements:

- ▶ Less than
- ▶ Less than or equal to
- ▶ Equal to
- ▶ Greater than or equal to
- ▶ Greater than

FIGURE 5.8 *The Processor Requirements box from the system requirements property page for application objects*

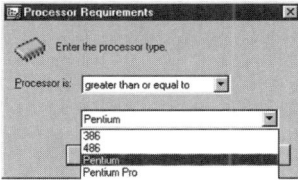

NOTE The Windows 3.x Application Programming Interface does not return values higher than 486. Therefore, if Application Launcher queries the processor type of a Windows 3.x workstation using a Pentium processor, Windows 3.x returns "486." In other words, even if you select the Pentium processor type for the Processor option, the application is displayed on 486 workstations running Windows 3.x.

Free Disk Space The System Requirements tab for application objects enables you to filter applications based on the amount of free disk space available to the client. You can filter disk space on local drives and mapped network drives, as well as the following specific locations:

- Windows system directory drive
- Windows directory drive
- Temp directory drive

To filter workstations by disk space available, click the Add button from the system requirements screen and then select Disk Space from the pop-up menu. A screen similar to the one in Figure 5.9 appears. From this screen, first select the location in which disk space is needed from the top drop-down list. Next, type in the MB of disk space needed to install and run the application. Then you have the option of specifying one of the following logical requirements:

- Less than
- Less than or equal to
- Equal to
- Greater than or equal to
- Greater than

The memory requirements box from the system requirements property page for application objects

You can specify multiple locations that require disk space by performing the same steps again.

An example of when to use this is when the application requires a minimum of 20MB free on the Windows directory drive, 10MB free on the Temp drive, and 80MB free on the D: drive. You can specify these settings, and the application object icon will only appear on workstations that contain enough free disk space in all three locations.

Environment Variables   The system requirements tab for application objects allows you to filter applications based on specific environment variable settings on the client. To filter workstations by environment variables, click the Add button from the system requirements screen and then select Environment Vars from the pop-up menu. A screen similar to the one in Figure 5.10 appears. From this screen, first type in the name of the variable and then type in the expected value.

The environment variable box from the system requirements property page for application objects

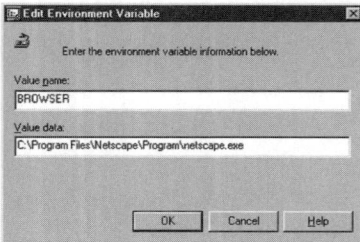

You can specify multiple environment variables to check for before displaying and installing the application, by following the same process again.

An example of when to use this is if some users use Netscape as their browser and some use Internet Explorer. If you only wanted users that used Netscape to receive the Netscape object, you could set up a browser environment variable on the workstations and then specify that variable be present from the system requirements property page.

Registry Entries The System Requirements tab for application objects enables you to filter applications based on specific Windows registry settings on the client. To filter workstations by registry settings, click the Add button from the system requirements screen and then select Registry from the pop-up menu. A screen similar to the one in Figure 5.11 appears. From this screen, first navigate the registry to find the specific registry key to filter on. Then you have the option to filter based on the following criteria:

▶ Key exists — Filter in if the key exists in the registry, by selecting this radial button.

▶ Key does not exist — Filter in if the key does not exist in the registry, by selecting this radial button.

▶ Value — You can check the value box and then indicate a specific value that is associated with the key.

▶ Value exists — If the value box is checked, then you can specify to filter the application in only if a value does exist for the selected key.

▶ Value does not exist — If the value box is checked, then you can specify to filter the application in only if a value does not already exist for the selected key.

▶ Data — If the value box is checked, a value is typed in, and the value exists option is set, then you can check the data box and specify a specific data sequence to associate with the value. You have the option of selecting whether the value equals or does not equal the data you specify.

You can specify multiple environment variables to check for before displaying and installing the application by following the same process again.

FIGURE 5.11
*The registry settings box from the system requirements
property page for application objects*

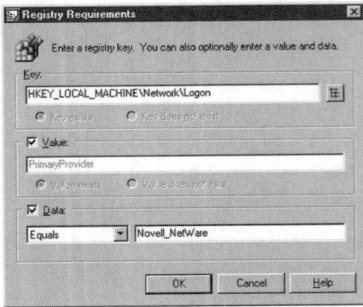

Files The System Requirements tab for application objects enables you to filter applications based on specific files installed on the client. To filter workstations by files, click the Add button from the system requirements screen and select Files from the pop-up menu. Then select one of the following filtering options:

▶ File Existence — The file existence option provides a window with two text boxes that enable you to specify the name and location of the file to filter on. At the bottom are two radial buttons that enable you to specify whether to filter if the file exists or does not exist.

▶ File Version — The file existence option provides a window with two text boxes that enable you to specify the name and location of the file to filter on. At the bottom of this window, you can input a specific version number to filter on, as well as the following logical operations: less than, less than or equal to, greater than, greater than or equal to, and equal to.

▶ File Date — The file existence option provides a window with two text boxes that enable you to specify the name and location of the file to filter on. At the bottom you can indicate a specific date for the file based on one of the following: before, on or before, on, on or after, and after.

Applications The system requirements tab for Application objects enables you to filter applications based on the existence of other applications on the client. To filter workstations by installed applications, click the Add button from the system requirements screen and then select Application from the pop-up menu. A window is displayed, allowing you to navigate the directory services tree to find specific applications that should or should not exist.

To filter on a specific application, simply navigate to that application in the NDS tree and select it. Click either the Application object exists option or the Application object does not exist option. You will want to use this option if an application is dependent on the existence of another one.

Schedule Availability

Another very useful advanced setting for application objects is to schedule the availability of the application object. You can use the Schedule property page to control when the application icon is available or when the users can install software.

This feature depends on the settings you have set up on the Launcher Configuration property page on a User, Workstation, Organizational Unit, Organization, or Country object. You should be aware of those settings before trying to set up scheduling for the Application object.

A good example of how to use the advanced feature is if you want to force run a virus detection application on users' workstations at a certain time, and only one time. You can force users to run the virus check by scheduling the appearance of the application using the Schedule property page, and designating the application as Force Run (see the Launcher Configuration property page).

> **Scheduling cannot deny access to an application outside of the schedule because file rights may still exist.**
>
> **NOTE**

To schedule application availability, use the following method:

1. Right-click the Application object and click Details.
2. Click the Schedule button.
3. From the Set schedule in drop-down list, select either Range of Days or Specified.

Set Schedule by Range of Days You can set a schedule by specifying a range of days to make the application available, as shown in Figure 5.12. An example would be if you select a start date of January 2, 1999 and an end date of January 9, 1999 with a start time of 8:00 a.m. and an end time of 5:00 p.m. The Application object icon would be visible to workstations from January 2nd at 8:00 a.m. until January 8th at 5:00 p.m.

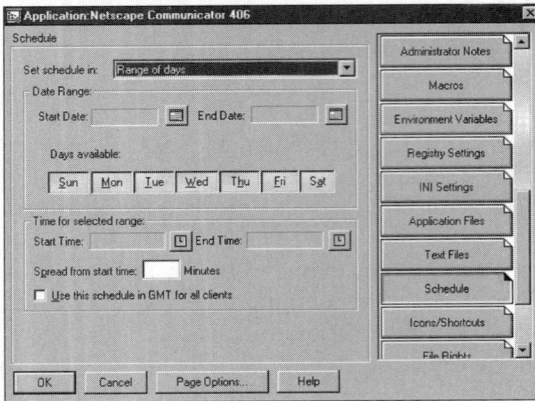

Another way to use the range of days option is to make applications available only on certain days of the week within a given range of dates. You do so by combining start and end dates and times with the Days available buttons.

For example, suppose you select the dates January 2, 1999, February 2, 1999, March 2, 1999, and May 2, 1999, and start and end times of 8:00 a.m. and 5:00 p.m. You also select the Tuesday and Thursday buttons. This combination makes applications available on all Tuesdays and Thursdays that fall within in the given date. Applications will be available on Tuesdays and Thursdays beginning at 8:00 a.m. until 5:00 p.m.

Set Schedule by Specified Days   You can also schedule application availability by selecting the Specified days option, as shown in Figure 5.13. This enables you to select specific dates during which you want the application to be available.

The application is only visible to users on the specific dates and times you indicate in this option. For example, if you select the dates January 2, 1999, February 2, 1999, March 2, 1999, and May 2, 1998, and start and end times of 8:00 a.m. and 5:00 p.m., this makes the application available from 8:00 a.m. to 5:00 p.m. on each of the days selected. The application is not available on any other days or at any other time. You select no more than 350 specific dates for this option.

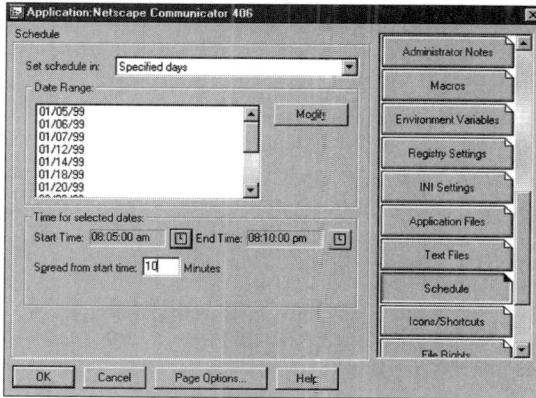

NOTE When scheduling applications, you can also force them to run at the scheduled time (in addition to merely displaying them). Because the Force Run option is available on a per-association basis, you must select it from the Applications property page located on a User, Group, Organization, or Organizational Unit object. If the association is not set up for a Force Run, the application icon is displayed according to the location specified by the association.

Spread from Start Time   You also have the option to specify a spread of time in which the application will become available to users. This is useful if you don't want all users to run the application at the same time for fear of bringing down the network because of the load and traffic. The spread option literally "spreads out" user access times over the number of minutes specified so they don't all run the application at once.

An example of how to use the spread from start time option is to set it to 120 minutes, so the application becomes available, on a random basis, between the hours of 10:00 a.m. and 12 noon. This spreads out the demand for the application over a longer period of time, and network traffic is minimized.

NOTE If users access applications after the spread time is expired but before the end time of the Application object, they access the application at that time and the spread variable has no effect.

GMT (Greenwich Mean Time) The final option you have available for the scheduling pages is to specify that all application scheduling you do with the Application property page is based on the workstation's time zone.

In other words, if your network spans different time zones and you schedule an application to run at 4:00 p.m., it would normally run at 4:00 p.m. in each time zone. If you select the GMT checkbox, however, workstations will run applications at the same time worldwide (according to GMT)—although you should be aware that the GMT time is not available if you are filtering out days of the week when in the Specified days mode.

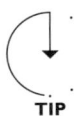

TIP Windows 3.x clients do not use a time zone concept. The only way Windows 3.x clients can use a time zone is if it is set in their environment. You can do this by placing the following command in the autoexec.bat file or login script: SET TZ=<TIMEZONE> (i.e. MST7DST for Mountain Daylight Savings).

Set Description for Users

Another advanced setting available for application objects is the capability to use the Description property page to give users more complete information than the application icon caption allows. Once the description is set, users can right-click an Application object in Application Launcher or Application Explorer to see details containing both the descriptive name of the application and the more lengthy description that you provide here.

An example of when to use the description option for application objects is if you have additional information that users need about the application, such as new features that are available.

NOTE The text you type in the Description property page is the same text the user sees if you have enabled the Prompt User Before Distribution option on the Distribution property page.

To create a description of the application, use the following method:

1. Right-click the application and click Details.

2. Click the Description button.

3. Write a description as needed and then click OK, as shown in Figure 5.14.

The description property page for application objects

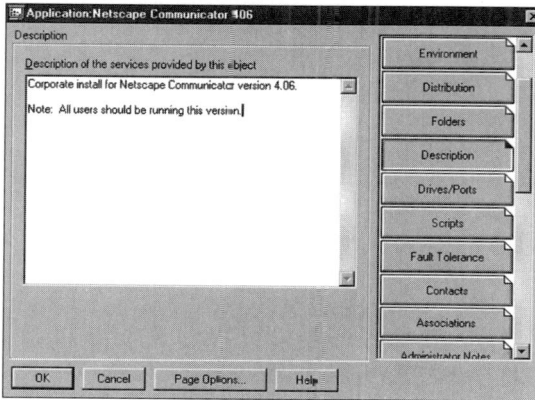

Set Termination Behavior

Another advanced setting available for application objects is the capability to determine the application termination behavior of the application on the workstation. Once the application has been executed at the workstation, you can specify the behavior associated with terminating the application.

To create a description of the application object, use the following method:

1. Right-click the application and click Details.

2. Click the Termination button, and a screen similar to the one in Figure 5.15 is displayed.

3. Select one of the following options as required, and then click OK.

None This option (the default) enables users to close the application on their own at will.

Send message to close application This option prompts users, at a specified interval, to close the application on their own, until the application closes by itself. For example, if you set an interval of five minutes, ZENworks will send a message (if one is active) to the user every five minutes until the application is closed.

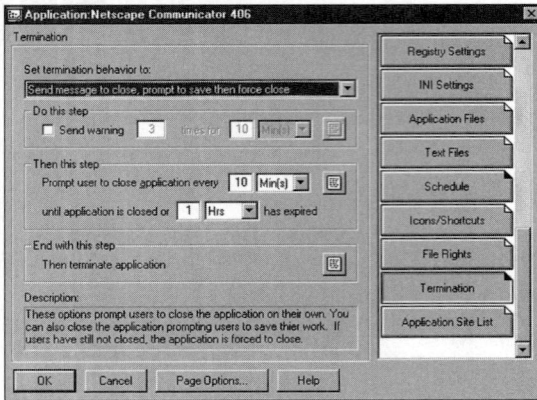

To set this option:

1. Specify the time interval in the text boxes provided.

2. Click the message button, and then click Use default to use the default system message.

3. Click Use custom, and then type the message you want your users to see.

4. Click None to send no message.

5. Click OK.

Send message to close then prompt to save data   This option allows users a specified period of time to close the application on their own (this action is optional). When that period of time expires, the Application Launcher will attempt to close the application. If users have not saved data, they will be prompted to save it. Users can choose not to close the application. If users have no unsaved data, the application will close. Once the application has closed, users will not be able to re-open it.

To set this option:

1. Select the checkbox next to Send warning, and specify the interval and period in the text boxes provided (optional). If you want to specify a custom message, click the message button and write one.

2. In the next group box, specify the time interval in the text boxes provided. If you want to specify a custom message for this action, click the message button and write one.

3. Click OK.

Send message to close, prompt to save, then force close   This option will prompt users, for a specified period of time, to close the application on their own. When that period of time expires, ZENworks can close the application after prompting users, at specified intervals, to save their work. If users have still not closed within a specified period of time, the application is forced to close. To set this option:

1. Select the checkbox next to Send warning, and specify the interval and period in the text boxes provided (optional). If you want to specify a custom message, click the message button and write one.

2. In the next group box, specify the message time interval and period in the text boxes provided. If you want to specify a custom message for this action, click the message button and write one.

3. In the last group box, click the message button and write a note to users explaining why the application terminated, and perhaps indicating when it will be available again.

4. Choose OK.

Send message to close then force close with explanation   This option will prompt users, for a specified period of time, to close the application on their own. When that period of time expires, the application is forced to close. To set this option:

1. Select the checkbox next to Send warning, and specify the interval and period in the text boxes provided (optional). If you want to specify a custom message, click the message button and write one.

2. In the last group box, click the message button and write a note to users explaining why the application terminated, and perhaps indicating when it will be available again.

3. Click OK.

Modify Application Files
Another advanced setting for application objects is the use of the Application Files property page to add, change, or delete application files and directories. You can also import new template information about files and

directories. This lets you instruct the Application object about what to do with the files and directories when the application distributes.

> **NOTE**
> If this is an Application object that has been distributed previously, note that before changes on this property page go into effect, you must change the version stamp value on the Distribution property page. Changing the version stamp value signals Application Launcher to redistribute the application.

To access the Application Files property page:

1. Right-click the Application object and click Details.
2. Click the Application Files button.
3. Once you are at the Application Files property page, you have the option of performing the following functions, as shown in Figure 5.16:
   - Add a file for consideration
   - Add a directory for consideration
   - Set a file as shared
   - Remove a file or folder from consideration
   - Import files and directory templates
   - Find a file or directory

► . . . . ◄

F I G U R E 5.16 *The application files property page for application objects*

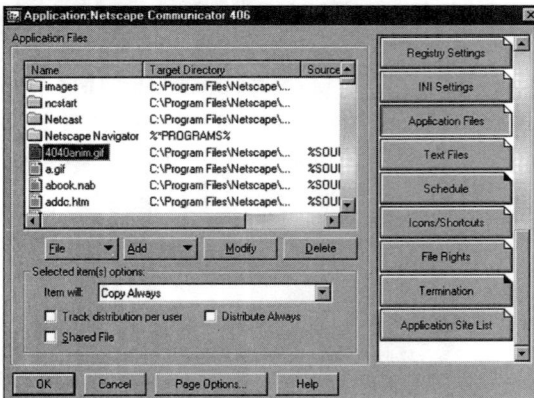

Modify Icons and Shortcuts

Another advanced setting for application objects is the use of the Icons/Shortcuts property page. This enables you to add, change, or delete the Program Groups, Program Group Items, and Explorer shortcut icons that appear in Program Manager (Windows 3.x) and Windows Explorer (Windows 95 and Windows NT 4.x) when the application distributes to workstations.

An example of when to modify the icons and shortcuts for an application object would be when using special icons for *all* applications that users run on their workstations. Using the Icons/Shortcuts property page for this Application object, you can change icons of other applications that may or may not have anything to do with this Application object.

NOTE If this Application object has been distributed previously, note that before changes on this property page go into effect, you must change the version stamp value on the Distribution property page. Changing the version stamp value signals Application Launcher to redistribute the application.

To access the Icons/Shortcuts property page:

1. Right-click the Application object and click Details.

2. Click the Icons/Shortcuts button.

3. Once you are at the Icons/Shortcuts property page, you can easily add, change, or delete specific icons, as shown in Figure 5.17. For example, if you need to adjust or even upgrade an application and icons are affected, you can reinstall the application, capture the changes in an Application object template (.AOT or .AXT) file using snAppShot, and then import that template into the Icons/Shortcuts property page.

Modify .INI Settings

Another advanced setting for application objects is the use of the INI Settings property page to add, change, and delete .INI files, sections, and values when the Application object distributes to the workstation. Not only can you order the changes within the .INI file, you can also import or export .INI files and settings using the .AOT or .AXT file format or the standard .INI file format.

► • ◄

F I G U R E   5.17   *The Icons/Shortcuts property page for application objects*

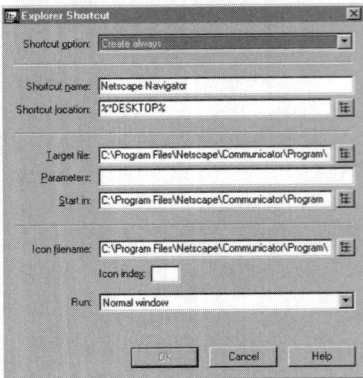

NOTE   Before changes on this property page go into effect, you must change the version stamp value on the Distribution property page. Changing the version stamp value signals Application Launcher to redistribute the application.

To access the INI Settings property page:

1. Right-click the Application object and click Details.

2. Click the INI Settings button.

3. Once at the INI Settings property page, you have the option of performing the following changes to the application object, as shown in Figure 5.18:

- Add an .INI setting for consideration
- Remove an .INI setting from consideration
- Modify an .INI setting
- Import and export .INI settings
- Find .INI settings

Modify Registry Setting

Another advanced setting for application objects is the use of the Registry Settings property page to add, change, and delete registry keys and values when the Application object distributes to the workstation. Several registry types are supported, including binary format, default strings, DWORD values, Expand Strings (REG_EXPAND_SZ), and Multi-Value Strings (REG_MULTI_SZ). You can import and export registry settings, either as .AOT or .AXT files, or using the standard registry (.REG) format.

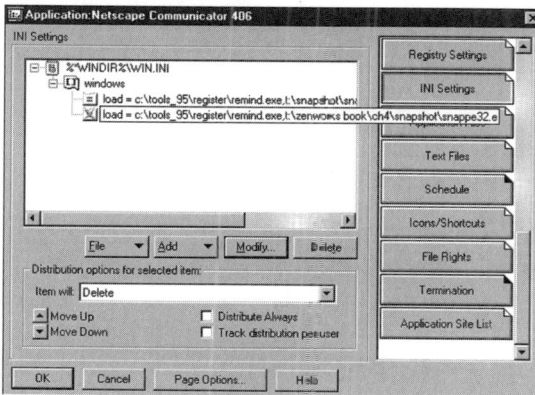

Before changes on this property page go into effect, you must change the version stamp value on the Distribution property page. Changing the version stamp value signals Application Launcher to redistribute the application.

NOTE

To access the Registry Settings property page:

1. Right-click the Application object and click Details.

2. Click the Registry Settings button.

3. Once at the Registry Settings property page, you have the option of performing the following changes to the application object:

   - Add a registry setting for consideration

   - Remove a registry setting from consideration

   - Modify a registry setting

   - Import and export registry settings

   - Find registry settings

F I G U R E 5.19 *The Registry Settings property page for application objects*

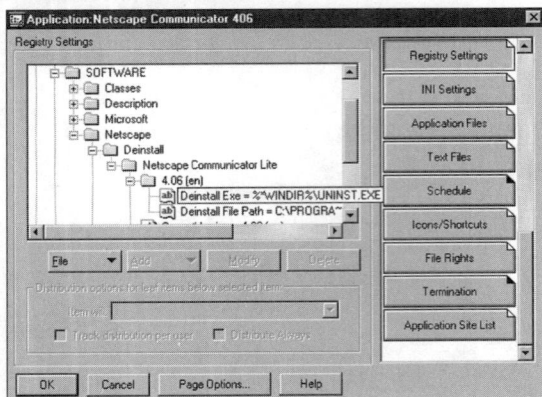

Modify Text Files

Another advanced setting for application objects is the use of the Text Files property page to add, change, or delete workstation text files (such as CONFIG.SYS and AUTOEXEC.BAT).

An example of when to use the Text Files properties page to modify the application object would be if users are experiencing problems due to an incorrect text string found in their workstation's CONFIG.SYS file. Rather than visit and change each workstation or run the risk of users incorrectly and inconsistently implementing a change, you can set up a text file that finds, deletes, modifies, or adds text strings to the text file of your choice. The text file implements the changes the next time the application runs.

> **NOTE**
>
> If this Application object has been distributed previously, note that before changes on this property page go into effect, you must change the version stamp value on the Distribution property page. Changing the version stamp value signals Application Launcher to redistribute the application.

To access the Text Files property page:

1. Right-click the Application object and click Details.
2. Click the Text Files button.

3. Once at the Text Files property page, you have the option of performing the following changes to the application object:

- Add a text file for consideration
- Add a text file setting for consideration
- Remove text files and settings from consideration
- Modify a text file in template
- Import text file templates
- No reboot needed if text file modified

NOTE

If you set the Prompt user for reboot setting on the Distribution property page to Always, that setting overrides the setting you make here.

Application Distribution Reporting

Another advanced feature ZENworks has introduced is application distribution reporting. When an application is distributed to the workstation, the application launcher will record whether the application was properly distributed. A successful distribution is recorded as well as any errors with the distribution. If any errors occurs, this will be recorded along with the reasons for the failure in the distribution.

This record of distribution will be recorded on a local file, and will also result in an event being sent to the centralized database that is also used for hardware and software inventory. These distributions can be set up through the Reporting property page in NWAdmin.

To access the Reporting property page:

1. Right-click the Application object and click Details.

2. Click the Reporting button.

3. Once at the Reporting property page, you have the option of performing the following changes to the application object, as shown in Figure 5.20:

- Enable Reporting — Select the Enable Reporting box to enable distribution reporting for the application object.
- Specifying the location of the log file — Select the Log File Path Box and specify a location in the text box to the location where reporting should log events.

- Enabling SNMP Traps — Select the Send SNMP Traps box if you wish to use ManageWise to be notified of application distribution events.

- Specifying Events to Report — In the Events to report section you have the option to report the following events: Launch Success, Launch Failure, Distribution Success, Distribution Failure, Filtering (Icon Hidden), and Filtering (Icon Shown).

F I G U R E 5.20 *The Reporting property page for application objects*

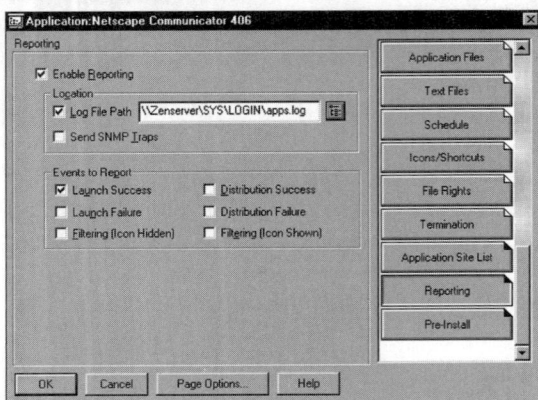

Setting Up Application Distribution

Once you have set up the properties for the application object, you need to set up the application distribution environment. This section covers using NWAdmin32 to set up application users to receive applications, application foldering, and automating application objects.

Setting Up Application Foldering

The first step in setting up the application environment is to set up application foldering. ZENworks offers powerful foldering capabilities that enable users to organize the applications you deliver to them with Application Launcher.

These folders appear in the Application Launcher and the Application Explorer browser view, as well as on the Start menu.

NOTE If two folders have the same name, their contents are merged together.

The following sections describe the four types of folders available to users in Application Launcher.

Application Folder Object

An Application Folder object is an independent object to which you associate Application objects. By linking many Application objects to one Application Folder object, you can manage the folder pathnames of many Application objects from one object. See the section "Create Application Folder Object and Associate with Application Objects" later in this chapter for more information.

Custom Folder

Custom folders are set up on the Application object's Folders property page and thus belong exclusively to the Application object. A custom folder cannot be shared with another Application object. You can name custom folders any way you please and set up folders within folders (subfoldering). Custom folders override any System folders that may exist as the result of Application-object-to-container associations. See the section "Create Custom Folders for Application Object" in this chapter for more information.

Personal Folder

Personal folders let users create and name their own folders and place Application Launcher-delivered applications in them. See the section "Enable Users to Create Personal Folders" in this chapter for more information.

System Folder

System folders appear in Application Launcher or Explorer when you associate an Application object with a User, Group, Organizational Unit, or Organization, or Country object, and you have not created any custom folders for that Application object or associated the Application object with a linked folder.

To set up application foldering to manage application objects, you need to perform the tasks described in the following sections.

Create Custom Folders for Application Object

The first step in setting up application foldering is to use the Folders property page to create custom folders in which to organize application objects. A custom folder is tied to one Application object. Using custom folders, you can achieve *subfoldering*, or placing folders within folders.

TIP

Suppose you have created a Folder object that contains several folders that are linked to several Application objects. You now would like to clear these folder-application links and start over. You could delete the Folder object, which converts all the linked folders to custom folders, which are then saved in all the relevant Application objects. In this case, you would have to open each Application object and delete the custom folders in them. A quicker method is to delete the folders and the linkages to Application objects from the Folder object, but not delete the Folder object itself. When the Folder object is empty, you can decide if you want to start over with new folders and links to Application objects, or you can delete the Folder object.

To create a custom folder for an application object, follow these steps:

1. From within NWAdmin32, right-click the Application object.

2. Click the Folders button, and a screen similar to the one in Figure 5.21 is displayed.

3. Click Add and select Custom to create a folder exclusively for this Application object, and then name the folder. Or, choose Linked to associate this Application object with a Folder object, which can be shared by this and other Application objects.

4. Highlight a folder and use the Modify or Delete buttons to change a folder's name or delete the folder.

5. Select Application Launcher and/or Start menu, depending on whether you want to display the folders in Application Launcher/Explorer browser view or on the Start menu.

In addition to custom folders, you also have the option of creating linked folders that can be shared by multiple application objects. To create a linked folder for an application object, follow these steps:

1. From within NWAdmin32, right-click the Application object.

2. Click the Folders button, and a screen similar to the one in Figure 5.21 will be displayed.

F I G U R E   5 . 2 1   *The Folders property page for application objects*

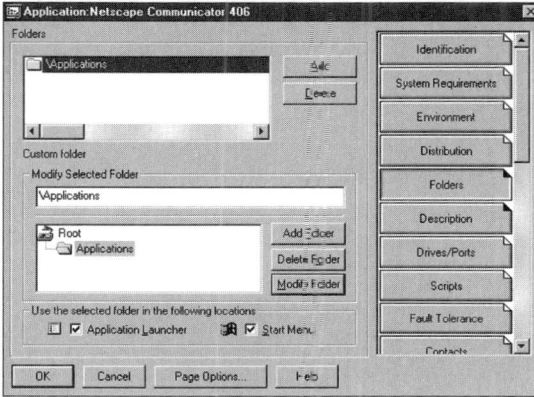

3. Click Add and select Linked to associate this Application object with a Folder object, which can be shared by this and other Application objects.

4. Highlight a folder and use the Modify or Delete buttons to change a folder's name or delete the folder.

5. Select Application Launcher and/or Start menu, depending on whether you want to display the folders in Application Launcher/Explorer browser view or on the Start menu.

Create Application Folder Object and Associate with Application Objects

The next step in setting up application foldering is to use the Folders property page on a folder object to create custom or linked folders in which to organize application objects

Custom folders are tied to one Application object. Linked folders, however, may contain many Application objects. All folders appear in Application Launcher or Explorer browser view and also in the Start menu.

To create a Folder object and link it to application objects, follow these steps:

1. Right-click the Organization Unit, Organizational, or Country object under which you want to create a Folder object.

2. Choose Create ➪ Application Folder, and then click OK.

3. Name the folder, select Define Additional Properties, and then choose OK.

4. Click the Folders button.

5. Click Add ⇨ Folder and then name the folder.

6. Click Add ⇨ Folder again and name the folder to put a folder within the folder you created in Step 5.

7. With a folder highlighted, click Add ⇨ Browse an Application object, and then choose OK, as shown in Figure 5.22. Repeat this process for all the Application objects you want to place in this folder.

8. Choose Application Launcher and/or Start menu depending on whether you want to display the folders in Application Launcher/Explorer browser view or on the Start menu.

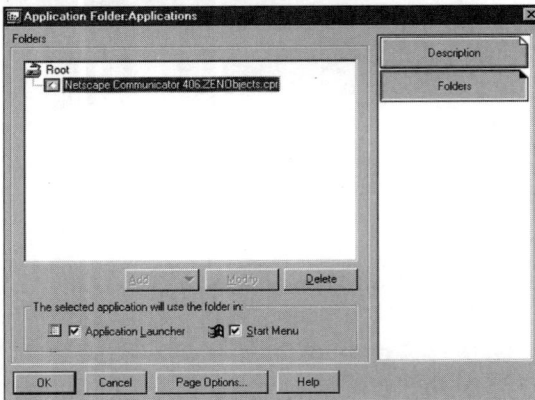

FIGURE 5.22 *Adding application objects in the Folders property page*

Customize Application Launcher Configurations Per User or Container

Once you have created the folder objects you need, you must customize the application launcher configurations. You have the option of configuring at a container level or at a user level to set the options described in the following sections.

Enable Users to View Folders (Default=Yes) For users to be able to see the folders you have created, you must make sure this option is enabled. You can enable it from the Launcher configuration page in a container or user details page in NWAdmin32. If Enable folder view is set to No, users see only the application icons available to them in Application Launcher.

Enable Users to Set Up Personal Folders (Default=No)   To allow users to create their own folders and move the icons around in them as they see fit, you need to enable this option. You can enable it from the Launcher configuration page in a container or user details page in NWAdmin32.

The icons must originate from an application associated with the user. A user cannot add a new, unassociated Application object using personal folders.

> **TIP**
>
> Use caution when offering the option to create personal folders. Users might forget where they have placed applications and call you for help. Not allowing personal folders may be a way to exert more strict control and thus reduce support calls.

Expand Folder View on Startup (Default=No)   Enabling the Expand Folder view on startup option expands the entire tree of folders when the Application Launcher starts

Rename System Folders with Full or Descriptive Names

Once you have created the application folders and customized the application launcher in NWAdmin32, you need to rename any system folders with more descriptive names. If you don't use a Custom or Linked folder, by default Application Launcher or Application Explorer puts applications in system folders that carry the NDS Distinguished Name (DN) of the associated Organization, Organizational Unit, or Country object.

> **NOTE**
>
> Because users cannot read the full or descriptive name attributes by default, you must explicitly grant them these rights. These names are read once at startup time, and are not updated until after Application Launcher or Application Explorer restarts.

To create a descriptive name for a system folder, follow these steps:

1. Right-click the User, Group, Organizational Unit, Organization, or Country object with which Application objects are associated.

2. Click Details.

3. From the Identification property page, type the descriptive name in the Full Name field (for User objects) or Description field (for Group, Organizational Unit. Organization, or Country objects).

> **NOTE**
> If you are creating a descriptive name for a User object, edit the Full Name field. If you are creating a descriptive name for a Group, Organizational Unit, Organization, or Country object, edit the Description field. If this field contains text, the text is used for the descriptive name. If this field is empty, the descriptive name that corresponds to the location in the NDS tree is used.

Setting Up Users to Receive Applications

Once you have set up application foldering, you need to set up users to receive applications via ZENworks. This section covers using NWAdmin32 to setup user objects to receive applications by associating their object with an application object, and by making Application Explorer and Application Launcher available to them and setting Application Launcher configurations.

Associate a User, Group, Workstation, or Container Object to Application Objects

The first step in setting up users to receive applications is to use the Applications property page to associate a User, Group, Workstation, Organizational Unit, Organization, or Country object to one or more Application objects. Unless you associate applications using one of these two methods, applications are not available to users.

In addition to associating applications with other objects, use the Applications property page to specify where and how users access applications on their workstations. For example, you can display application icons in Application Launcher, Application Explorer, Windows Explorer, Start menu, Desktop, and System Tray (or in all of these areas). You can also force applications to launch when Windows starts.

> **NOTE**
> The default method of access is App Launcher, meaning that users see the application only in the Application Launcher and Application Explorer browser view (depending on what you have made available).

To specify who sees the application and where it is displayed on workstations, use the following method:

1. Right-click the User, Group, Organizational Unit, Organization, or Country object, and then click Details.

2. Click the Applications button.

3. Click Add, browse and select the Application object, and then click OK. Specify how and where you want the application to work by checking the appropriate checkbox and then clicking OK, as shown in Figure 5.23.

F I G U R E   5.23 *The application property page for user, group, or container objects*

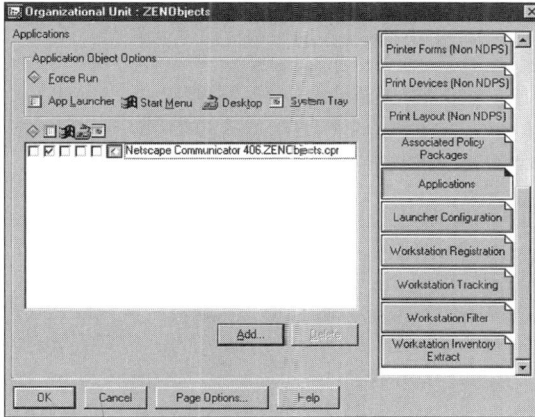

Force Applications to Run The Force Run option runs applications immediately when Application Launcher or Application Explorer starts and the application is available. You can use the Force Run option in conjunction with several other Application object settings to achieve unique behaviors.

For example, if you set an application as Run Once (on the Application object's Identification property page) and Force Run (on the User, Group, or container object's Applications property page), the application will run immediately one time (if available).

Put Applications in the Application Launcher or Explorer Browser View The App Launcher option displays application icons in Application Launcher and Application Explorer (browser view), depending on which one you make available to your users.

Put Applications on the Start Menu When Application Explorer is enabled, the Start Menu option displays icons on the Windows 95 or Windows NT Start menu under Novell Application Launcher.

Put Applications on the Desktop   When Application Explorer is enabled, the Desktop option displays icons on the Windows 95 or Windows NT desktop area.

Put Applications on the System Tray   The System Tray option displays icons on the System Tray, an area on the Windows 95 or Windows NT 4.0 Taskbar where small icons, representing applications, are placed for easy access. The Application Explorer can display or remove applications on the System Tray at any time.

Make Application Explorer Available to Users

Once you have associated the Application object with the users you wish to receive it, you need to make Application Explorer available to them. Application Explorer is software that runs on users' Windows 95 or Windows NT 4.0 workstations. It displays the applications that you distribute to users, using an Application Launcher snap-in. You can specify to what degree users control the options in Application Explorer by using a User, Organizational Unit, Organization, or Country object's Launcher Configuration property page.

Application Explorer displays application icons in a special Application Explorer window, Windows Explorer, Start menu, System Tray, or Desktop. Use the User, Group, Organizational Unit, Organization, or Country object's Applications property page to set up the different Application Explorer access points, as discussed earlier in this chapter.

> Application Explorer is a 32-bit application and should not be run under Windows 3.1x or DOS.
>
> **IMPORTANT**

To make Application Explorer available to users:

I. Ensure that NALEXPLD.EXE is in a network directory (such as SYS:\PUBLIC) where users have rights and access. The Application Explorer is installed to the SYS:\PUBLIC directory when ZENworks is installed on a server, but you may need to copy it to the public directory on other servers that do not have ZENworks installed on them.

2. Add the following command to the User or Organizational Unit object's login script:

```
if platform = "w95" then

        @\\servername\sys\public\nalexpld.exe
```

```
end

if platform = "wnt" then

      if os_version = "v4.00" then

            @\\servername\sys\public\nalexpld.exe

      end

end
```

Make Application Launcher Available to Users

Once you have associated the application object with the users you wish to receive it, you also need to make Application Launcher available to them. Application Launcher is software that runs from users' workstations. It displays the applications that you distribute to them using an Application Launcher snap-in. Using a User, Organizational Unit, Organization, or Country object's Launcher Configuration property page, you can specify to what extent users can control the options in Application Launcher.

For example, you can allow them to create personal folders (in which to store the applications you assign to them), refresh icons, or exit Application Launcher.

In addition to following the steps below, you also need to enable the Application Launcher option on a User, Group, Organizational Unit, Organization, or Country object's Applications property page so users can see applications in Application Launcher, as discussed earlier in this chapter. This option is turned on by default.

To make Application Launcher available to users:

1. Ensure that NAL.EXE is in a network directory (such as SYS:\PUBLIC) where users have rights and access.

2. Add the one of the following commands to the login script of the User object or the users' Organizational Unit:

```
#\\servername\sys\public\nal.exe
```

```
or
```

```
@\\servername\sys\public\nal.exe
```

NOTE The # command requires the external command to complete before executing the next line in the login script. The @ command allows the login script to continue processing while the external command is processed. We recommend using the @ symbol for faster script execution. Do not equate NAL.EXE, a "wrapper" executable that does not stay in memory, with NALWIN32.EXE or NALW31.EXE. If you use # with NALWIN32.EXE or NALW31.EXE, any scripts will wait until the user exits Application Launcher.

Customize Application Launcher Configurations Per User or Container

Once you have associated the application object with the users and provided the users with access to Application Launcher and Application Explorer, use the Launcher Configuration dialog box to specify configurations that dictate how users view and work with Application Launcher and Application Explorer desktop software.

NOTE This dialog box is available for User, Organizational Unit, Organization, and Country objects only. It is not available for Group objects.

To access the Launcher Configuration property page:

1. Right-click a User, Organizational Unit, Organization, or Country object and click Details.

2. Click the Launcher Configuration button.

3. Choose View/edit object's custom settings from the Mode drop-down list, and then choose Edit.

4. Choose the User, Window, Explorer, or Workstation tab to specify settings for the following options, as shown in Figure 5.24.

Specify E-mail Attribute (Default=Mailbox ID) This option lets you specify the NDS attribute that you want to use to display an e-mail name in the Help Contacts tab (when the user right-clicks an application icon and chooses Properties). If users have problems with applications, they can contact people by e-mail to get help. The e-mail name that appears is pulled from the NDS attribute you specify here.

FIGURE 5.24 *The launcher configuration property page for user, group, or container objects*

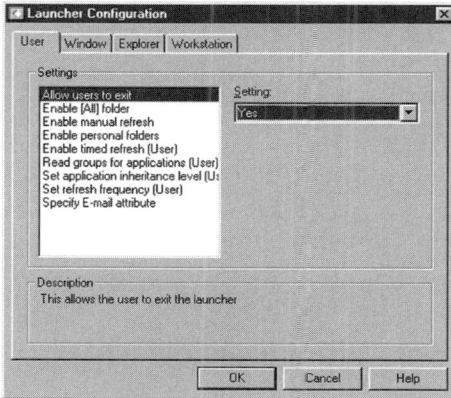

Enable Timed Refresh (User) (Default=No)   The Enable Timed Refresh option refreshes the application icons automatically without the user having to choose File ⇨ Refresh or press F5 to manually refresh icons. The Timed Refresh setting affects settings such as the Force Run feature.

Set Timed Refresh Frequency (User) (Default=3600 Seconds)   The Set refresh frequency option lets you specify the frequency in seconds.

For example, if you set the refresh to 300 seconds, Application Launcher or Application Explorer updates applications from the network automatically every five minutes, and may even run some applications, depending on how you have set them up.

> **TIP**   A short timed refresh interval is very useful in situations where you want changes to refresh quickly. However, a short timed refresh interval can cause higher network traffic. The Refresh Icons option and Timed Refresh options are not connected in any way except that they both control refresh. One option does not have to be selected for the other to work.

Allow Users to Exit (Default=Yes)   The Allow users to exit option determines whether or not users can exit Application Launcher or Explorer.

An example of when to use this would be if you are running software at a conference where workstations are available for the attendees of the conference to use. If you do not want users to exit Application Launcher and change settings on the hard disk drive, set this option to No.

Set Application Inheritance Level (User) (Default=1) The set application inheritance level option specifies how many parent Organization or Organizational Unit objects up the NDS tree Application Launcher or Application Explorer should search for applications.

An example of this would be if a user object's Distinguished Name is user1.dev.la.acme and this option is set to a value of 2, then Application Launcher or Application Explorer would look at the Organization or Organizational Unit object dev and la for Application objects, but would ignore acme. A value of −1 instructs Application Launcher or Application Explorer to search all the way up the NDS tree.

Enable Users to Refresh Icons Manually (Default=Yes) The Enable Manual Refresh option lets users refresh Application Launcher or Application Explorer manually. This displays any Application objects that were delivered since the last refresh.

Read Group Objects for Applications (User) (Default=Yes) If a Group object has been associated with Application objects, users who are members of that Group can run Application objects by virtue of their membership. While this is a convenient way of indirectly associating users with applications, it can also decrease performance. If you want to increase performance, set this option to No.

Enable Users to Set Up Personal Folders (Default=No) If Enable personal folders is set to Yes, users can create their own folders and move the icons around in them as they see fit. However, the icons must originate from an application associated with the user. A user cannot add a new, unassociated Application object using personal folders.

Use caution when offering the option to create personal folders. Users may forget where they have placed applications and call you for help. Not allowing personal folders may be a way to exert more strict control and thus reduce support calls.

Enable Users to View Folders (Default=Yes) The folder view in Application Launcher may be confusing to some users. By setting Enable folder view to No, users see only the application icons available to them in Application Launcher.

Enable Users to Login (Default=Yes)   Setting the Enable login option to Yes activates the Login option found on Application Launcher's File menu. The user can use this option to run the GUI Login software and log in to the network. This option is not available for Application Explorer.

NOTE   When this option is selected, and the user is not logged in, Application Launcher searches for the Login executable in the path, and if it is found, displays a Login icon in Application Launcher. If the Login executable cannot be found, or if the user is already logged in, the Login option is grayed. Ensure that Application Launcher can find the login program (LOGINW31.EXE, LOGINW95.EXE, or LOGINWNT.EXE) on the client workstation before you select the Login option.

Expand Folder View on Startup (Default=No)   The Expand folder view on startup option enables you to specify whether the user can view folders. This option expands the entire tree of folder when the Application Launcher starts.

Save Window Size and Position (Default=Yes)   The Save window size and position option enables you to set whether or not to save window size and position settings on a local drive. If you set this option to Yes, Application Launcher is always displayed in the same position for every user.

Display Start Menu in Application Launcher (Default=Show When Not Authenticated)   The Display Start Menu option copies the current Windows 95 or Windows NT Start menu organization (including Programs and above) into the Application Launcher. You can specify settings such as Never Show, Show Always, or Show When Authenticated.

Display Icon on Desktop (Default=Yes)   The Display icon on desktop option enables you to specify whether you want the Application Explorer icon to appear on the user's desktop. When enabled, an Application Explorer icon appears on both the desktop and the System Tray.

Name Icon on Desktop (Default=Application Explorer)   The Name icon on desktop option enables you to change the name of the icon that opens the Application Explorer browser view. For example, you could name it something such as "Corporate Applications."

Enable Helper (Workstation)   The Enable Helper option enables the helper DLL by loading and adding it to the WM scheduler for the workstations.

Enable Timed Refresh (Workstation) (Default=No)   The Enable Timed Refresh option refreshes the application icons automatically without the user having to choose File ⇨ Refresh or press F5 to manually refresh icons. The Timed Refresh option affects settings such as the Force Run feature.

Read Group Objects for Applications (Workstation) (Default=Yes)   If a Group object has been associated with Application objects; users who are members of that Group can run Application objects by virtue of their membership. While this is a convenient way of indirectly associating users with applications, it can also decrease performance. If you want to increase performance, set this option to No.

Set Application Inheritance Level (Workstation) (Default=1)   The Set application inheritance level option specifies how many parent Organization or Organizational Unit objects up the NDS tree Application Launcher or Application Explorer should search for applications.

An example of this would be if a user object's Distinguished Name is user1.dev.la.acme and this option is set to a value of 2, then Application Launcher or Application Explorer would look at the Organization or Organizational Unit object dev and la for Application objects, but would ignore acme. A value of –1 instructs Application Launcher or Application Explorer to search all the way up the NDS tree.

Set Timed Refresh Frequency (Workstation) (Default=3600 Seconds) The Set refresh frequency option lets you specify the frequency in seconds.

For example, if you set the refresh to 300 seconds, Application Launcher or Application Explorer updates applications from the network automatically every five minutes, and may even run some applications, depending on how you have set them up.

Automating Application Objects

The final step in setting up the application distribution environment is automating Application objects. Automating application objects is the process of setting up scripting, scheduling, and macros to remove required interaction with Application object distribution. This step is completely optional, however; you may wish to use some of the following options to make the application distribution completely seamless for users.

Manage Application Object Macros

One way to automate application objects is to use the Macros property page to manage the Application object macros that you create expressly for this Application object, and that are used on other property pages of the Application object. You can use all types of macros (including Application object macros) in the following Application object locations:

- ▶ Path to Executable (Identification property page)
- ▶ Command Line (Environment property page)
- ▶ Working Directory (Environment property page)
- ▶ Mapping Path (Drives/Ports property page)
- ▶ Capture Port Path (Drives/Ports property page)
- ▶ Registry Settings Property Page: Key, Name, Value (String only)
- ▶ .INI Settings Property Page: Group, Name, Value
- ▶ Application Files Property Page: Source/Target, Directory
- ▶ Text Files Property Page: Find and Add String
- ▶ Icons/Shortcuts Property Page: All locations

TIP

You can put macros within macros. For example:
`%TARGET_PATH%=%*WINDISK%\Program Files` **or**
`EMAIL_ADDRESS=%CN%@acme.com.`

To access the Macros property page, use the following steps from within NWAdmin32:

1. Right-click the Application object and click Details.

2. Click the Macros button.

3. Click Import, browse and highlight the Application Object Template (.AOT or .AXT) file that you created with snAppShot, and then click Open.

   Or, highlight a Macro template entry and click Modify to edit its name and value. For example, you can change the value of the %SOURCE_PATH% to \\<servername>\<volumename>\apps\netscape.

   Or, click Add to create a new Macro template entry. Name the macro and include a value, and then click OK.

NOTE For best results, we recommend using a UNC pathname for the source path rather than a mapped drive. If you use a mapped drive letter as the source drive, some files may not copy correctly.

Prompted Macros

One way to automate application objects is to use the Macros property page to set up special prompted macros. At times, the end user has a different system setup than what is expected by the administrator.

For example, users may want to put an application on a different drive than what was described in the application object. Prompted macros allow the administrator to request that the user be prompted for the information. By using the prompted macros feature, the administrator could have the destination drive requested of the end user, and the resulting distribution will go to the specified drive.

To set up prompted macros, access the Macros property page by following these steps from within NWAdmin32:

1. Right-click the Application object and click Details.

2. Click the Macros button.

3. Click Add.

4. Select Prompted from the drop-down menu.

5. Select either Drive or String, depending on whether you wish to prompt for a location or a string.

A window similar to the one shown in Figure 5.25 is displayed. From the prompted macro window, you can set up the following options for the macro:

▶ Prompt text — Textual information to be displayed for the user when prompting for the macro.

▶ Macro name — Name setup for the macro for install scripts and such.

▶ Default Value — You can specify a default value for the macro for users to use if they have no need to specify otherwise.

▶ Minimum disk space — You can specify a minimum amount of disk space required in setting the macro.

▶ Maximum String len — You can use this option to specify the maximum number of characters allowed for string macros.

Prompted Macros

Enter the string macro information:

Prompt text: [Enter the username:]

Macro name: [USER_NAME]

Default Value: [admin]

Minimum disk space: [0]   MB

Maximum string len: [256]   characters

[OK]   [Cancel]   [Help]

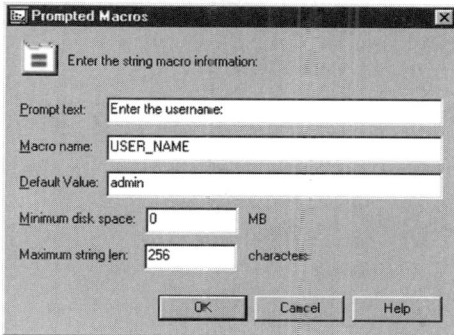

Special Windows Macros

Another way to automate application distribution is by using special Windows macros. A special Windows macro is one that defines Windows 3.*x*, 95, and NT directories. The typical paths listed below are based on default installations and may or may not match your specific setup. On Windows 95 workstations, macros behave differently if User Profiles are enabled.

The following macros are very helpful for redirecting application files that expect Windows directories to be in a particular location:

```
%*WinDir%      Windows directory, typically c:windows or
               c:winnt

%*WinSysDir%   Windows system directory, typically
               c:\windows\system or c:\winnt\system32

%*WinDisk%     Drive letter (plus colon) for Windows
               directory, typically c:

%*WinSysDis<%  Drive letter (plus colon) for Windows
               system directory c:

%*WinSys16Dir% Windows NT** 16-bit system directory
               (c:\winnt\system)

%*TempDir%     Windows temporary directory
               (c:\windows\temp)
```

> The asterisk character (*) is a required syntax for these macros. Don't confuse these asterisk characters with the Novell trademark asterisk.
>
> **NOTE**

Login Script Variables

Another way to automate application distribution is by using login script variables. Application Launcher supports the familiar or traditional login script variables; however, not all login script variables are supported.

The following is a list of supported login script macros and what they mean. Alternate macro names are shown in parentheses.

DAY	Numeric day of the month. For example: 01, 10, 15, and so on.
FILESERVER (FILE_SERVER)	Name of the NetWare file server of NDS monitored connection. For example: APPS_PROD.
FULL_NAME	Full name attribute of the User object. For example: Jane Doe.
HOUR24 (24HOUR)	Time of the day according to a 24-hour clock. For example: 02, 05, 14, 22, and so on.
HOUR (HOURS)	Hour of the day. For example: 0 = 12, 13 = 1, and so on.
LAST_NAME	Last name of the current user (also known as the user's NDS Surname attribute).
LOGIN_NAME	First eight bytes of the user's NDS object name. For example: jsmith.
MINUTE (MINUTES)	Current minute. For example: 02, 59, and so on.
MONTH	Current month number. For example: 01 for January, and so on.
NDAY_OF_WEEK	Numeric day of the week. For example: 1 for Sunday, and so on.
NETWORK (NETWORK_ADDRESS)	Workstation network address. For example: 01010120

OS_VERSION	Version of the OS. For example: v5.00 (Win3 show DOS version, Win 95 and NT show Windows version).
OS	OS type. For example: MSDOS, WIN95, WINNT, and so on. (Win3 shows MSDOS.)
PLATFORM	Platform running. For example: WIN, W95, WNT, and so on.
PHYSICAL_STATION (P_STATION)	MAC address. For example: 0000C04FD92ECA.
REQUESTER_CONTEXT	Context of the requester (for the selected tree).
SECOND (SECONDS)	Number of seconds. For example: 03, 54, and so on.
SHORT_YEAR	Short year number. For example: 97, 00, and so on.
WINVER	Windows version. For example: v3.11, v4.00, and so on.
YEAR	Full year number. For example: 1997, and so on.

NDS Attribute Macros

Another useful tool in automating application distribution is the use of NDS attribute macros. Application Launcher supports macros that pull information from the attributes of the currently logged-in user, the current Application object, or from the attributes of other NDS objects.

An example of using NDS attribute macros would be a GroupWise Application object that runs ofwin.exe with a command line parameter:

`/@U-@USERNAME@`

USERNAME can be replaced with a macro that uses a user's NDS common name (CN):

`/@U-@%CN%@`

If the NDS object name is the same as the e-mail login for GroupWise, every user who runs the application has the correct username passed in to GroupWise.

The following are variables defined by an attribute in an NDS object that can be used as NDS attribute macros:

%CN%	Common Name (user's object name or login name)
%DN%	User's Full Distinguished Name (used with Application Launcher only)
%Given Name%	Given Name
%Surname%	Last Name
%Full Name%	Full Name
%Telephone Number%	Telephone
%Home Directory%	Home Directory
%Email Address%	E-mail Address
%Mailbox ID%	Mailbox ID

Environment Variables

Another useful tool in automating application distribution is using environment variables. The following are some examples of environment variables that Application Launcher will support:

- ► %NWLANGUAGE%
- ► %TEMP%
- ► %PATH%

> The value of the variable must not exceed the length of the Application object name; otherwise, the variable fails.
>
> **NOTE**

Schedule Application Availability

Another useful tool in automating application distribution is to schedule application availability. Earlier in this chapter, we discussed using the Scheduling property page for Application objects to set schedules of when the application will be available. You can use this to help automate when users will be able to access the application object.

Create Application Scripts

Another useful tool available to automate application distribution is the use of the Scripts property page to set up scripts that are executed automatically each time the application is launched and closed. Unlike environment parameters, scripts can overwrite existing drive mappings and printer ports.

The two types of application scripts are the Startup script and the post-termination script. Run before Launching (or Startup) scripts are executed after the environment is set and before the application is launched. Run after Termination (or post-termination) scripts are executed after the application is closed and before the network resources are cleaned up.

The following are some examples of what you can use application scripts for:

▸ Provide extra mappings beyond those defined on the Drives/Ports property page

▸ Provide a mapping to override another mapping

▸ Run other applications

▸ Log in to other servers or NDS trees

▸ Terminate applications under certain circumstances

The following is an example of script syntax:

▸ #calc.exe — Run the Calculator application, pausing the script processing until Calculator returns control.

▸ @calc.exe — Run the Calculator application concurrently with the remainder of the script processing.

To create application object scripts, use the following steps:

1. Right-click the Application object and click Details.

2. Click the Scripts button.

3. Type the appropriate commands in either the Run before Launching or Run after Termination text boxes.

TIP Commands for cleaning up the changes made by the pre-launch script should be placed in the post-termination script. The post-termination script is run after Application Launcher detects that the application has terminated.

The following is a list of scripting commands that Application Launcher does not support:

▸ CLS

▸ DISPLAY

▸ EXIT

▸ FDISPLAY

- ▶ INCLUDE
- ▶ LASTLOGINTIME
- ▶ NO_DEFAULT
- ▶ NOSWAP
- ▶ PAUSE
- ▶ PCCOMPATIBLE
- ▶ SCRIPT_SERVER
- ▶ SET_TIME
- ▶ SWAP
- ▶ WRITE

The following is a list of scripting commands that Application Launcher scripting does not do:

- ▶ Output anything to the screen
- ▶ Display errors
- ▶ Pause

Distribute the Applications

Once you have created the application object, set up the properties for the object, and set up the distribution options, the final step is to actually distribute the application to users. To accomplish this, you actually do nothing. That is what ZENworks application distribution is all about. Once you have it all set up, ZENworks will automatically distribute the application for you according to your application object settings.

CHAPTER 6

Setting Up User Policies

This chapter discusses the use and creation of User policies. User policies are associated with users and affect their working environment.

Relationship of User Policies to Users

Users are associated with User policies in any of three ways: 1) Policies can be associated with the user object directly, 2) Policies can be associated with a parent container of the user object, and 3) Policies can be associated with a group of which the user is a member.

When a user logs into the tree, a ZENworks agent (Workstation Manager Service) will walk up the tree looking for the first User policy package it can find that is associated with the user. Like all agents associated with ZENworks, the order in which the tree is searched is dependent on standard Novell Directory Services behavior and any search policies that may be in the tree. When a policy is being searched from the tree, the Workstation Manager agent will walk the tree until it finds the root of the tree or a search policy that limits its searching. All of the applicable user policies will be merged together, and the culmination will be applied to the workstation. If there are any conflicts with the policies (for example, two user policies both affect the same parameter), then the parameter setting in the first policy found will be applied.

The remote control policy can be created for both the user and the workstation. In the instances when there is a remote control policy for both the user and the workstation, the remote control subsystem takes the most restrictive combination of the policies. For example, if one policy says to prompt the user for permission and the other does not, then the system will prompt the user.

Advantages of Platform-Specific Policies

ZENworks allows the administration of specific policies for each platform that is supported in the ZENworks system. By having a policy that is categorized for each type of platform, the administrator can make unique policies for each system. Regardless of the users logged into the system, each workstation will find the policies associated with it and execute the administrative configurations for that platform.

On occasion, you may want to associate a particular, unique policy to a set of workstations that may be contained in containers along with other workstations of the same type. You can then create a group of workstations and associate specific policies to those workstations. Consequently, these workstations will receive the policies from this group rather than from the container.

Creating a Windows 3.1 User Policy Package

In order to have a policy that affects users who are logging into the tree through workstations that are running the Windows 3.1 operating system, you must create a Windows 3.1 User policy package. Use the following steps to create a Windows 3.1 User policy package. Figure 6.1 shows the dialog box for creating an object within a container.

Dialog box for creating an object within a container. The Policy Package object is selected.

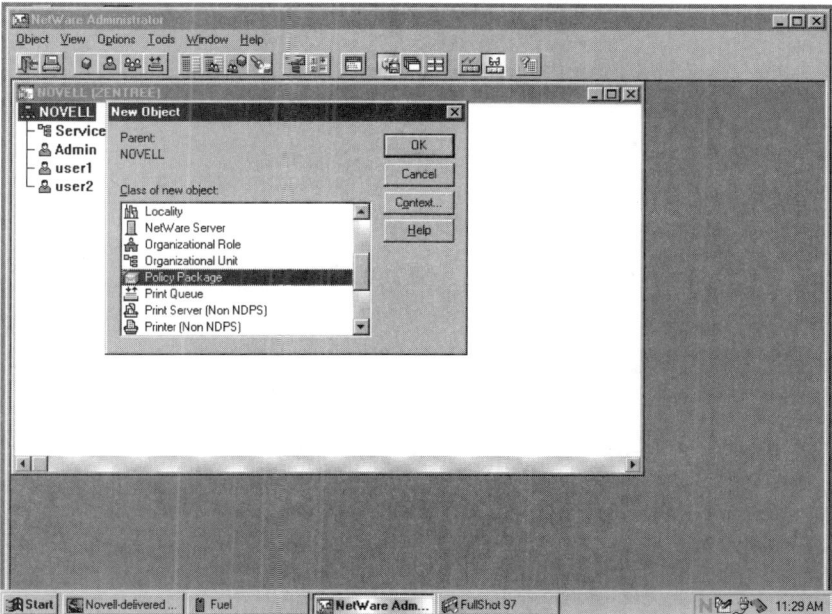

1. Start NWAdmin32

2. Browse to the container where you would like to have the policy package. Remember that you do not have to create the policy package

in the container where you are doing the associations. You can associate the same policy package to many containers in your tree.

3. Create the policy package by clicking the right mouse button and choosing Create.

4. Select the Policy Package object in the list of objects that can be created in the selected container.

5. In the Create Policy Package dialog box, select the type of package to be a Windows 3.1 User policy package and name the object. Also, select the Define Additional Attributes checkbox so you can define policies.

6. Press OK. Next, NWAdmin32 displays a dialog box that enables you to create policies for this policy package.

7. Check and set any policies you desire for this Windows 3.1 User policy package and press OK.

Policies Page

Once you have created a Windows 3.1 User policy package, you can activate policies that will be used for all Windows 3.1 users that were associated with the policy package. If you click a policy within the policy package, that policy becomes active. An active policy is designated by a check in the checkbox. The details of any particular policy can be modified by selecting the policy and pressing the Details button, or by double-clicking the policy itself. Figure 6.2 shows the screen for the Windows 3.1 policy package.

F I G U R E   6 . 2   *Windows 3.1 User policy package policies dialog page*

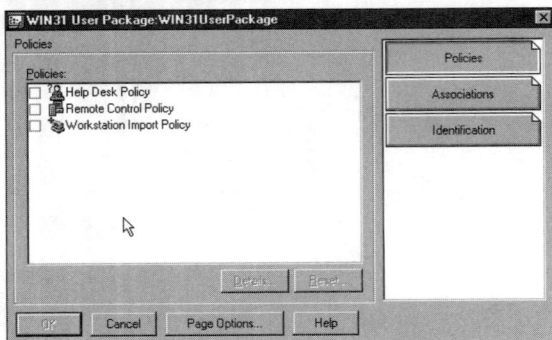

The Reset button on the policy page will reset the selected policy back to the system defaults for that policy.

Associations page

The Associations page of the Windows 3.1 User policy package displays all the locations in the tree (containers) where the policy package has been placed. The Windows 3.1 users that are in or below those containers will have this policy package enforced.

Identification Page

The Identification page of the Windows 3.1 User policy package simply enables users to enter additional description information to help users understand the purpose of the particular policy package.

Adding a Help Desk Policy

The Help Desk policy sets the features associated with the Help Request system that is provided with the ZENworks system. The Help Request system includes a program that can be presented to all users in the tree through the ZENworks Application Launcher. When ZENworks is installed, it creates an Application Object that is associated with the Help Request program. When you associate this application object to users, groups, or containers, end users are presented with this program on their desktop.

When the Help Request program is launched, it checks to see if there is a policy package associated with the currently logged in user; if there is, a Help Desk policy is enabled. If there is a Help Desk policy, then the program launches on the desktop. The interface presented through the Help Requester is fully configured by the Help Desk policy and is described below with each page of the policy.

The Help Desk Policy is the same for all platforms and the administrator is presented with the same interface regardless of the individual policy package. Although the interface is the same, each individual Help Desk Policy is unique and independent for each policy package.

A Help Desk policy is activated for this policy package by either double-clicking the Help Desk policy or selecting the checkbox on the Help Desk policy. Once this is selected, then this Help Desk Policy is activated for all Windows 3.1 users who are associated with the Windows 3.1 policy package.

Information Page

The Information page enables you to enter a selected set of information to have displayed through the Help Request system presented to the end user. When the Help Request system is launched on an individual's desktop, the user is presented with this contact information. Figure 6.3 shows the Information page for the Help Desk policy.

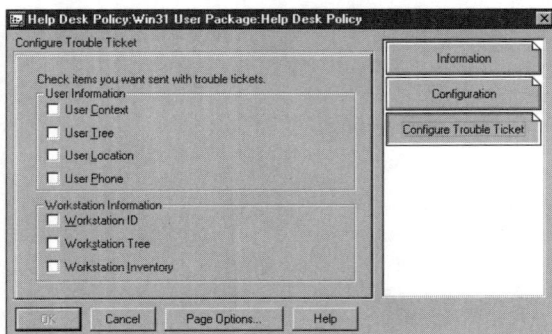

FIGURE 6.3   *Information page of the Help Desk policy within a Windows 95/98 User policy package*

The contact name should be the name of the help desk personnel or service, such as "PC Repair services." The Telephone Number field is also presented to the end user of the Help Request application, and should be the help number that the user can call for assistance. The e-mail address is the electronic mail address of the person or organization to be contacted when the Help Request system is launched. Trouble tickets generated by the Help Request system are automatically sent to this e-mail address.

Configuration Page

The Configuration page of the Help Desk policy enables you to administer the behavior of the Help Request system. By checking the Allow user to launch the Help Requester field, you activate the Help Request system for all Windows 3.1 users who are associated with this policy package. Until this box is checked, any user who launches the Help Request system will be denied access. Once this box is checked, the Help Request system is activated. Figure 6.4 shows the Configuration page of the Help Desk policy.

Help Desk policy configuration page of a Windows 3.1 User policy package

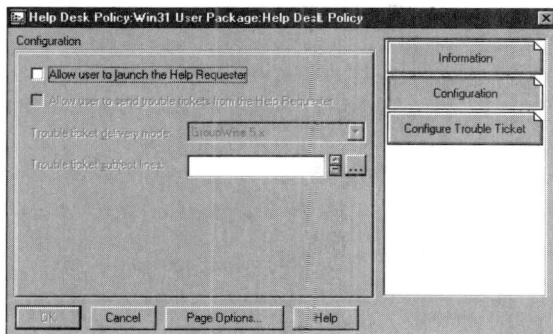

The Allow user to send trouble tickets from the Help Requester field is only activated when you check the box that enables users to launch the Help Requester. Before this box is checked, the user may only use the information and call buttons on the Help Requester system. These buttons only provide information about the user and workstation objects and the contact information that was administered on the Information page of the Help Desk policy.

The Trouble ticket delivery mode field identifies for the system the method that should be used by the Help Requester application for sending generated trouble tickets. Currently, the choices for this mode are GroupWise 5.x and MAPI. By checking the GroupWise 5.x system, the Help Requester application will assume that the GroupWise 5.0 or greater libraries are present on the end user's workstation and will make the calls necessary to send the automatically created trouble tickets to the Contact Name e-mail address via these GroupWise calls. If the MAPI option is chosen, then the same attempt is made, only using standard Windows MAPI calls to activate the e-mail system.

The Trouble ticket subject lines field enables you to enter as many trouble ticket subjects lines as you wish. By pressing the ... button, you are given a prompt to enter text for your subject line. These subject lines are presented to the end user via the Help Requester system. The end user may select which subject line to associate with the help request. This is also placed as the subject line in the e-mail message of the trouble ticket.

Configure Trouble Ticket Page

The Configure Trouble Ticket page enables you to specify the information you want stored in the trouble ticket about the user and the workstation that is issuing the ticket. Figure 6.5 shows this page.

FIGURE 6.5 *Help Desk Policy Configure Trouble Ticket page of a Windows 3.1 User policy package*

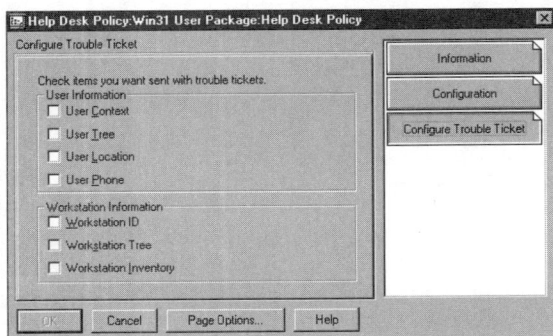

The following fields can be checked in the Configure Trouble Ticket to signal that the information should be included in the ticket. The information included is either related to the current user that is logged into the tree or to the workstation.

- ► User Context — This will include the tree context (for example, .user1.novell) of the user object of the user who is logged into the workstation when the trouble ticket is sent.

- ► User Tree — This will include the tree name in the ticket.

- ► User Location — This will include the value in the location field of the user object for the current user.

- ► User Phone — This will include the phone number field of the user object for the current user.

- ► Workstation ID — This will be the workstation object name of the workstation (for example, workstation1.workstations.novell).

- ► Workstation Tree — This will specify the tree name where the workstation object is located.

▶ Workstation Inventory — This will include inventory information about the workstation. This information includes the following: Computer Type, Computer Model, Serial Number, Asset Tag, OS Type, OS Version, Novell Client version, NIC Type, Video Type, BIOS Type, Processor, Memory Size, Disk Info, MAC Address, Subnet Address, and IP Address. This is basically the same information that is stored in the workstation object in the tree.

Adding a Remote Management Policy

A Remote Management policy is activated for this policy package by either double-clicking the Remote Management policy or selecting the checkbox on the Remote Management policy. Once this is selected and a check is displayed in the checkbox, this Remote Management policy is activated for all Windows 3.1 users who are associated with the Windows 3.1 Policy package.

The Remote Management policy controls the features of the Remote Management subsystem that is shipped with the ZENworks package and is not shipped with the ZENworks Starter Pack. The Remote Management system is composed of two parts: Remote Management Session Manager, which makes the connection and is used by the administrator and the Remote Management Agents that are installed on the end user's workstation. The remote control agents may be installed onto the workstation when the client that is shipped with ZENworks is installed, or the agents may be installed on the workstation through the remote control application objects that were added to your tree when you installed ZENworks. You would need to simply associate these application objects to the users and then have the ZENworks Application launcher install these agents automatically on the workstation. For more information, see Chapter 5.

The Remote Management system will make a peer-to-peer connection between the administrator's workstation and the remote workstation. This may be done using either the IPX or the TCP/IP protocol. In this policy, you may specify the preferred protocol for the connection. This protocol is attempted first, but if the connection cannot be made, then the alternate protocol will be used.

Remote controlling a workstation via ZENworks also requires rights within the Workstation Object that represents the workstation you want to be controlled. Without these rights, the administrator will be denied access to the remote control subsystem. Both the session manager and the agents validate that the user has rights to remote control the workstation. You assign the remote control rights either through the Remote Management Rights Wizard or in the workstation object in the Remote Operators page.

Remote Management Policy Page

The Remote Management Policy page identifies the features that you want to be activated with the Remote Management system. Figures 6.6 through 6.8 show the Remote Management Policy page and the tabbed values of the policy.

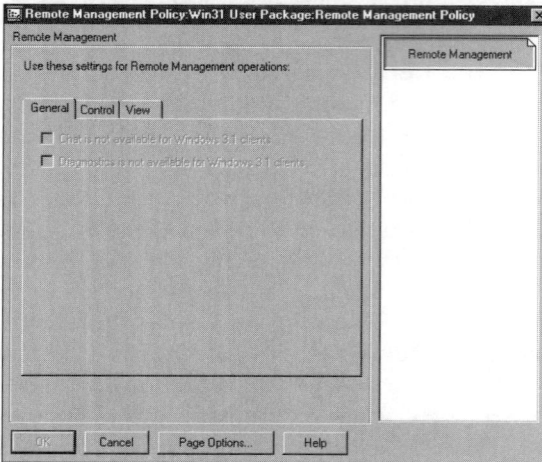

FIGURE 6.6 *Remote Management Policy page, General tab*

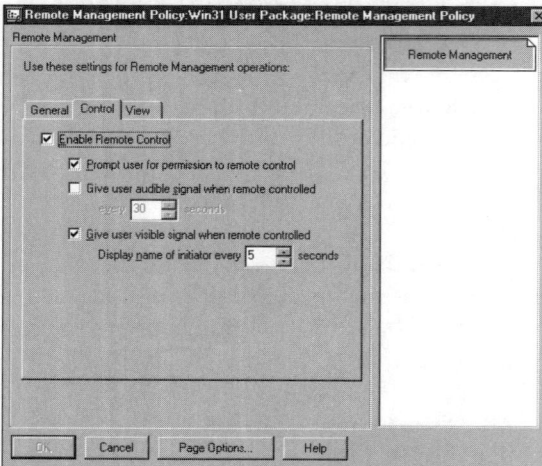

FIGURE 6.7 *Remote Management Policy page, Control tab*

FIGURE 6.8 *Remote Management Policy page, View tab*

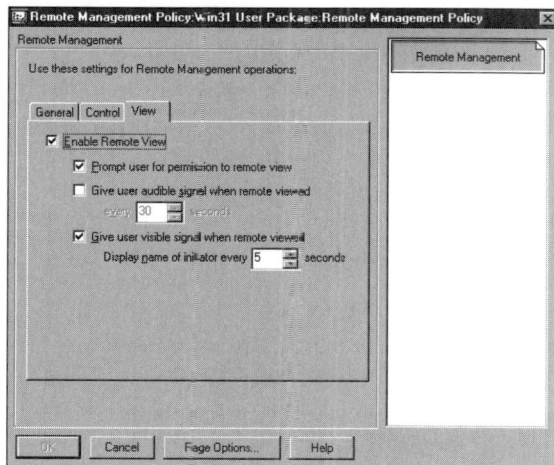

The following describes each of the options available under each tab of the Remote Management policy:

► General Tab — This tab has options on general system functions:

   • Enable Chat — The chat feature is not available for Windows 3.1 so this field is disabled.

   • Enable Diagnostics — The diagnostics is not available for Windows 3.1 so this field is grayed.

► Control Tab — This tab describes the feature enabling of remote control functions:

   • Enable Remote Control — When this option is enabled, the remote control subsystem can be activated. Without this setting on, no one can remote control the workstations where the currently logged in user has this policy associated with his or her user object.

   • Prompt user for permission to remote control — This option will cause a dialog box to be displayed on the end user's machine when a remote control session is started. The end user has the option of accepting or denying the remote control request. Within this dialog box, the user is told who wants to remote control his or her machine, and asks if this is approved. If the user denies the remote control session, then the session is terminated and the administrator cannot remote control the workstation.

- Give user audible system when remote controlled — This option periodically provides the end user with a tone while the remote control session is active. You can also set the number of seconds between each beep.

- Give user visible signal when remote controlled — This option displays a dialog box on the end user's desktop while the remote control session is active. The dialog box indicates that the workstation is being remote controlled, and also displays the NDS name of the user who is remote controlling the workstation. You can set the number of seconds you want to have between flashing of the name of the user who is initiating the remote control session.

▶ View Tab — This tab describes the feature enabling of the remote view functions. Remote view gives the administrator the capability to view the remote windows screen of the target machine, without being able to control the mouse or keyboard of the machine.

- Enable Remote View — When this option is enabled, the remote view subsystem can be activated. Without this setting on, no one may remote view the workstations where the currently logged in user has this policy associated with his or her user object.

- Prompt user for permission to remote view — This option will cause a dialog box to be displayed on the end user's machine when a remote view session is started. The end user has the option of accepting or denying the remote view request. Within this dialog box, the user is told who wants to remote view his or her machine, and asks if this is approved. If the user denies the remote view session, then the session is terminated and the administrator cannot remote view the workstation.

- Give user audible system when remote viewed — This option periodically provides the end user with a tone while the remote view session is active. You can also set the number of seconds between each beep.

- Give user visible signal when remote viewed — This option displays a dialog box on the end user's desktop while the remote view session is active. The dialog box indicates that the workstation is being remote viewed, and also displays the NDS name of the user who is remote viewing the workstation. You can set the number of seconds you want to have between flashing of the name of the user who is initiating the remote view session.

Adding a Workstation Import Policy

This policy governs the behavior of the import process, which imports workstations into the tree and associates the physical workstation device to the workstation object in the tree. This policy describes how a workstation object should be named, and where in the tree the workstation object should be created.

The import process is accomplished in four steps:

1. A Workstation Import policy must be created and associated with the first user who is logged in to the workstation.

2. When the first user logs in to the tree, a registration process is activated that places some information about the user and the workstation into the immediate container of the user.

3. The administrator must execute the workstation import program, which imports information from the registration stored in the user's container and creates the workstation object using the information given in the registration process.

4. The next user to log in to the system after the import process is completed will cause the system to detect that a workstation object has been created for that particular device. Once the object is discovered, the NDS name of the workstation object is stored in the workstation registry, and the workstation now can connect to the system via that workstation object.

Once the workstation object has been associated with a physical device (the import process described above has been completed), then that workstation object will receive all information about the workstation and will represent that workstation in the tree. Associations of policies with that workstation object, workstation container, or workstation group will govern behavior of the systems on that workstation.

You may activate a workstation import policy by going to the details of the Windows 3.1 Workstation Package object. Within that policy package, you may select and activate the workstation import policy. All users who are associated with that package will now use that import policy to describe how the import policy should behave.

Workstation Location Page

This page enables the administrator to identify the container in the tree that should hold the workstation object when it is created during the import process. Figure 6.9 shows this screen.

F I G U R E   6 . 9 *Workstation Import policy, workstation location*

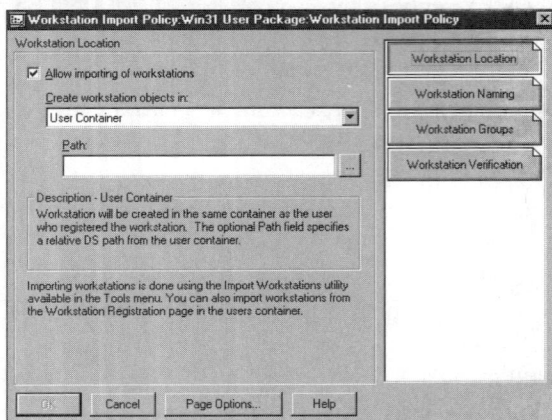

The Allow importing of workstations option enables or disables the capability to import workstations from this user. Once this option is activated, the other fields of the page are usable.

The Create workstation objects in drop-down box provides the administrator with various objects for locating the container to place the workstation objects. The options are as follows:

▶ User Container — This signals that the container that holds the user object of the user that had logged into the system when the registration of the workstation occurred will be the container that also will hold the workstation object. Remember, the first user who connects to the system will have the association to the workstation. A path may be specified in the path field considered to be relative to the user's container. The path field is constructed by entering a relative path. This relative path is constructed by a series of dots and container names. For each dot in the path, the system will move up one level from the associated object container. For example, the path of ..Workstations indicates for the system to go up two levels and then to a container called Workstations at that level. If an alternate user is desired, you must run the un-registration tool described in Chapter 10.

▸ Associated Object Container — This signals that the container that has the policy package associated with it will be used as the starting container in which to place the workstation object. If a path is specified, then the associated container is used as the base, and the path is considered a relative path. The path field is constructed by entering a relative path. This relative path is constructed by a series of dots and container names. For each dot in the path, the system will move up one level from the associated object container. For example, the path of ..Workstations means for the system to go up two levels and then to a container called Workstations at that level.

▸ Selected Container — This identifies that the specified path is an absolute container path in the tree. The Path field is required with this selection, and must identify the specific container that will hold the workstation object.

Workstation Naming Page

On this page, the administrator can describe how the import process should use the information in the registration to craft the name of the workstation object. Figure 6.10 presents an image of the naming page.

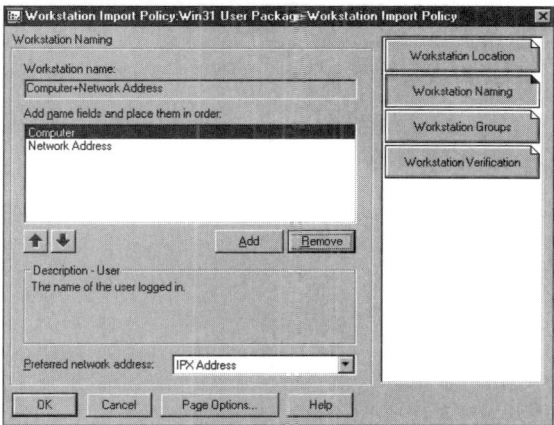

F I G U R E   6 . 1 0   *Workstation Import policy, Workstation Naming page*

The Workstation name field displays the final combination of registration information that will be combined into the name. In the preceding example, the workstation object name will be the computer name followed by the network address. This is confirmed by the fact that the Workstation name field has Computer+Network Address. If the computer name were Rtanner and the network address of the NIC card were 12345, then the workstation object name would be Rtanner12345.

The Add name fields and place them in order field displays the various components that are put together to form the workstation name. Each line displayed in this field represents a value that will be part of the name. The order of the lines from top to bottom represent the order in which they will appear in the name. The options that can be placed in the names are as follows:

▶ <User Defined> — This represents an administrator defined string. When this field is chosen, the administrator is prompted to enter a string into the dialog box. This string will be placed into the name. This can be any combination of standard ASCII visible characters, including white space characters.

▶ Computer — This represents the name that was given to the computer, usually during installation of the operating system.

▶ Container — This represents the name of the container into which the workstation object is placed. This name will then be included in the workstation name.

▶ CPU — This value represents the CPU type of the machine. Currently this attribute has no value for Windows 3.1 and DOS machines, and retrieves its information in the Windows 95/98 and NT environment from the operating system. The possible values are 386, 486, and PENTIUM.

▶ DNS — This represents the DNS (Domain Name Services) name of the computer.

▶ Network Address — This represents the address of the machine when it is first registered with the tree. The other field, Preferred network address, represents the two addresses that represent the network address for the workstation. These addresses can either be the IPX address (which actually uses the MAC address of the NIC card), or the IP address of the machine.

▶ OS — This represents the operating system type of the machine. The expected values would be WINNT, WIN95, WIN31, for example.

▶ Server — This represents the name of the current server. If the user login has not occurred and the preferred server has not been indicated, then this server could simply be the first server to respond with a connection. In WINNT systems, where the registration is running as part of a service, this server will be the first server to respond to the request for the connection and not necessarily the preferred server of the user.

▶ User — This is the login name of the user who was connected to the tree when the registration process first executed.

As an example, let's assume that a workstation had been registered with the following values:

```
CPU = PENTIUM
DNS = zen.novell.com
IPX address = 01010430:00600803c2e7
TCP/IP address = 137.65.61.99
OS = WINNT
Server = ZENSERVER
User = rtanner
Computer = RonComputer
```

If you were to administer the workstation import policy with the following naming attributes, the corresponding workstation name would be created, assuming pieces that are in quotes are a user defined string:

```
UserOS = rtannerWINNT
DNSCPU = zen.novell.comPENTIUM
User" "Network Address = rtanner 00600803c2e7
```

You must remember that these values are only used at workstation object creation time. Once the object is created, its name never changes. Therefore, if you replace the NIC card (although the address of the workstation changed, the name of the workstation does not), and if the name includes the NIC address, then the workstation would retain the name with the old NIC address.

Workstation Groups

The Workstation Groups page enables you to specify into which groups you would like to place the workstation object when it is created. By placing the workstation object into a specific group, you can automatically provide policies or rights to the workstation through group associations. Figure 6.11 shows the Workstation Groups page.

► ◦ ◀

FIGURE 6.11 *Workstation Import policy, Workstation Groups page*

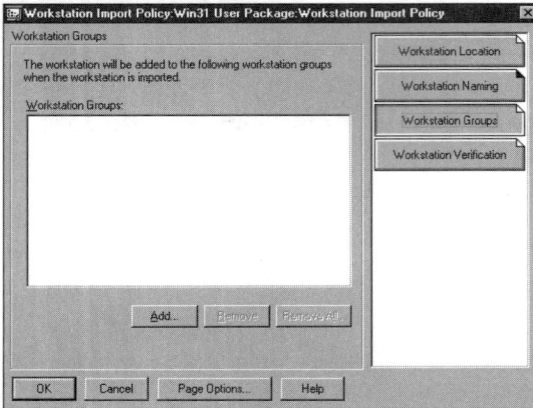

In the workstation groups page, you may add and remove groups in the list, and the workstation will be placed in as a member of each group. The following list describes the behavior of each button on the screen:

- Add — Press this button to add a group to the list. When this button is pressed, a dialog box is presented that enables you to browse the tree to identify the group. You browse the tree in the right pane and select the group in the left pane. Once a group is selected, it is added and displayed to the list.

- Remove — This button is activated when a group in the window is highlighted by pressing the left mouse button when the cursor is over the desired group. When a group is selected and this button is pressed, the group is removed from the list.

- Remove All — This button will completely remove all groups from the list and remove the set from consideration.

- Remember that this policy is only activated when a new workstation is imported into the tree. If a workstation that was created with this policy is associated with a group, and you go into the import policy and change the group memberships, the workstations that have already been created will retain their group memberships. Only the new workstations created after the change will be affected.

Workstation Verification

This field enables you to specify the length of time that the agents on the workstation should wait between cycles when they check for the existence of the workstation object and the modification of policies associated with the object. Figure 6.12 shows this screen.

Workstation Import policy, Workstation Verification page

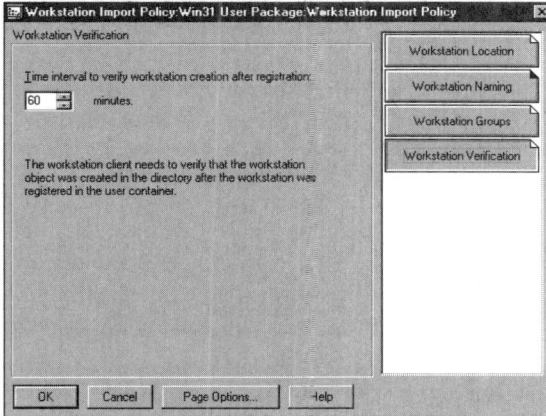

Creating a Windows 95/98 User Policy Package

In order to have a policy that affects users who are logging into the tree through workstations that are running the Windows 95 or Windows 98 operating systems, you must create a Windows 95/98 User policy package. To create a Windows 95/98 User policy package follow these steps:

1. Start NWAdmin32.

2. Browse to the container where you would like to have the policy package. Remember that you do not have to create the policy package in the container where you are doing the associations. You can associate the same policy package to many containers in your tree.

3. Create the policy package by clicking the right mouse button and choosing Create.

4. Select the Policy Package object in the list of objects that can be created in the selected container.

5. In the Create Policy Package dialog box, select the type of package you want to be a Windows 95 User Package, and name the object. Also, select the Define Additional Attributes checkbox so you can define policies.

6. Click OK. Next, NWAdmin32 displays a dialog box that enables you to create policies for this policy package.

7. Check and set any policies you desire for this Windows 95/98 User Policy package, and Click OK.

Policies Page

Once you have created a Windows 95/98 User policy package, you can activate policies that will be used for all Windows 95 and Windows 98 users who were associated with the policy package. If you click a policy within the policy package, that policy becomes active. An active policy is designated by a check in the checkbox next to it. The details of any particular policy can be modified by selecting the policy and pressing the Details button, or by double-clicking the policy itself. Figure 6.13 shows this policy screen.

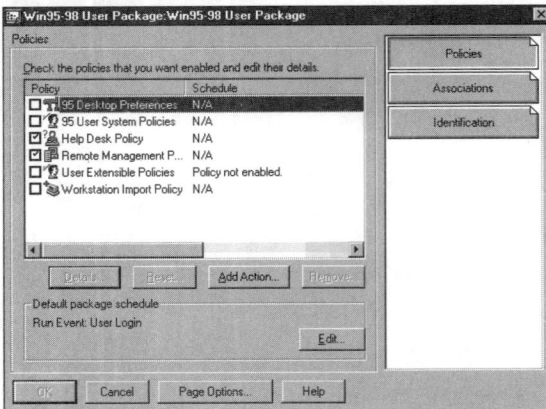

F I G U R E   6 . 1 3   *Windows 95/98 policy package Policies page*

The Reset button on the Policies page will reset the selected policy back to the system defaults for that policy.

Associations Page

The Associations page of the Windows 95/98 User Policy Package displays all the locations in the tree (containers) where the policy package has been placed. The Windows 95 and Windows 98 users who are in or below those containers will have this policy package enforced. Pressing the Add or Remove buttons enables you to add or remove containers in the list that are associated with this policy.

Identification Page

The Identification page of the Windows 95/98 User policy package simply enables you to enter additional description information to help users understand the purpose of the particular policy package.

Adding a 95 Desktop Preferences Policy

This policy enables you access to the ZAW/ZAK features that are exposed by the Microsoft Windows system. Within the ZENworks system, these ZAW/ZAK policies are divided into their logical parts: Desktop Preferences, User System Policies, and Workstation Policies. This policy enables the administrator to set the desktop preferences for any Windows 95 or Windows 98 system to which the user is currently connected. This policy follows users as they move from workstation to workstation.

Microsoft provides a tool called *poledit* that enables an administrator to construct some registry setting (ZAW/ZAK features) and have those settings saved in a .POL file. This .POL file can then be applied to any workstation by having the system look for these files on the server. The problem here is that these policy files must be located on every server any user may use as an initial connection. With ZENworks, this information is stored in these policies and in Novell Directory Services, thus making it always accessible to every user who connects to the system, without your having to place these policy files on every server.

Control Panel Page

The Control Panel page enables you to set the characteristics of several desktop items, including Accessibility, Display, Keyboard, Mouse, and Sounds. Figure 6.14 shows the Control Panel page.

► . . . . ◄

| F I G U R E   6.14 | *Windows 95/98 Desktop Preferences policy of the Windows 95 User Policy package* |

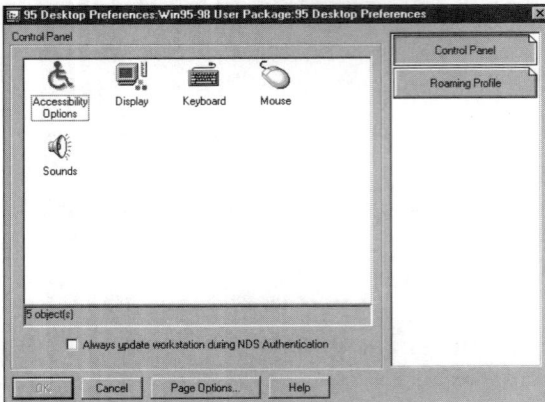

By double-clicking each of the icons presented in the Control Panel page of the Windows 95/98 Desktop Preferences policy, an administrator can configure the properties of each of these Control Panel items.

The standard scenario is that the agent will search the tree for this policy and apply it during the login of the user. This schedule can be changed in the policy package to be another scheduled time or event. To ensure that these preferences are always applied when the user logs into the tree, regardless of the schedule in the policy, you need to check the Always update workstation during NDS Authentication checkbox.

Accessibility Options   By double-clicking this icon, you are presented with a tabbed dialog box that gives you the capability to set the following properties:

► Keyboard page — Enables you to set the standard Windows 95/98 Accessibility Options for StickyKeys, FilterKeys, and ToggleKeys.

► Sound page — Enables you to set the SoundSentry and ShowSounds.

► Mouse page — Enables you to configure the MouseKeys.

► General page — Enables you to configure Automatic reset, Notification, and SerialKey devices.

You cannot set the Display properties through this policy.

Display   Double-clicking this icon brings up the property page that enables you to make the following configurations:

- ▶ Background tab — Allows setting of the wallpaper. You can specify that no wallpaper be presented, or specify a filename of the .BMP file to be displayed for the wallpaper.

- ▶ Screen Saver page — Enables you to configure whether a screen saver should be available. You may also specify a particular .SCR or .EXE to be executed for the screen saver. In addition to the screen saver program, you can specify whether the screen should be password protected. Also, on this page you may specify the capability to use the energy-saving features of your monitor.

- ▶ Appearance tab — Enables you to specify the color scheme you want applied for this user. You can set the color scheme to any of the following choices: Windows Standard, Brick, Desert, Eggplant, High Contrast Black, High Contrast White, Lilac, Maple, Marine (high color), Plum (high color), Rainy Day, Red White and Blue (VGA), Rose, Slate, Spruce, Storm (VGA), Teal (VGA), or Wheat.

- ▶ Plus page — Enables you to set some basic features of the Plus! Package. These features include: Use large icons, Show window contents while dragging, Smooth edges of screen fonts, Show icons using all possible colors, and Stretch desktop wallpaper to fit the screen.

Keyboard   This icon lets you indicate the Speed setting for the user. You can specify character repeat rates and the cursor blink rate.

Mouse   This icon brings up the property page of the mouse system for the user. From this property page, you can set the following features:

- ▶ Buttons tab — Provides you with the following features: Button configuration for left or right handed mouse, and Double-click speed.

- ▶ Pointers tab — Enables you to configure the mouse cursor to be used: 3D Pointers, Animated Hourglasses, Windows Standard, Windows Standard (extra large), or Windows Standard (large).

- ▶ Motion property tab — Gives you the capability to set the pointer speed and the pointer trail speed.

Sounds   This icon enables you to specify the sound scheme be one of the following for these users: No Sounds, Jungle Sound Scheme, Windows Default, Musica Sound Scheme, Robotz Sound Scheme, or Utopia Sound Scheme.

Roaming Profile Page

The Roaming Profile page allows you to specify if roaming profiles should exist in the system and where the information about them should be stored. Windows 95, Windows 98, and Windows NT store desktop information in profiles on the workstation. One method to allow the user's desktop to follow them from one workstation to another is to save this profile on a server. Then, when the user logs in to the system through any workstation, this profile can be found on the server and downloaded into the workstation at login time. This way the user's profile is all set up on the workstation as if it were the user's normal machine.

Another way to have a desktop follow the user is to use the ZENworks Application Launcher desktop features. This allows you to describe the desktop in NDS, and this will follow the user anywhere in the system without your having to keep a copy of Windows profile files on a server.

Figure 6.15 displays a screen capture of a Windows 95/98 Roaming Profile page.

F I G U R E   6.15   *Windows 95/98 Roaming Profile page*

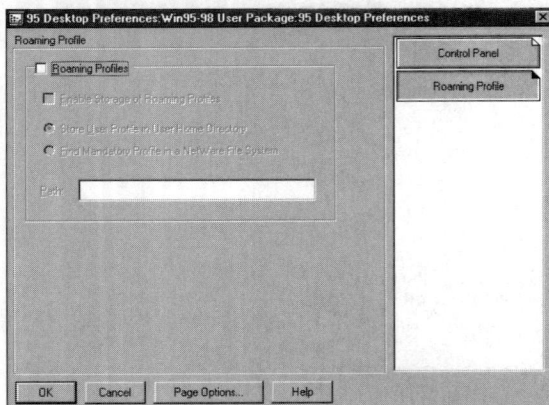

The following fields are available on this screen:

- ▶ Roaming Profiles — This flag must be set in order for the Roaming Profile feature to be activated on the system for the associated users. If this flag is not turned on, then roaming profiles will not be available.

- ▶ Enable Storage of Roaming Profiles — This flag will turn on the storing of profile files on the network. If this flag is not set, then the profiles are not copied to and from a network server.

▶ Store User Profile in User Home Directory — If this option is left on, then a directory will be created in the user's home directory, and all of the profiles will be copied to and from that location.

▶ Find Mandatory Profile in a NetWare File System — This will give users a company profile that is stored on a server, rather than giving them a personal profile.

Adding 95 User System Policies

This policy allows you access to the ZAW/ZAK features that are exposed by the Microsoft Windows system. Within the ZENworks system, these ZAW/ZAK policies are divided into their logical parts: Desktop Preferences, User System Policies, and Workstation Policies. This policy allows the administrator to set the system policies for any Windows 95 or Windows 98 system to which the user is currently connected. This policy follows users as they move from workstation to workstation.

Microsoft provides a tool called *poledit* that allows an administrator to construct some registry settings (ZAW/ZAK features) and have those settings saved in a .POL file. This .POL file can then be applied to any workstation by having the system look for these files on the server. The problem here is that these policy files must be located on every server any user may use as an initial connection. With ZENworks, this information is stored in these policies and into Directory Services, thus making it always accessible to every user who connects to the system, without your having to place these policy files on every server. To make the system more familiar, ZENworks has mimicked the user interface of the poledit program.

95 User System Policies Page

This page allows you to specify the specific registry settings for the users associated with this policy. Figure 6.16 displays a snapshot of one of these screens.

You edit the user system policy simply by clicking the tree components and then clicking the checkbox next to each item to enable, disable, or ignore the workstation setting. In some respects, this can be very confusing interface, but you need to keep in mind that you are choosing to either: 1) Enable — a check is present and provides this capability to the user, 2) Disable — a check is not present and you are turning off this capability for the user, or 3) Ignore — a grayed box appears, meaning that you want to leave the setting as it already is in the registry on the workstation. (For example, if the feature is turned off, it will be left off; if it is already turned on, it will be left on.)

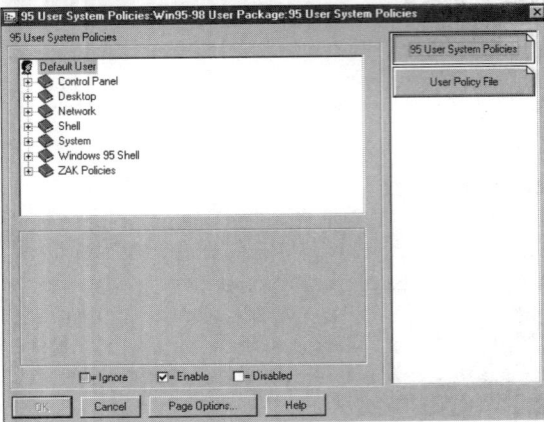

FIGURE 6.16 *Windows 95/98 user system policy*

Remember that the user policies are an accumulation of all the user policies found in the tree associated with the user or the containers, walking up the tree until the root is found or a search policy restricts the searching. Consequently, if there are several User System policies in the tree that are associated with the user, then the first policy found that has a setting of Enable or Disable for the particular attribute of the policy will be used. Should the attribute be set to Ignore, then a setting of Enable or Disabled in another policy may be applied.

You can administer each of the settings by simply walking the expanding book folders presented in the policy page. Once the folder is expanded and the final attribute is displayed, you may cycle through the Ignore, Enable, and Disabled settings by clicking the checkbox associated with each attribute.

User Policy File Page

This page gives you the additional option of specifying a .POL file that holds the ZAW/ZAK setting. When you use Microsoft tools such as poledit to construct the registry settings, this outputs a .POL file. You can use this page to identify a path to a .POL file that you want to use for the users associated with this policy. Figure 6.17 shows the User Policy File page.

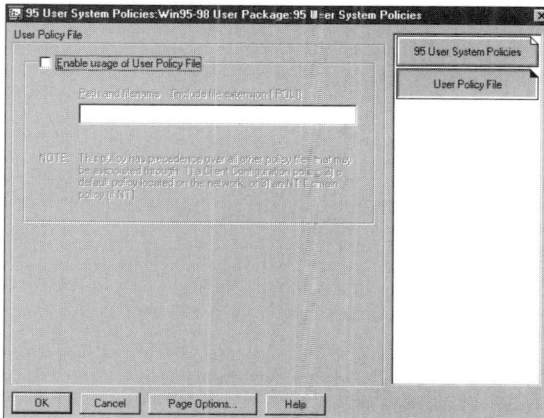

From within the User Policy File page, you can activate the feature by selecting the Enable usage of User Policy File flag and then specifying where the .POL file is located by typing a UNC path into the provided field.

Adding a Help Desk Policy

The Help Desk policy sets the features associated with the Help Request system that is provided with the ZENworks system. The Help Request system includes a program that can be presented to all users in the tree through the ZENworks Application Launcher. When ZENworks is installed, it creates an Application object that is associated with the Help Request program. If you associate this application object to users, groups, or containers, the end user is presented with this program on their desktop.

When the Help Request program is launched, it checks to see that there is a policy package associated with the currently logged in user, and if there is, a Help Desk policy is enabled. If there is a Help Desk policy, then the program launches on the desktop. The interface presented through the Help Requester is fully configured by the Help Desk policy (each page of the policy is described in the next sections).

The Help Desk Policy is the same for all platforms, and the administrator is presented with the same interface regardless of the individual policy package. Although the interface is the same, each individual Help Desk Policy is unique and independent for each policy package.

A Help Desk policy is activated for this policy package by either double-clicking the Help Desk policy or selecting the checkbox for the Help Desk policy. Once this is selected and a check is displayed in the checkbox, the Help Desk Policy is activated for all Windows 95 and Windows 98 users that are associated with the Windows 95/98 policy package.

Information Page

The Information page enables you to enter a selected set of information to have displayed through the Help Request system presented to the end user. When the Help Request system is launched on an individual's desktop, users are presented with this contact information. Figure 6.18 shows the Information page.

F I G U R E   6.18 *Information page of the Help Desk policy*

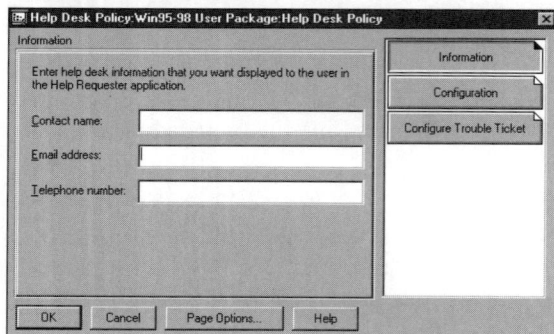

The Contact Name should be the name of the help desk personnel or service, such as PC Repair Services. The Telephone Number field is also presented to the end user of the Help Request application and should be the help number that the user can call for assistance. The E-mail address is the electronic mail address of the person or organization to be contacted when the Help Request system is launched. Trouble tickets generated by the Help Request system are automatically sent to this e-mail address.

Configuration Page

The Configuration page of the Help Desk policy enables you to administer the behavior of the Help Request system. By checking the Allow user to launch the Help Requester field, you activate the Help Request system for all Windows 95 and Windows 98 users who are associated with this policy package. Until this box is checked, any user who launches the Help Request system will be denied access. Once this box is checked, the Help Request system is activated. The Configuration page is reflected in Figure 6.19.

F I G U R E   6 . 1 9 *Configuration page of the Help Desk Policy*

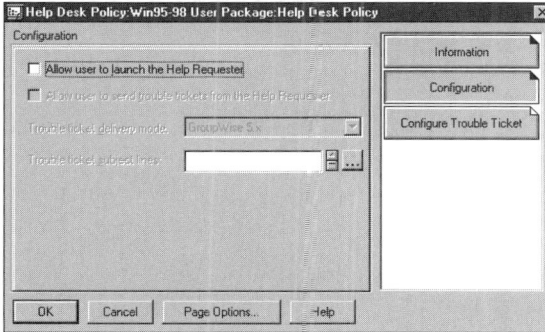

The Allow user to send trouble tickets from the Help Requester field is only activated when you check the box that enables users to launch the Help Requester. Before checking this box, the user may only use the information and call buttons on the Help Requester system. These buttons only provide information about the User and Workstation objects and the contact information that was administered on the Information page of the Help Desk policy.

The Trouble ticket delivery mode identifies for the system the method that should be used by the Help Requester application for the sending of generated trouble tickets. Currently, the choices for this mode are Groupwise 5.x and MAPI. By checking the GroupWise 5.x system, the Help Requester application will assume that the GroupWise 5.0 or greater libraries are present on the end users' workstations and will make the calls necessary to send the automatically created trouble tickets to the Contact Name e-mail address via these GroupWise calls. If the MAPI option is chosen, the same attempt is made, only using standard Windows MAPI calls to activate the e-mail system.

The Trouble ticket subject lines field enables you to enter as many trouble ticket subject lines as you wish. When you press the ... button, you are prompted to enter text for your subject line. These subject lines are presented to the end user via the Help Requester system. The end user may select which subject line to associate with the help request. This is also placed as the subject line in the e-mail message of the trouble ticket.

Configure Trouble Ticket Page

The Configure Trouble Ticket page enables you to specify the information you want stored in the trouble ticket about the user and the workstation that is issuing the ticket. Figure 6.20 shows this page.

▶ . . . . ◀

F I G U R E   6 . 2 0   *Help Desk Policy Configure Trouble Ticket page*

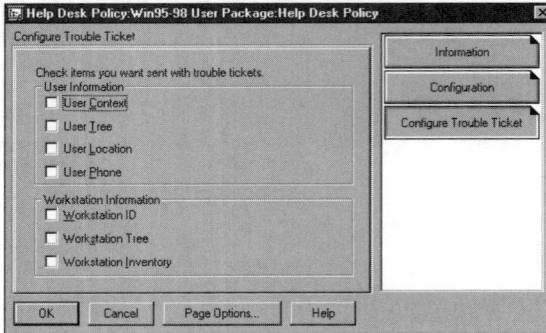

The following fields can be checked in the Configure Trouble Ticket to signal that the information should be included in the ticket. The information included is related either to the current user who is logged in to the tree, or to the workstation.

- ▶ User Context — This includes the tree context (for example, .user1.novell) of the user object of the user who is logged in to the workstation when the trouble ticket is sent.

- ▶ User Tree — This includes the tree name in the ticket.

- ▶ User Location — This includes the value in the location field of the user object for the current user.

- ▶ User Phone — This includes the phone number field of the user object for the current user.

- ▶ Workstation ID — This is the workstation object name of the workstation (for example, .workstation1.workstations.novell).

- ▶ Workstation Tree — This specifies the tree name where the workstation object is located.

▶ Workstation Inventory — This includes inventory information about the workstation. This information includes the following: Computer Type, Computer Model, Serial Number, Asset Tag, OS Type, OS Version, Novell Client version, NIC Type, Video Type, BIOS Type, Processor, Memory Size, Disk Info, MAC Address, Subnet Address, and IP Address. This is basically the same information that is stored in the workstation object in the tree.

Adding a Remote Management Policy

A Remote Management policy is activated for this policy package by either double-clicking the Remote Management policy or selecting the checkbox on the Remote Management policy. Once this is selected and a check is displayed in the checkbox, this Remote Management Policy is activated for all Windows 95/98 users who are associated with the Windows 95/98 policy package.

The Remote Management policy controls the features of the Remote Management subsystem that is shipped with the ZENworks package, and is not shipped with the ZENworks Starter Pack. The Remote Management system is composed of two parts: Remote Management Session Manager, which makes the connection and is used by the administrator; and the Remote Management Agents, which are installed on the end users' workstations. The remote control agents may be installed onto the workstation when the client that is shipped with ZENworks is installed, or the agents may be installed on the workstation through the remote control application objects that were added to your tree when you installed ZENworks. You would need to simply associate these application objects to the users and then have the ZENworks Application launcher install these agents automatically on the workstation. For more information, see Chapter 5.

The Remote Management system will make a peer-to-peer connection between the administrator's workstation and the remote workstation. This may be done using either the IPX or the TCP/IP protocol. In this policy, you may specify the preferred protocol for the connection. This protocol is attempted first, but if the connection cannot be made, then the alternate protocol will be used.

Remote controlling a workstation via ZENworks also requires rights within the Workstation object that represents the workstation you want to be controlled. Without these rights, the administrator will be denied access to the remote control subsystem. Both the session manager and the agents validate that the user has rights to remote control the workstation. You assign the remote control rights through the Remote Management Rights wizard or in the workstation object in the Remote Operators page.

Remote Management Page

The Remote Management page identifies the features that you want to be activated with the Remote Management system. Figures 6.21 through 6.24 show the Remote Management page and the tabbed values of the policy.

► . . . . ◄

FIGURE 6.21 *Remote Management policy page, General tab*

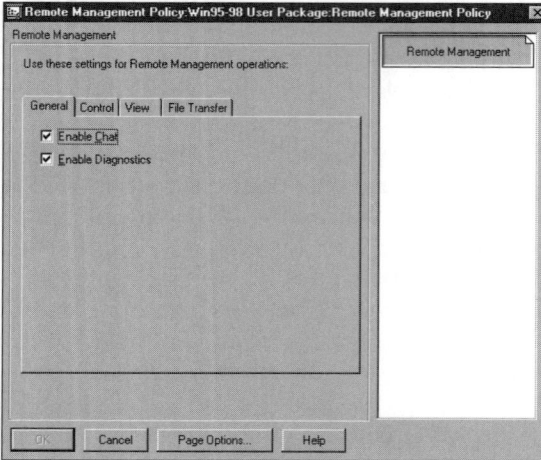

► . . . . ◄

FIGURE 6.22 *Remote Management policy page, Control tab*

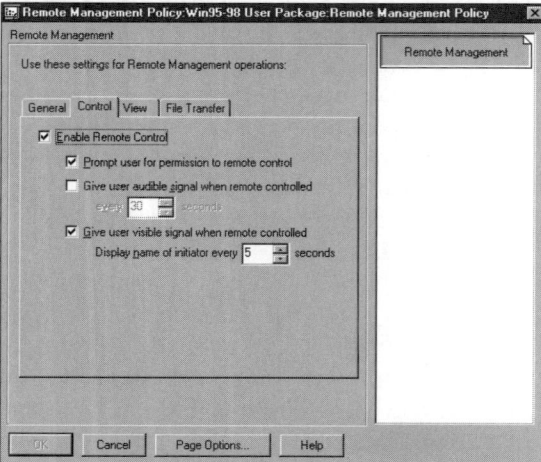

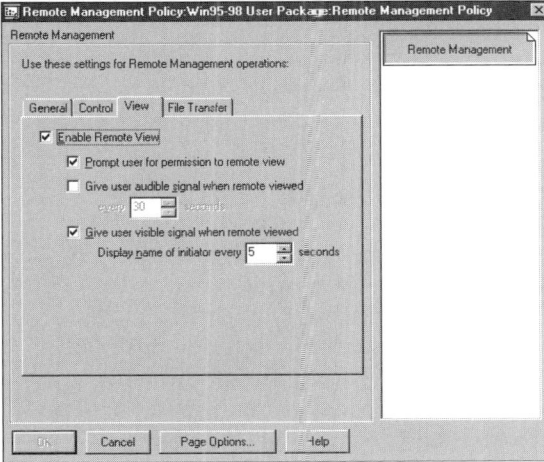

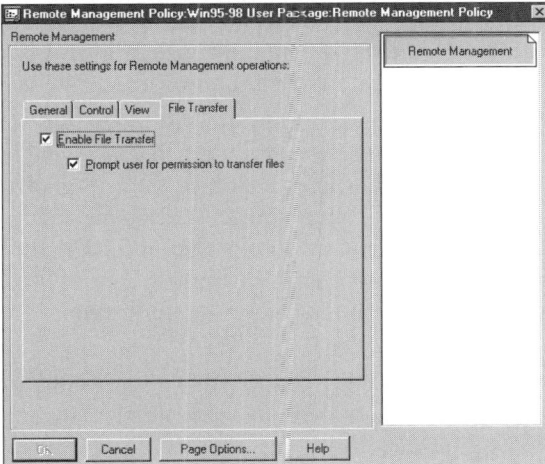

The following list describes each of the options available under each tab of the Remote Management policy:

► General Tab — This tab has options for general system functions:

- • Enable Chat — This enables users who have this policy associated with them to accept a chat request. Chat sets up a communication system between the initiator and the receiver, and allows them to type and send messages to one another.

- • Enable Diagnostics — This allows the agent on the workstations to perform a diagnostics report. This can be done from the Tools ⇨ ZENworks Remote Management menu. The Diagnostics utility will perform some basic queries on the system and return the information about the workstation. This information includes memory, environment, and processes running. Additionally, it would include NDS and NetWare connection information, client information, network drives, and open file lists, as well as printers, Network protocols, and network services that are active.

► Control Tab — This tab describes the feature enabling of remote control functions:

- • Enable Remote Control — When this option is enabled, the remote control subsystem can be activated. Without this setting on, no one may remote control the workstations where the currently logged in user has this policy associated with his or her user object.

- • Prompt user for permission to remote control — This option will cause a dialog box to be displayed on the end user's machine when a remote control session is started. The end user has the option of accepting or denying the remote control request. Within this dialog box, users are told who wants to remote control their machine, and are asked if they approve. If the user denies the remote control session, the session is terminated and the administrator cannot remote control the workstation.

- • Give user audible system when remote controlled — This option will periodically provide the end user with a tone while the remote control session is active. You can also set the number of seconds between each beep.

- Give user visible signal when remote controlled — This option will display a dialog box on the end user's desktop while the remote control session is active. The dialog box indicates that the workstation is being remote controlled, and also displays the NDS name of the user that is remote controlling the workstation. You can set the number of seconds that you want to have between the flashing of the name of the user that is initiating the remote control session.

▶ View Tab — This tab describes the feature enabling of the remote view functions. Remote view is the capability for the administrator to view the remote windows screen of the target machine, without being able to control the mouse or keyboard of the machine:

- Enable Remote View — When this option is enabled, the remote view subsystem can be activated. Without this setting on, no one may remote view the workstations where the currently logged in user has this policy associated with his or her user object.

- Prompt user for permission to remote view — This option will cause a dialog box to be displayed on the end user's machine when a remote view session is started. The end user has the option of accepting or denying the remote view request. Within this dialog box, users are told who wants to remote view their machine, and are asked if they approve. If the user denies the remote view session, the session is terminated and the administrator cannot remote view the workstation.

- Give user audible system when remote viewed — This option will provide the end user with a tone periodically while the remote view session is active. You can also set the number of seconds between each beep.

- Give user visible signal when remote viewed — This option will display a dialog box on the end user's desktop while the remote view session is active. The dialog box indicates that the workstation is being remote viewed, and also displays the NDS name of the user who is remote viewing the workstation. You can set the number of seconds you want to have between the flashing of the name of the user who is initiating the remote view session.

▶ File Transfer Tab — This tab describes the feature enabling of the file transfer system. This will enable you to send files to the remote workstation.

- Enable File Transfer — When this option is enabled, the file transfer subsystem can be activated. Without this setting on, no one may send files to the workstations where the currently logged in user has this policy associated with his or her user object.

- Prompt user for permission to transfer files — This option will cause a dialog box to be displayed on the end user's machine when a file transfer session is started. The end user has the option of accepting or denying the file transfer request. Within this dialog box, users are told who wants to perform the file transfer to their machine and are asked if they approve. If the user denies the file transfer session, the session is terminated and the administrator cannot send the files to the workstation.

Adding a User Extensible Policy

Microsoft has required that software packages that bear the Windows approved logo provide capabilities to be configured through .POL files. The poledit program enables you to edit these "extensible policies" and include them into the system .POL file. ZENworks also allows the policies that are stored in NDS to accept these additional "extensible polices" and provide them to all the users who are associated with these policies.

The User Extensible policy will allow you to import these special .ADM files into the NDS tree and have them administered and dispersed to the users associated with the policy package. Once these .ADM files have been imported into the tree, they can be administrated and associated to users in the NDS tree. These settings will be applied like the User system policies.

Extensible Policies

When you first bring up the User Extensible Policies dialog box, you are presented with a scheduled page as well as the Extensible Policies page. This page is displayed in Figure 6.25.

▶ . . . . ◀

FIGURE 6.25 *Extensible Policies page of the User Extensible Policies policy*

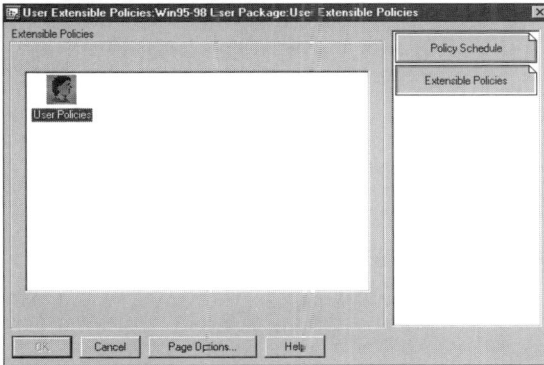

From the Extensible Policies page, you can double-click the User Policies icon. This launches a program to import the .ADM files. The window that is displayed from the program is shown in Figure 6.26.

FIGURE 6.26 *User policies import program initial screen*

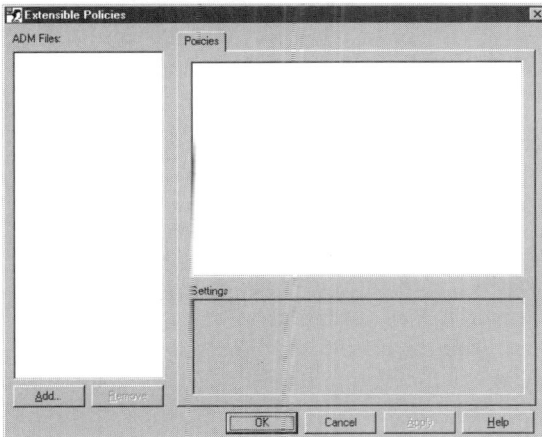

When the import program screen is brought up, you must specify the .ADM file that you want to import into the policy. Pressing the Add button brings up a dialog box enabling you either to specify the .ADM file or to browse to the location of the file. Once the file is specified, press OK to bring it into the Extensible Policies system. Figure 6.27 shows the screen after a sample Windows NT .ADM file has been brought into the system and a few folders have been opened.

► · ◄

F I G U R E   6 . 2 7   *User policies import program with an imported .ADM file*

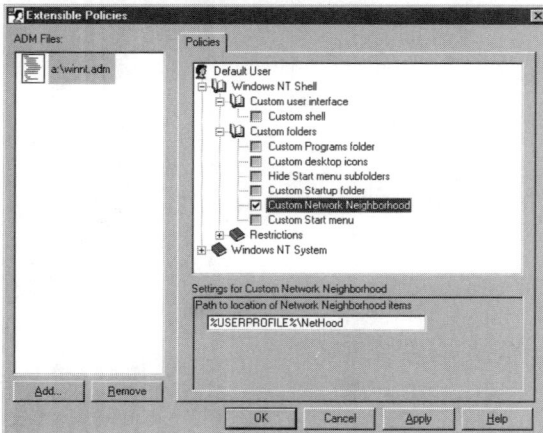

The Settings for Custom Network Neighborhood area of the screen displays the key that is being modified with the checkbox setting. By browsing through the settings, you can set the keys just as you do in poledit.exe.

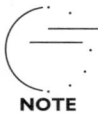

NOTE

The .ADM file must be stored on a server to which users have access. The policy will reference the .ADM file and will need to retrieve it to apply it to the users and to allow the administrators to modify the settings. We recommend, therefore, that you use a UNC path in specifying the location of the file.

Adding a Workstation Import Policy

This policy governs the behavior of the import process, which imports workstations into the tree and associates the physical workstation device to the workstation object in the tree. This policy describes how a workstation object should be named and where in the tree the workstation object should be created.

The import process is accomplished in four steps:

1. A Workstation Import policy must be created and associated with the first user who logs in to the workstation.

2. When the first user logs in to the tree, a registration process is activated that places some information about the user and the workstation into the immediate container of the user.

3. The administrator must execute the workstation import program, which imports information from the registration stored in the user's container and creates the workstation object using the information given in the registration process.

4. The next user to log in to the system after the import process is completed will cause the system to detect that a workstation object has been created for that particular device. Once the object is discovered, the NDS name of the workstation object is stored in the workstation registry, and the workstation can connect to the system via that workstation object.

When the workstation object has been associated with a physical device (that is, the import process described above has been completed), then that workstation object will receive all information about the workstation and will represent that workstation in the tree. Associations of policies with that workstation object, workstation container, or workstation group will govern behavior of the systems on that workstation.

You may activate a workstation import policy by going to the details of the Windows 95/98 Workstation Package object. Within that policy package, you may select and activate the workstation import policy. All users who are associated with that package will now use that import policy to describe how the import policy should behave.

Workstation Location Page

This page enables you to identify the container in the tree that should hold the workstation object when it is created during the import process. Figure 6.28 shows this screen.

Workstation import policy, workstation location

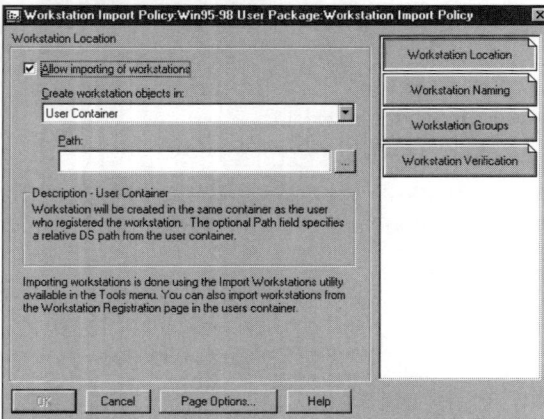

The Allow importing of workstations option enables or disables the capability to import workstations from this user. Once this is activated, the other fields of the page are usable.

The Create workstation objects in drop-down box provides you with various objects for locating the container in which to place the workstation objects. The options are as follows:

▶ User Container — This signals that the container that holds the user object of the user that had logged into the system when the registration of the workstation occurred will be the container that also will hold the workstation object. Remember, the first user who connects to the system will have the association to the workstation. A path may be specified in the path field that would be considered to be relative to the user's container. The path field is constructed by entering a relative path. This relative path is constructed using a series of dots and container names. For each dot in the path, the system will move up one level from the associated object container. For example, the path of ..Workstations means for the system to go up two levels and then to a container called Workstations at that level. If an alternate user is desired, you must run the un-registration tool described in Chapter 10.

▶ Associated Object Container — This signals that the container that has the policy package associated with it will be used as the starting container to place the workstation object. If a path is specified, then the associated container is used as the base and the path is considered a relative path. The path field is constructed by entering a relative path. This relative path is constructed with a series of dots and container names. For each dot in the path, the system will move up one level from the associated object container. For example, the path of ..Workstations means for the system to go up two levels and then to a container called Workstations at that level.

► Selected Container — This indicates that the specified path is an absolute container path in the tree. The Path field is required with this selection and must identify the specific container that will hold the workstation object.

Workstation Naming Page

On this page, the administrator can describe how the import process should use the information in the registration to craft the name of the work-station object. Figure 6.29 shows the naming page.

F I G U R E   6 . 2 9 *Workstation Import Policy, Workstation Naming page*

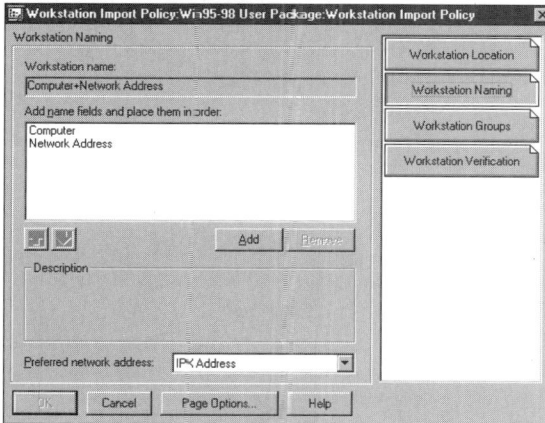

The Workstation name field displays the final combination of registration information that will be incorporated into the name. In the preceding example, the workstation object name will be the computer name followed by the network address This is confirmed by the fact that the workstation name field is shown as Computer+Network Address. If the computer name were Rtanner and the network address of the NIC card were 12345, then the workstation object name would be Rtanner12345.

The Add name fields and place them in order field displays the various components that are put together to form the workstation name. Each line displayed in this field represents a value that will be part of the name. The order of the lines from top to bottom represent the order in which they will appear in the name. The options that can be placed in the names are as follows:

▶ <User Defined> — This represents an administrator-defined string. When this field is chosen, the administrator is prompted to enter a string into the dialog box. This string will be placed into the name. This can be any combination of standard ASCII visible characters, including white space characters.

▶ Computer — This represents the name that was given to the computer, usually during installation of the operating system.

▶ Container — This represents the name of the container into which the workstation object is placed. This name will be included in the workstation name.

▶ CPU — This value represents the CPU type of the machine. Currently, this attribute has no value for Windows 3.1 and DOS machines, and retrieves its information in the Windows 95/98 and NT environment from the operating system. The possible values are 386, 486, and PENTIUM.

▶ DNS — This represents the DNS (Domain Name Services) name of the computer.

▶ Network Address — This represents the address of the machine when it is first registered with the tree. The other field, Preferred network address, contains the two addresses that represent the network address for the workstation. These addresses can either be the IPX address (it actually uses the MAC address of the NIC card) or the IP address of the machine.

▶ OS — This represents the operating system type of the machine. The expected values would be WINNT, WIN95, and WIN31, for example.

▶ Server — This represents the name of the current server. If the user login has not occurred and the preferred server has not been specified, then this server could simply be the first server that responded with a connection. In WINNT systems, where the registration is running as part of a service, this will be the first server to respond to the request for the connection, and not necessarily the preferred server of the user.

▶ User — This is the login name of the user who was connected to the tree when the registration process first executed.

As an example, let us assume that a workstation had been registered with the following values:

```
CPU = PENTIUM
DNS = zen.novell.com
IPX address = 01010480:00600803c2e7
TCP/IP address = 137.65.61.99
OS = WINNT
Server = ZENSERVER
User = rtanner
Computer = RonComputer
```

If we were to administer the workstation import policy with the following naming attributes, then the corresponding workstation name would be created, assuming pieces that are in quotes are a user-defined string:

```
UserOS = rtannerWINNT
DNSCPU = zen.novell.comPENTIUM
User" "Network Address = rtanner 00600803c2e7
```

You must remember that these values are only used at workstation object creation time. Once the object is created, its name never changes. Therefore, if you replace the NIC card (even though the address of the workstation changed, the name of the workstation does not), and if the name includes the NIC address, then the workstation would retain the name with the old NIC address.

Workstation Groups

The Workstation Groups page enables you to specify into which groups you would like to place the workstation object when it is created. By placing the workstation object into a specific group, you can automatically provide policies or rights to the workstation by group associations. Figure 6.30 shows the Workstation Groups page.

Workstation Import Policy Workstation Groups page

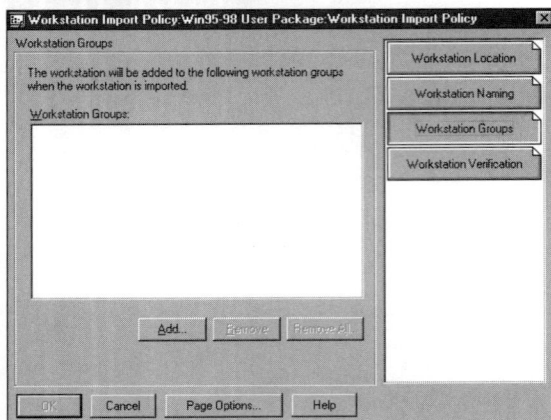

In the Workstation Groups page, you may add and remove groups in the list, and the workstation will be placed in as a member of each group. The following describes the behavior of each button on the screen:

- ▶ Add — Press this button to add a group to the list. When the button is pressed, a dialog box is presented that enables you to browse the tree to identify the group. You browse the tree in the right pane and select the group in the left pane. Once a group is selected, it is added and displayed in the list.

- ▶ Remove — This button is activated when a group in the window is highlighted by pressing the left mouse button when the cursor is over the desired group. When a group is selected and this button is pressed, the group is removed from the list.

- ▶ Remove All — This button will completely remove all groups from the list and clean the set from consideration.

- ▶ Remember that this policy is only activated when a new workstation is imported into the tree. If a workstation that was created with this policy is associated with a group, and you go into the import policy and change the group memberships, the workstations that have already been created will retain their group memberships. Only the new workstations created after the change will be affected.

Workstation Verification

This field enables you to specify the length of time that the agents on the workstation should wait between cycles when they check for the existence of the workstation object and the modification of policies associated with the object. Figure 6.31 shows this screen.

FIGURE 6.31 *Workstation Import Policy Workstation Verification page*

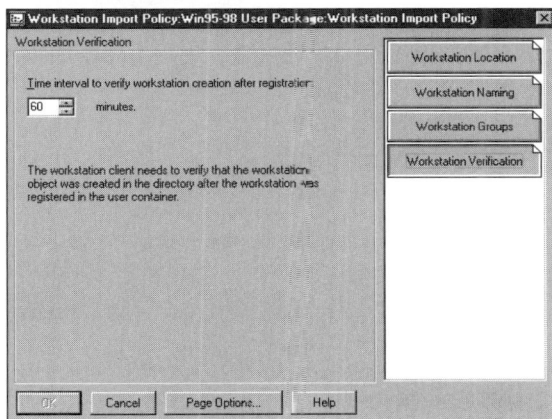

Creating a Windows NT User Policy Package

To have a policy that affects users who are logging in to the tree through workstations that are running the Windows NT operating system, you must create a Windows NT User policy package. To create a Windows NT User policy package, do the following:

1. Start NWAdmin32.

2. Browse to the container where you would like to have the policy package. Remember that you do not have to create the policy package in the container where you are doing the associations. You can associate the same policy package to many containers in your tree.

3. Create the policy package by clicking the right mouse button and choosing Create.

4. Select the Policy Package object in the list of objects that can be created in the selected container.

5. In the Create Policy Package dialog box, select the type of package you want to be a Windows NT User Package and name the object. Also, select the Define Additional Attributes checkbox so you can define policies.

6. Click OK. Next, NWAdmin32 displays a dialog box that enables you to create policies for this policy package.

7. Check and set any policies you desire for this Windows NT User policy package and click OK.

Policies Page

Once you have created a Windows NT User policy package, you can activate policies that will be used for all Windows NT users that were associated with the policy package. If you click a policy within the policy package, that policy becomes active. An active policy is designated by a check in the check box. The details of any particular policy can be modified by selecting the policy and pressing the Details button, or by double-clicking the policy itself. Figure 6.32 shows the Windows NT User policy package.

▶ . . . . ◀
F I G U R E   6 . 3 2   *Windows NT Policy Package Policies page*

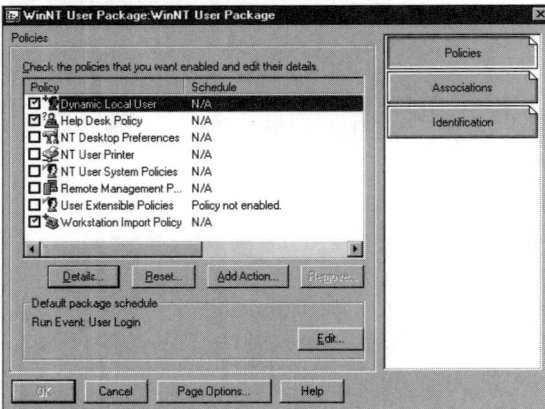

The Reset button on the policies page will set the selected policy back to the system defaults for that policy.

Associations Page

The Associations page of the Windows NT User policy package displays all the locations in the tree (containers) where the policy package has been placed. The Windows NT users who are in or below those containers will have this policy package enforced.

Identification Page

The Identification page of the Windows NT User policy package simply allows users to enter additional description information to help others understand the purpose of the particular policy package.

Adding a Dynamic Local User Policy

Often, several users within a company may have access to shared Windows NT workstations, and it would be an administrative nightmare to have to keep up accounts for all users of these shared systems. Consequently, ZENworks has the capability to dynamically create accounts on the local NT workstation while the user is logging in to the system. The local account is literally created at login time.

By having the system automatically create the account at the time that the user is authenticated to the Novell Directory Services tree, any of these users can log in to any Windows NT workstation and have a local account automatically created on that workstation. To prevent the system from allowing any user to log in to a specific workstation, administer the Restrict Login policy in the Windows NT Workstation policy package. The Restrict Login policy enables you to specify which users can or cannot log in to the specific workstation. Figure 6.33 shows the Dynamic Local User policy page.

Checking the Enable Dynamic Local User option will allow the system to start creating accounts on the local system. The following options may be set in this policy:

▶ Manage Existing NT account (if any) — When checked, this allows the ZENworks agents to manage a previously existing account for this user through the Dynamic Local User system. If this option is checked, then any previously generated account will be subject to the properties that you administer in this policy.

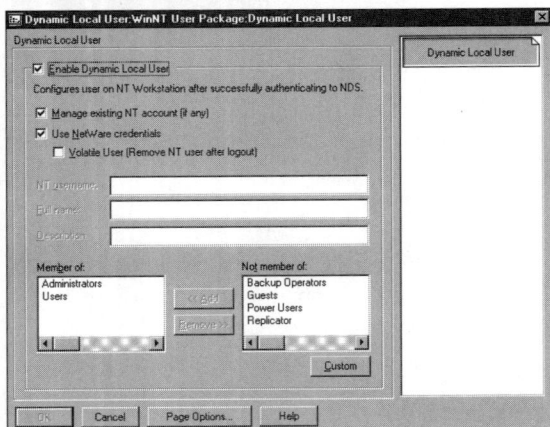

▶ Use NetWare credentials — When this is enabled, the system will use the password that is used for the Novell Directory Services as the password for the local account.

▶ Volatile User (Remove NT user after logout) — This checkbox is only accessible if you have checked the Use NetWare credentials box. This checkbox enables the system to remove the local account that was used for the dynamic user when the user logs out of the system. Having this feature enabled, in conjunction with enabling the Manage Existing NT account (if any) options, will cause a previously created local account to become volatile and be removed when that person logs out of the workstation.

▶ NT username — This field is only accessible if the Use NetWare credentials option is disabled. The system will use the specified name for the local account when any Novell Directory Services user logs in to the system.

▶ Full name — This field is only accessible if the Use NetWare credentials option is disabled. The system will use the specified full name for the local account when any Novell Directory Services user logs in to the system.

▶ Description — This field is only accessible if the Use NetWare credentials option is disabled. The system will use the given description for the local account when any Novell Directory Services user logs into the system.

▶ Member of/Not member of — This list allows you to specify that the local account created or used for these users be a member of certain local NT groups.

▶ Custom — This button enables you to create new custom groups to the list in order to make the dynamic local users members of these groups.

If the NetWare credentials are not used for the Dynamic Local User policy, causing the NT username, Full name, and Description to be used, then this account will always be volatile and will be created and removed each time a user logs in to and out of the workstation.

Additionally, if *any* password restrictions (such as Minimum Password Age, or Length, or Uniqueness) have been placed in the local workstation policy, then the Dynamic Local User system will not be activated for that workstation. A dialog box notifying the user that Dynamic Local User features have been disabled will be displayed whenever anyone attempts to log in to the workstation.

Adding a Help Desk Policy

The Help Desk policy sets the features associated with the Help Request system that is provided with the ZENworks system. The Help Request system includes a program that can be presented to all users in the tree through the ZENworks Application Launcher. When ZENworks is installed, it creates an Application object that is associated with the Help Request program. When you associate this Application object to users, groups, or containers, end users will be presented with this program on their desktop.

When the Help Request program is launched, it checks to see if there is a policy package associated with the currently logged in user, and if there is, then a Help Desk policy is enabled. If there is a Help Desk policy, the program launches on the desktop. The interface presented through the Help Requester is fully configured by the Help Desk policy; each page of the policy is described in the next few sections.

The Help Desk policy is the same for all platforms, and the administrator is presented with the same interface regardless of the individual policy package. Although the interface is the same, each individual Help Desk policy is unique and independent for each policy package.

You activate a Help Desk policy for this policy package by either double-clicking the Help Desk policy or selecting the checkbox on the Help Desk policy. Once this is selected and a check is displayed in the checkbox, this Help Desk policy is activated for all Windows NT users that are associated with the Windows NT policy package.

Information Page

The Information page enables you to enter a selected set of information to have displayed through the Help Request system presented to the end user. When the Help Request system is launched on an individual's desktop, the user is presented with this contact information. Figure 6.34 shows the Information page.

► · ◄

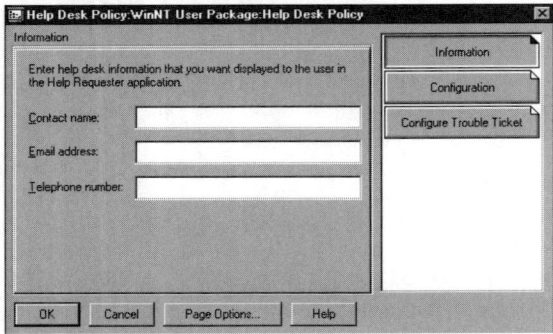

FIGURE 6.34 *Information page of the Help Desk policy*

The Contact Name should be the name of the help desk personnel or service, such as PC Repair Services. The Telephone Number field is also presented to the end user of the Help Request application, and should give the help number that the user can call for assistance. The E-mail address is an electronic mail address of the person or organization to be contacted when the Help Request system is launched. Trouble tickets that are generated by the Help Request system are automatically sent to this e-mail address.

Configuration Page

The Configuration page of the Help Desk policy enables you to administer the behavior of the Help Request system. By checking the Allow user to launch the Help Requester field, you activate the Help Request system for all Windows NT users who are associated with this policy package. Until this box is checked, any user who launches the Help Request system will be denied access. Once this box is checked, the Help Request system is activated. The Configuration page is reflected in Figure 6.35.

► . . . . ◄

F I G U R E   6 . 3 5   *Configuration page of the Help Desk policy*

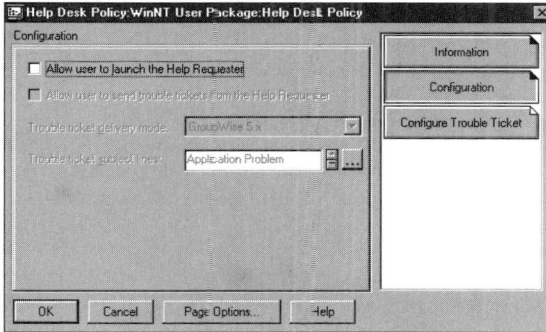

The Allow user to send trouble tickets from the Help Requester field is only activated when you check the box that enables the users to launch the Help Requester. Before checking this box, the user may only use the information and call buttons on the Help Requester system. These buttons only provide information about the user and workstation objects and the contact information that was administered on the Information page of the Help Desk policy.

The Trouble ticket delivery mode identifies for the system the method that should be used by the Help Requester application for the sending of generated trouble tickets. Currently, the choices for this mode are Groupwise 5.x and MAPI. By checking the GroupWise 5.x system, the Help Requester application assumes that the GroupWise 5.0 or greater libraries are present on the end user's workstation and will make the calls necessary to send the automatically created trouble tickets to the Contact Name e-mail address via these GroupWise calls. If the MAPI option is chosen, then the same attempt is made, only using standard Windows MAPI calls to activate the e-mail system.

The Trouble ticket subject lines field enables you to enter as many trouble ticket subject lines as you wish. When you press the ... button, you are prompted to enter text for your subject line. These subject lines are presented to the end user via the Help Requester system. The end user may select which subject line to associate with the help request. This is also placed as the subject line in the e-mail message of the trouble ticket.

Configure Trouble Ticket Page

The Configure Trouble Ticket page allows you to specify the information you want stored in the trouble ticket about the user and the workstation that is issuing the ticket. Figure 6.36 shows this page.

► . . . . ◄

F I G U R E 6 . 3 6 *Help Desk Policy Configure Trouble Ticket page*

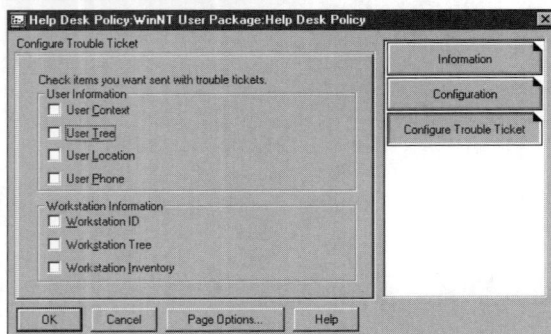

The following fields can be checked in the Configure Trouble Ticket page to signal that the information should be included in the ticket. The information included is either related to the current user who is logged in to the tree or the workstation.

► User Context — This includes the tree context (for example, .user1.novell) of the user object of the user who is logged in to the workstation when the trouble ticket is sent.

► User Tree — This includes the tree name in the ticket.

► User Location — This includes the value in the location field of the user object for the current user.

► User Phone — This includes the phone number field of the user object for the current user.

► Workstation ID — This will be the workstation object name of the workstation (for example, .workstation1.workstations.novell).

▶ Workstation Tree — This specifies the tree name where the workstation object is located.

▶ Workstation Inventory — This includes inventory information about the workstation. This information includes the following: Computer Type, Computer Model, Serial Number, Asset Tag, OS Type, OS Version, Novell Client version, NIC Type, Video Type, BIOS Type, Processor, Memory Size, Disk Info, MAC Address, Subnet Address, and IP Address. This is basically the same information that is stored in the workstation object in the tree.

Adding NT Desktop Preferences Policy

This policy enables you access to the ZAW/ZAK features that are exposed by the Microsoft Windows system. Within the ZENworks system, these ZAW/ZAK policies are divided into their logical parts: Desktop Preferences, User System Policies, and Workstation Policies. This policy allows the administrator to set the desktop preferences for any Windows NT system to which the user is currently connected. This policy follows users as they move from workstation to workstation

Microsoft provides a tool called *poledit*, which allows an administrator to construct some registry settings (ZAW/ZAK features) and have those settings saved in a .POL file. This .POL file can then be applied to any workstation by having the system look for these files on the server. The problem here is that these policy files must be located on every server that any user may use as an initial connection. With ZENworks, this information is stored in these policies and in the Novell Directory Services, thus making it always accessible to every user who connects to the system, without your having to place these policy files on every server.

The NT Desktop Preferences allow you to set Control Panel features as well as Roaming Profile configurations.

Control Panel Page

By double-clicking each of the icons presented in the Control Panel page of the Windows NT Desktop Preferences policy, the administrator can configure the properties of each of these control panel items. Figure 6.37 displays the Control Panel page.

FIGURE 6.37
Control Panel page of a Windows NT Desktop Preferences policy

The standard scenario is that the agent will search the tree for this policy and apply it during login of the user. This schedule can be changed in the policy package to be another scheduled time or event. To ensure that these preferences are always applied when the user logs in to the tree, regardless of the schedule in the policy, you need to check the Always update workstation during NDS Authentication checkbox.

Accessibility Options By double-clicking on the Accessibility Options icon, you are presented with a tabbed dialog box giving you the capability to set the following properties:

► Keyboard page — Allows you to set the standard Windows NT Accessibility Options for StickyKeys, FilterKeys, and ToggleKeys.

► Sound page — Allows you to set SoundSentry and ShowSounds.

► Mouse page — Allows you to configure the MouseKeys.

► General page — Allows you to configure Automatic reset, Notification, and SerialKey devices.

You cannot set the Display properties through this policy.

Console   This icon will bring up the property page that enables you to configure the properties of the console window (for example, DOS box) for the Windows NT system. The Console Windows properties allow you to set the following:

▶ Options tab — Allows the setting of console options such as Cursor Size, Display Options, Command History sizes and buffers, QuickEdit Mode, and Insert Mode.

▶ Layout tab — Provides the configuration for the Screen Buffer Size, Window Size, and the Window Position.

▶ Colors tab — Provides for the setting of the Console colors for the text and backgrounds.

From this policy, you cannot set the font properties of the console window.

Display   Double-clicking on this icon brings up the property page that enables you to make the following configurations:

▶ Background tab — Allows setting of the wallpaper. You can specify that no wallpaper be presented, or specify the name of the .BMP file to be displayed for the wallpaper.

▶ Screen Saver page — Allows you to configure whether a screen saver should be available. You may also specify a particular .SCR or .EXE file to be executed for the screen saver. In addition to the screen saver program you can specify whether the screen should be password protected. Also, on this page, you may specify the capability to use the energy-saving features of your monitor.

▶ Appearance tab — Allows you to specify the color scheme you want applied for this user. You can set the color scheme to any of the following choices: Windows Standard, Brick, Desert, Eggplant, High Contrast Black, High Contrast White, Lilac, Maple, Marine (high color), Plum (high color), Rainy Day, Red White and Blue (VGA), Rose, Slate, Spruce, Storm (VGA), Teal (VGA), or Wheat.

▶ Plus page — Allows you to set some basic features of the Plus! Package. These features include: Use large icons, Show window contents while dragging, Smooth edges of screen fonts, Show icons using all possible colors, and Stretch desktop wallpaper to fit the screen.

Keyboard   This icon allows you to indicate the Speed setting for the user. You can specify character repeat rates and the cursor blink rate.

Mouse   This icon will bring up the property page of the mouse system for the user. From this property page, you can set the following features:

▶ Buttons tab — Provides you with the following features: Button configuration for left or right handed mouse and Double-click speed.

▶ Pointers tab — Allows you to configure the mouse cursor to be used: 3D Bronze, 3D-White, Conductor, Dinosaur, Hands 1, Hands 2, Magnified, Old Fashioned, Variations, Windows Animated, or Windows Default.

▶ Motion property tab — Gives you the capability to set the pointer speed and the pointer trail speed.

Sounds   This icon enables you to specify the sound scheme be one of the following for these users: No Sounds, Jungle Sound Scheme, Windows Default, Musica Sound Scheme, Robotz Sound Scheme, or Utopia Sound Scheme.

Roaming Profile Page

The settings for any particular desktop, such as the desktop icons, screen colors, and task bar selections are stored in profiles. With the Roaming Profile feature, these profiles can be placed into the file system on the network. This way, if users who have their profiles saved on the network log in to any NT workstation, their profiles will be retrieved from the network and brought to that workstation. This presents the user with a consistent look and feel for the workstation, regardless of which actual workstation he or she is using. Any changes to the desktop or preferences will be stored on the network and there-fore reflected the next time the user logs in to any NT workstation. Figure 6.38 shows a screen image from the Roaming Profile page.

In the Roaming Profile page, the administrator can determine whether Roaming Profiles are available. If they are available, then you will also want to check the Enable Storage of Roaming Profiles checkbox. This will allow the profiles to be stored on a network server for access from any NT workstation.

Roaming Profile page of a Windows NT Desktop Preferences policy

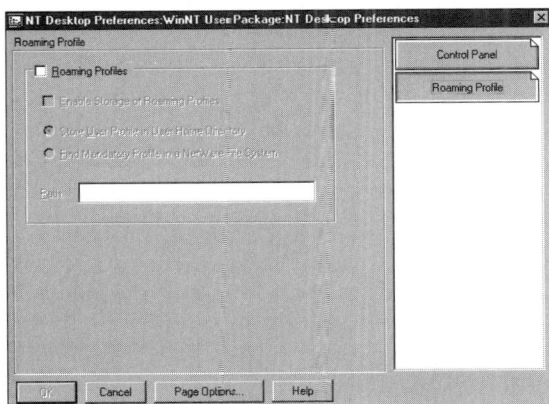

Once storage has been enabled, you have the choice of allowing the profiles to be stored either in the Users home directory or in a specified file system directory. By specifying that the profiles be stored in the User's home directory, a subdirectory called Windows NT 4.0 Workstation Profile is created in the user's home directory. Within that directory, the profile information will be stored and maintained. If you identify a specific directory, all users who log in to the NT workstation with that policy will store the desktop information directly in that directory and will share the profiles with all users who log in to that workstation. This is why storage in a specific directory is recommended for mandatory profiles only.

Adding NT User Printer Policy

This policy allows the administrator to set up network printers on the local Windows NT desktop. In order to add printers to the policy, you must have already set up some printers into your NetWare system, and have corresponding printer and print queue objects in your Novell Directory Services tree. Figure 6.39 shows the policy screen.

Windows NT User Printer policy

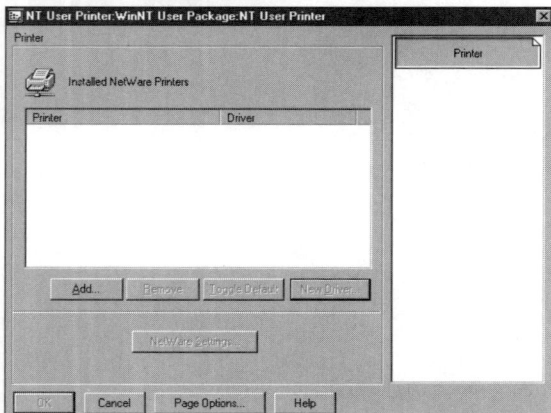

Perform the following steps to add a printer to the printer policy:

1. Click the Add button.

2. Browse through the dialog box and select the Printer or Print Queue object that you want to deliver to the users associated with the policy.

To remove a printer from the policy, simply highlight the printer in the list and click the Remove button.

Any printers that have been added to this list will be added to users' desktops automatically when they first log in to the system. When the printer is removed from this list, it is removed from the local system account the next time the user logs in to the workstation.

Adding NT User System Policies

This policy allows you access to the ZAW/ZAK features that are exposed by the Microsoft Windows system. Within the ZENworks system, these ZAW/ZAK policies are divided into their logical parts: Desktop Preferences, User System Policies, and Workstation Policies. This policy allows the administrator to set the system policies for any Windows NT system to which the user is currently connected. This policy follows users as they move from workstation to workstation.

Microsoft provides a tool called *poledit* that allows an administrator to construct some registry setting (ZAW/ZAK features) and have those settings saved in a .POL file. This .POL file can then be applied to any workstation by having the system look for these files on the server. The problem here is that these policy files must be located on every server that any user may use as an initial connection. With ZENworks, this information is stored in these policies and in Directory Services, thus making it always accessible to every user who connects to the system without your having to place these policy files on every server. To make the system more familiar, ZENworks has mimicked the user interface of the poledit program.

NT User System Policies Page
This page allows you to administer the ZAW/ZAK features. Figure 6.40 shows this screen.

FIGURE 6.40 *Windows NT User System Policies*

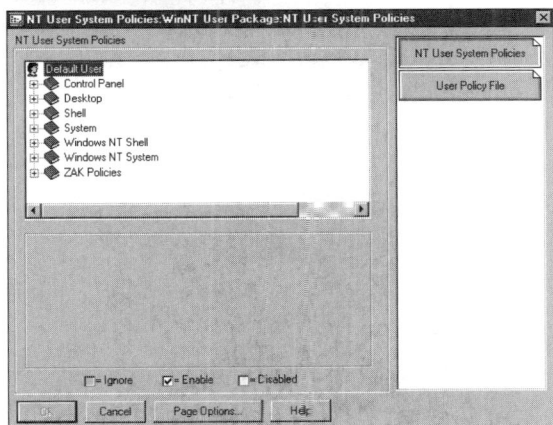

You would edit the above user system policy by simply clicking the tree components and then clicking on the checkbox next to each item to enable, disable, or ignore the workstation setting. In some respects, this can be very confusing interface, but you need to keep in mind that you are choosing to either: 1) Enable — a check is present and allows this capability to the user, 2) Disable — a check is not present and you are turning off this capability for the user, or 3) Ignore — a grayed box meaning that you want to leave the setting as it already is in the registry on the workstation (for example, if the feature is turned off it will be left off, or if it is already turned on it will be left on).

Remember that the user policies are an accumulation of all of user policies found in the tree associated with the user or the containers, walking up the tree until the root is found or a search policy restricts the searching. Consequently, if there are several User System policies in the tree that are associated with the user, the first policy found that has a setting of Enable or Disable for the particular attribute of the policy will be used. Should the attribute be set to Ignore, then a setting of Enable or Disable in another policy may be applied.

You can administer each of the settings by simply walking the expanding book folders presented in the policy page. Once the folder is expanded and the final attribute is displayed, you may cycle through the Ignore, Enable, and Disable settings by clicking the checkbox associated with each attribute.

User Policy File Page

This page gives you the additional option of specifying a .POL file that holds the ZAW/ZAK setting. When you use a Microsoft tool such as poledit to construct the registry settings, it outputs a .POL file. You can use this page to identify a path to a .POL file that you want to use for the users associated with this policy. Figure 6.41 shows the User Policy File page.

► .   .   .   .   ◄

F I G U R E   6 . 4 1   *Windows NT User Policy File page*

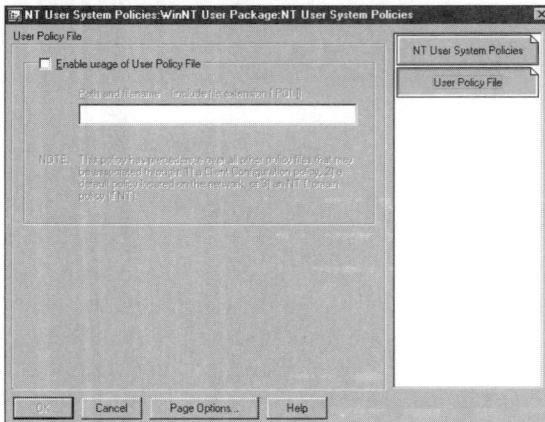

From within the User Policy File page, you can activate the feature by selecting the Enable usage of User Policy File flag, and then specify where the .POL file is located by typing a UNC path into the provided field.

Adding a Remote Management Policy

A Remote Management policy is activated for this policy package by either double-clicking the Remote Management policy or selecting the checkbox on the Remote Management policy. Once this is selected and a check is displayed in the checkbox, this Remote Management policy is activated for all Windows NT users who are associated with the Windows NT policy package.

The Remote Management policy controls the features of the Remote Management subsystem that is shipped with the ZENworks package and is not shipped with the ZENworks Starter Pack. The Remote Management system is composed of two parts: Remote Management Session Manager, which makes the connection and is used by the administrator, and the Remote Management Agents, which are installed on the end user's workstation. The remote control agents may be installed on the workstation when the client that is shipped with ZENworks is installed, or the agents may be installed on the workstation through the remote control application objects that were added to your tree when you installed ZENworks. You would simply need to associate these application objects to the users, and then have the ZENworks Application launcher install these agents automatically on the workstation. For more information, see Chapter 5.

The Remote Management system will make a peer-to-peer connection between the administrator's workstation and the remote workstation. This may be done using either the IPX or TCP/IP protocol. In this policy, you may specify the preferred protocol for the connection. This protocol is attempted first, but if the connection cannot be made, then the alternate protocol will be used.

Remote controlling a workstation via ZENworks also requires rights within the Workstation Object that represents the workstation you want to be controlled. Without these rights, the administrator will be denied access to the remote control subsystem. Both the session manager and the agents validate that the user has rights to remote control the workstation. You assign the remote control rights through the Remote Management Rights Wizard, or in the workstation object in the Remote Operators page.

Remote Management Page

The Remote Management page identifies the features that you want to be activated with the Remote Management system. Figures 6.42 through 6.45 show the Remote Management page and the tabbed values of the policy.

FIGURE 6.42 *Remote Management Policy page, General tab*

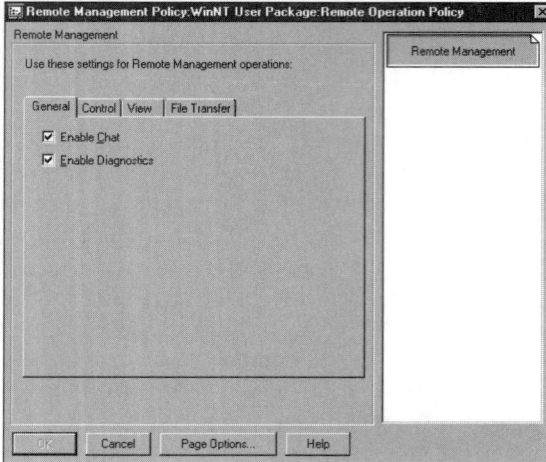

FIGURE 6.43 *Remote Management Policy page, Control tab*

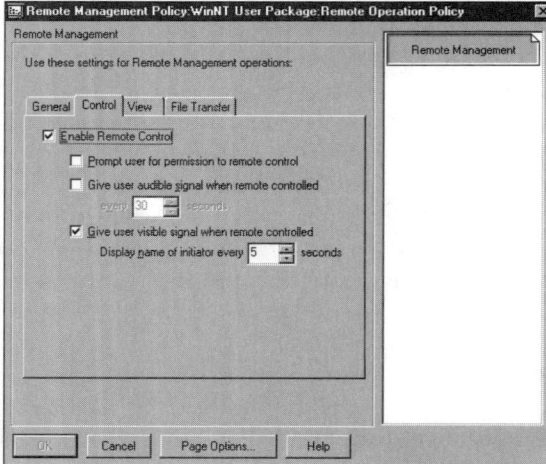

F I G U R E   6.44 *Remote Management Policy page, View tab*

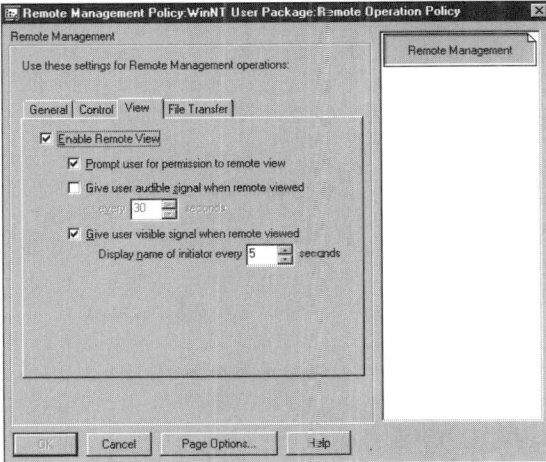

F I G U R E   6.45 *Remote Management Policy page, File Transfer*

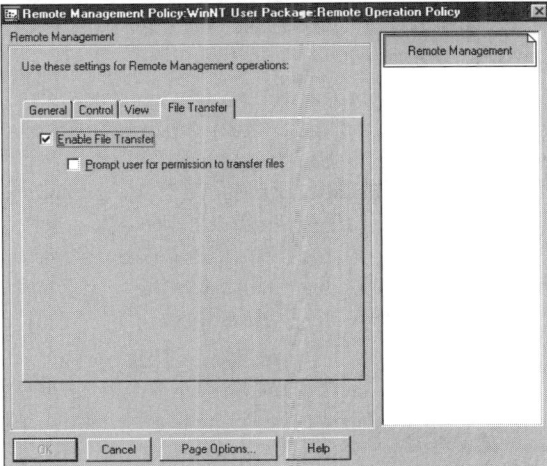

The following describes each of the options available under each tab of the Remote Management policy:

- ▶ General Tab — This tab has options on general system functions:

  - Enable Chat — This enables those who have this policy associated with them to accept a chat request. Chat sets up a communication system between the initiator and the receiver and allows them to type and send messages to one another.

  - Enable Diagnostics — This allows the agent on the workstations to perform a diagnostics report. This can be done from the Tools ⇨ ZENworks Remote Management menu. The Diagnostics utility will perform some basic queries on the system and return the information about the workstation. This information includes memory, environment, and processes running. Additionally, it would include NDS and NetWare connection information, client information, network drives, and open file lists, as well as printers, network protocols, and network services that are active.

- ▶ Control Tab — This tab describes the feature enabling of remote control functions:

  - Enable Remote Control — When this option is enabled, the remote control subsystem can be activated. Without this setting on, no one may remote control the workstations where the currently logged in user has this policy associated with his or her user object.

  - Prompt user for permission to remote control — This option will cause a dialog box to be displayed on the end user's machine when a remote control session is started. The end user has the option of accepting or denying the remote control request. Within this dialog box, the user is told who wants to remote control his or her machine and is asked if this is approved. If the user denies the remote control session, the session is terminated and the administrator cannot remote control the workstation.

  - Give user audible system when remote controlled — This option will periodically provide the end user with a tone while the remote control session is active. You can also set the number of seconds between each beep.

  - Give user visible signal when remote controlled — This option will display a dialog box on the end user's desktop while the remote control session is active. The dialog box indicates that the workstation is being remote controlled, and also displays the NDS name of the user who is remote controlling the workstation. You can set the number of seconds you want to have between the flashing of the name of the user who is initiating the remote control session.

▶ View Tab — This tab describes the feature enabling of the remote view functions. Remote view is the capability for the administrator to view the remote windows screen of the target machine, without being able to control the mouse or keyboard of the machine.

• Enable Remote View — When this option is enabled, the remote view subsystem can be activated. Without this setting on, no one may remote view the workstations where the currently logged in user has this policy associated with his or her user object.

• Prompt user for permission to remote view — This option will cause a dialog box to be displayed on the end user's machine when a remote view session is started. The end user has the option of accepting or denying the remote view request. Within this dialog box, the user is told who wants to remote view his or her machine and is asked if this is approved. If the user denies the remote view session, the session is terminated and the administrator cannot remote view the workstation.

• Give user audible system when remote viewed — This option will periodically provide the end user with a tone while the remote view session is active. You can also set the number of seconds between each beep.

• Give user visible signal when remote viewed — This option will display a dialog box on the end user's desktop while the remote view session is active. The dialog box indicates that the workstation is being remote viewed, and also displays the NDS name of the user who is remote viewing the workstation. You can set the number of seconds you want to have between the flashing of the name of the user who is initiating the remote view session.

▶ File Transfer Tab — This tab describes the feature enabling of the file transfer system. This enables you to send files to the remote workstation.

• Enable File Transfer — When this option is enabled, the file transfer subsystem can be activated. Without this setting on, no one may send files to the workstations where the currently logged in user has this policy associated with his or her user object.

- Prompt user for permission to transfer files — This option will cause a dialog box to be displayed on the end user's machine when a file transfer session is started. The end user has the option of accepting or denying the file transfer request. Within this dialog box, the user is told who wants to perform the file transfer on his or her machine and is asked if this is approved. If the user denies the file transfer session, the session is terminated and the administrator cannot send the files to the workstation.

Adding a User Extensible Policy

Microsoft has required that software packages that bear the Windows approved logo provide capabilities to be configured through .POL files. The poledit program allows you to edit these "extensible policies" and include them in the system .POL file. ZENworks also allows the policies that are stored in NDS to accept these additional "extensible polices" and provides them to all the users who are associated with these policies.

The User Extensible policy will allow you to import these special .ADM files into the NDS tree and have them administered and dispersed to the users associated with the policy package. Once these .ADM files have been imported into the tree, they can be administered and associated to users in the NDS tree. These settings will be applied like the User System policies.

Extensible Policies

When you first bring up the User Extensible Policies dialog box, you will be presented with a scheduled page as well as the Extensible Policies page. This page is shown in Figure 6.46.

From the Extensible Policies page, you can double-click the User Policies icon. This will launch a program to import the .ADM files. The window that is displayed from the program is shown in Figure 6.47.

When the import program is brought up, you must specify the .ADM file that you want to import into the policy. Pressing the Add button will bring up a dialog box enabling you either to specify the .ADM file or to browse to the location of the file. Once the file is specified, click OK to bring it into the Extensible Policies system. Figure 6.48 displays the screen after a sample Windows NT .ADM file has been brought into the system and a few folders have been opened.

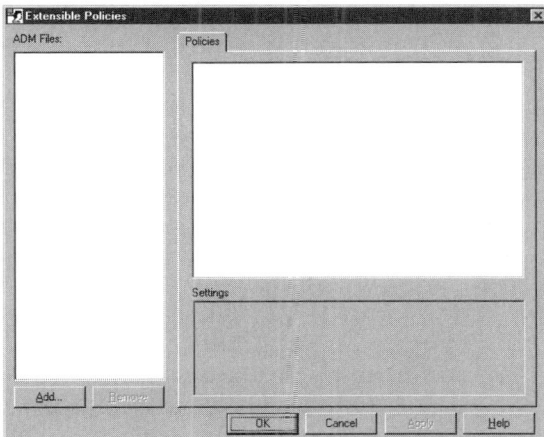

FIGURE 6.46 *Extensible Policies page of the User Extensible Policies policy*

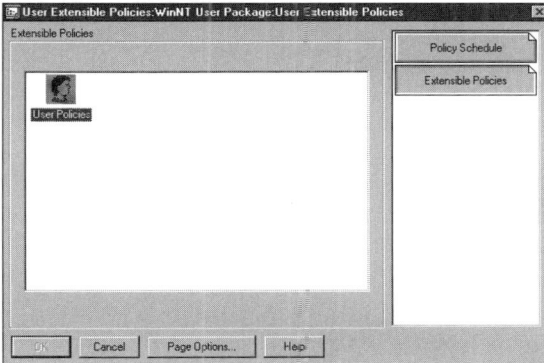

FIGURE 6.47 *User policies import program initial screen*

▶ · ◀

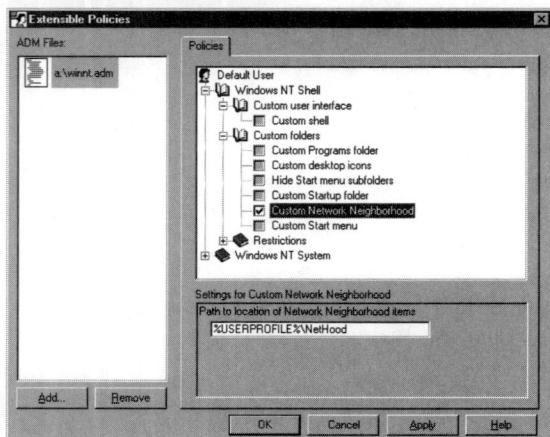

The Settings for Custom Network Neighborhood area of the screen will display the key that is being modified with the checkbox setting. By browsing through the settings, you can set the keys just as you do in POLEDIT.EXE.

NOTE

The .ADM file must be stored on a server to which users have access. The policy will reference the .ADM file and will need to retrieve it to apply it to the users and to allow the administrators to modify the settings. We would recommend, therefore, that you use a UNC path in specifying the location of the file.

Adding a Workstation Import Policy

This policy governs the behavior of the import process, which imports workstations into the tree then and associates the physical workstation device to the workstation object in the tree. This policy describes how a workstation object should be named, and where in the tree the workstation object should be created.

The import process is done in four steps:

I. A Workstation Import policy must be created and associated with the first user who logs in to the workstation.

2. When the first user logs in to the tree, a registration process is activated that places some information about the user and the workstation into the immediate container of the user.

3. The administrator must execute the workstation import program that imports information from the registration stored in the user's container, and creates the workstation object using the information given in the registration process.

4. The next user to log in to the system after the import process is completed will cause the system to detect that a workstation object has been created for that particular device. Once the object is discovered, the NDS name of the workstation object is stored in the workstation registry and the workstation now can connect to the system via that workstation object.

Once the workstation object has been associated with a physical device (the import process described above has been completed), that workstation object will receive all information about the workstation and will represent that workstation in the tree. Associations of policies with that workstation object, workstation container, or workstation group will govern behavior of the systems on that workstation.

You may activate a workstation import policy by going to the details of the Windows NT Workstation Package object. Within that policy package, you may select and activate the workstation import policy. All users who are associated with that package will now use that import policy to describe how the import policy should behave.

Workstation Location Page

This page allows the administrator to identify the container in the tree that should hold the workstation object when it is created during the import process. Figure 6.49 shows this screen.

The flag Allow importing of workstations enables or disables the capability to import workstations from this user. Once this flag is activated, the other fields of the page are usable.

The Create workstation objects in drop-down box provides the administrator with various objects for locating the container in which to place the workstation objects. The options are as follows:

▶ User Container — This signals that the container that holds the user object of the user who had logged in to the system when the registration of the workstation occurred will be the container that also will hold the workstation object. Remember the first user who connects to the system will have the association to the workstation. A path may

Workstation Import policy, workstation location page

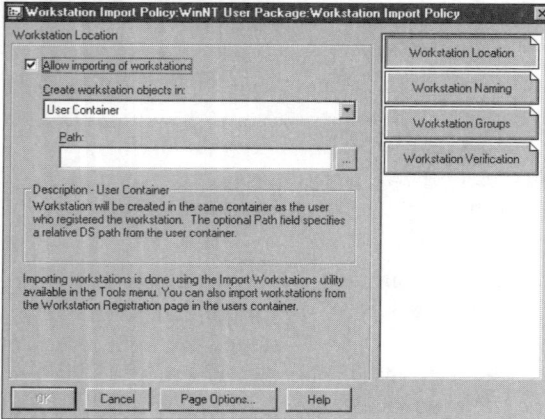

be specified in the path field that would be considered to be relative to the User's container. The path field is constructed by entering a relative path. This relative path is constructed with a series of dots and container names. For each dot in the path, the system will move up one level from the associated object container. For example, the path of ..Workstations means for the system to go up two levels and then to a container called Workstations at that level. If an alternate user is desired, you must run the un-registration tool described in Chapter 10.

▶ Associated Object Container — This signals that the container that has the policy package associated with it will be used as the starting container to place the workstation object. If a path is specified, then the associated container is used as the base and the path is considered a relative path. The path field is constructed by entering a relative path. This relative path is constructed with a series of dots and container names. For each dot in the path, the system will move up one level from the associated object container. For example, the path of ..Workstations means for the system to go up two levels and then to a container called Workstations at that level.

▶ Selected Container — This identifies that the specified path is an absolute container path in the tree. The Path field is required with this selection and must identify the specific container that will hold the workstation object.

Workstation Naming Page

On this page, the administrator can describe how the import process should use the information in the registration to craft the name of the workstation object. Figure 6.50 presents an image of the naming page.

F I G U R E   6 . 5 0   *Workstation Import policy, Workstation Naming page*

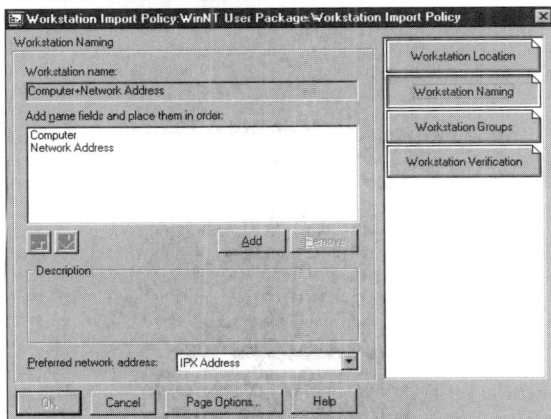

The Workstation name field displays the final combination of registration information that will be combined into the name. In the preceding example, the workstation object name will be the computer name followed by the network address. This is confirmed by the fact that the Workstation name field appears as Computer+Network Address. If the computer name were Rtanner and the network address of the NIC card were 12345, then the workstation object name would be Rtanner12345.

The Add name fields and place them in order field displays the various components that are put together to form the workstation name. Each line displayed in this field represents a value that will be part of the name. The order of the lines from top to bottom represent the order in which they will appear in the name. The options that can be placed in the names are as follows:

- ▶ <User Defined> — This represents an administrator defined string. When this field is chosen, the administrator is prompted to enter a string into the dialog box. This string will be placed into the name. This can be any combination of standard ASCII visible characters, including white space characters.

▶ Computer — This represents the name that was given to the computer, usually during installation of the operating system.

▶ Container — This represents the name of the container into which the workstation object is placed. This name will be included in the workstation name.

▶ CPU — This value represents the CPU type of the machine. Currently, this attribute has no value for Windows 3.1 and DOS machines, and retrieves its information in the Windows 95/98 and NT environment from the Operating System. The possible values are 386, 486, and PENTIUM.

▶ DNS — This represents the DNS (Domain Name Services) name of the computer.

▶ Network Address — This represents the address of the machine when it is first registered with the tree. The other field, Preferred network address, contains the two addresses that represent the network address for the workstation. These addresses can either be the IPX address (which actually uses the MAC address of the NIC card) or the IP address of the machine.

▶ OS — This represents the operating system type of the machine. The expected values would be WINNT, WIN95, WIN31, for example.

▶ Server — This represents the name of the current server. If the user login has not occurred and the preferred server has not been specified, then this server could simply be the first server that responded with a connection. In WINNT systems, where the registration is running as part of a service, this server will be the first server to respond to the request for the connection, and not necessarily the preferred server of the user.

▶ User — This is the login name of the user who was connected to the tree when the registration process first executed.

As an example, let us assume that a workstation had been registered with the following values:

```
CPU = PENTIUM
DNS = zen.novell.com
IPX address = 01010480:00600803c2e7
```

```
TCP/IP address = 137.65.61.99

OS = WINNT

Server = ZENSERVER

User = rtanner

Computer = RonComputer
```

If we were to administer the workstation import policy with the following naming attributes, the corresponding workstation name would be created, assuming pieces that are in quotes are a user defined string:

```
UserOS = rtannerWINNT

DNSCPU = zen.novel.comPENTIUM

User" "Network Address = rtanner 00600803c2e7
```

You must remember that these values are only used at workstation object creation time. Once the object is created, its name never changes. Therefore, if you replace the NIC card (although the address of the workstation changed, the name of the workstation does not), and if the name includes the NIC address, then the workstation retains the name with the old NIC address.

Workstations Groups

The workstation groups page allows you to specify into which groups you would like to place the workstation object when it is created. By placing the workstation object into a specific group, you can automatically provide policies or rights to the workstation by group associations. Figure 6.51 shows the Workstation Groups page.

In the workstation groups page, you may add and remove groups in the list, and the workstation will be placed in as a member of each group. The following describes the behavior of each button on the screen:

▶ Add — Press this button to add a group to the list. When the button is pressed, a dialog box is presented that allows you to browse the tree to identify the group. You browse the tree in the right pane and select the group in the left pane. Once a group is selected, it is added and displayed in the list.

FIGURE 6.51 *Workstation Import policy, Workstation Groups page*

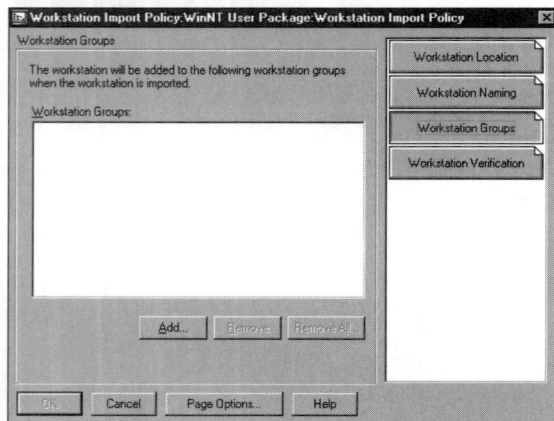

- ▶ Remove — This button is activated when a group in the window is highlighted by clicking the left mouse button when the cursor is over the desired group. When a group is selected and this button is pressed, the group will be removed from the list.

- ▶ Remove All — This button will completely remove all groups from the list and clean the set from consideration.

- ▶ Remember that this policy is only activated when a new workstation is imported into the tree. If a workstation that was created with this policy is associated with a group and you go into the import policy and change the group memberships, the workstations that have already been created will retain their group memberships. Only the new workstations created after the change will be affected.

Workstation Verification

This field allows you to specify the length of time that the agents on the workstation should wait between cycles when they check for the existence of the workstation object and the modification of policies associated with the object. Figure 6.52 displays a printout of this screen.

FIGURE 6.52 *Workstation Import policy, Workstation Verification page*

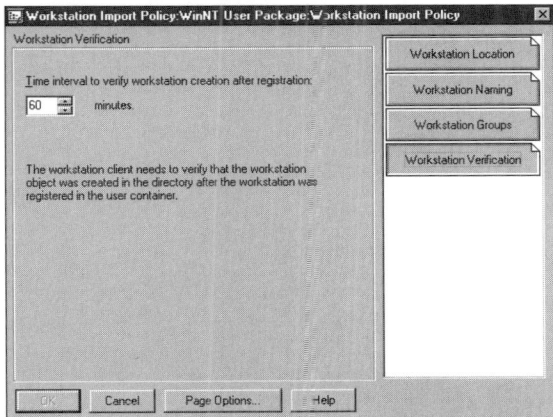

CHAPTER 7

Setting Up a Computer Policy Package

This chapter will discuss the use and creation of Workstation policies. Workstation policies are associated with workstations and workstation groups and affect their working environment.

► • ◄

Relationship of Computer Policies to Workstations

Workstations are associated with Computer Policies in any of these three ways: 1) Policies can be associated with the workstation object directly, 2) Policies can be associated with a parent container of the workstation object, and, 3) Policies can be associated with a workstation group to which the workstation is a member.

The ZENworks Workstation Manager agent is activated on a workstation at user login for Windows 3.1, Windows 95, and Windows 98 systems; on Windows NT systems it is activated when the service is started. Once the ZENworks Workstation Manager agent is activated, it logs into the tree as the workstation and walks up the tree looking for the first Computer Policy Package it can find that is associated with the workstation. Like all ZENworks agents, the order that the tree is searched is dependent on standard Novell Directory Services behavior and any Search Policies that may be in the tree. All of the applicable workstation policies are merged together and then the culmination is applied to the workstation. If there are any conflicts with the policies (e.g., two computer policies which both affect the same parameter) then the parameter setting in the first policy found is applied.

The remote control policy can be created for both the user and the workstation, and in these instances the remote control subsystem will take the most restrictive combination of the policies. For example, if one policy says to prompt the user for permission and the other does not — then the system will prompt the user.

► • ◄

Advantages of Platform-Specific Policies

ZENworks allows the administration of specific policies for each platform that is supported in the ZENworks system. By having a policy that is categorized for each type of platform, the administrator can make unique policies for each system. No matter which users are logged into the system, each workstation will find the policies associated with it and execute the administrative configurations for that platform.

There are occasions when you may want to associate a particular, unique policy to a set of workstations, which are found in containers along with other workstations of the same type. You can then create a group of workstations and associate specific policies to those workstations. Consequently, these workstations will receive the policies from this group rather than from the container.

Creating a Windows 3.1 Workstation Policy Package

If you want to have a policy that affects workstations, is connected to the tree, and runs the Windows 3.1 operating system, you must create a Windows 3.1 Workstation Policy Package. Use the following steps to create a Windows 3.1 Workstation Policy Package. Figure 7.1 shows the dialog box for creating an object within a container.

FIGURE 7.1 Dialog box for creating an object within a container. The Policy Package object is selected.

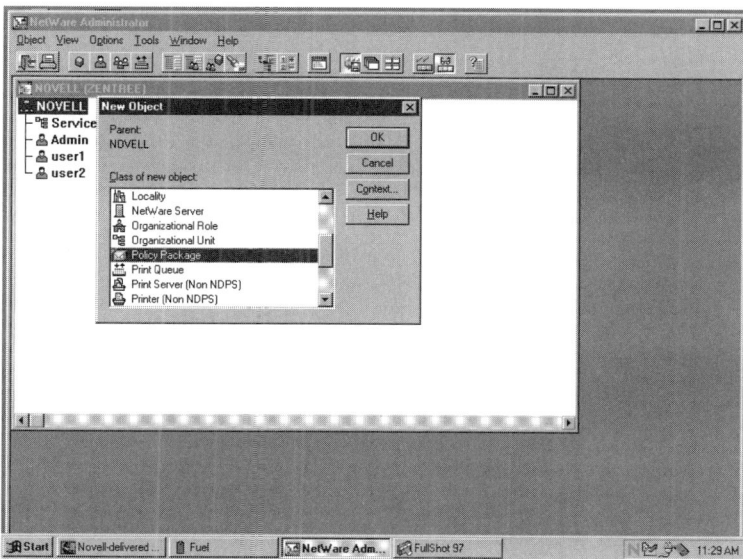

1. Start NWAdmin32.

2. Browse to the container where you would like to have the policy package. Remember that you do not have to create the policy package in the container where you are doing the associations. You can associate the same policy package to many containers in your tree.

3. Create the policy package by pressing the right mouse button and choosing Create.

4. Select the Policy Package object in the list of objects that can be created in the selected container.

5. In the Create Policy Package dialog select the type of package to be a Windows 3.1 Workstation Policy Package and name the object. Also, select the Define Additional Attributes checkbox so you can define policies.

6. Press OK. Next, NWAdmin32 will display a dialog box that allows you to create policies for this policy package.

7. Check and set any policies you desire for this Windows 3.1 Workstation Policy package and press OK.

Policies Page

Once you have created a Windows 3.1 Workstation Policy Package you can activate policies that will be used for all Windows 3.1 workstations that were associated with the policy package. When you click on a policy within the policy package, it becomes active. An active policy is designated by a check in the check box. The details of any particular policy can be modified by selecting the policy and pressing the Details button, or by double-clicking on the policy itself. Figure 7.2 shows the policy page.

The Reset button on the policies page will reset the selected policy back to the system defaults for that policy.

Associations Page

The Associations page of the Windows 3.1 Workstation Policy Package displays all of the locations in the tree (containers) where the policy package has been placed. The Windows 3.1 workstations that are in or below those containers will have this policy package enforced.

FIGURE 7.2 Windows 3.1 Workstation Package policy page

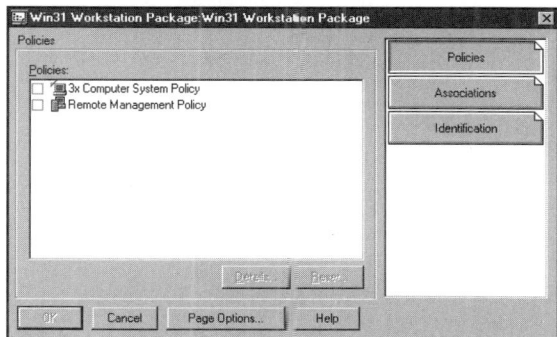

Identification Page

The Identification page of the Windows 3.1 Workstation Policy Package allows users to enter additional description information to help convey the purpose of the particular policy package.

Adding a Windows 3.x Computer System Policy

This policy allows you to automatically download specific files to the Windows 3.x workstation as you (the user) log into the system and activate the ZENworks agents.

Remember, this policy is a simple method of moving files to the desktop. A much more robust method, ZENworks Application Launcher, will allow you to keep files on the local workstation current with files on the network.

Figure 7.3 displays the policy package. From this page you can manage the files on the workstation.

The following fields are used to manage the files on the Windows 3.x system:

▶ Managed files — This is a list of the files that are to be managed on the workstation.

▶ Edit — This allows you to edit the selections on the files list. By highlighting the line in the managed files list you can press this button to edit the source and destination paths of the binary files, or the context of the text files.

▶ . . . . ◀

| F I G U R E   7 . 3 | *Windows 3.x Computer System Policy within a Windows 3.x Workstation Package policy package* |

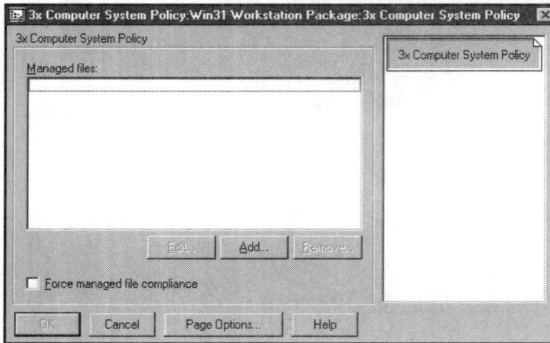

- ▶ Add — This button adds a file to the managed list. When pressed this button presents a dialog box allowing you to select whether the file is a binary or ASCII text file. If the file is a binary file then the dialog box will next ask you for the destination of the file on the workstation (be sure and include the file name) and the source of the file (you may enter a UNC path for the file on the server). If the file is a text file you are prompted for the destination path with the file name, and then you are given a simple editor that allows you to enter the actual text of the ASCII file.

- ▶ Remove — By highlighting an entry in the managed files list and pressing this button the file will be removed from the managed files list.

- ▶ Force managed file compliance — This allows you to specify whether the user can bypass the updating of these files or not.

Adding a Remote Management Policy

A Remote Management Policy is activated for this policy package by either double clicking the Remote Management Policy or selecting the check box on the Remote Management Policy. Once this is done, the Remote Management Policy is activated for all Windows 3.1 workstations that are associated with the Windows 3.1 Workstation Policy package.

The Remote Management Policy controls the features of the Remote Management subsystem that is shipped with the ZENworks package (remember, it is *not* shipped with the ZENworks Starter Pack). The Remote

Management system is composed of two parts: a Remote Management Session Manager that makes the connection and is used by the administrator and the Remote Management Agents that are installed on the end-user's workstation. The remote control agents may have been installed onto the workstation at the same time that the client shipped with ZENworks was installed. The other option would be if the agents are installed on the workstation through the remote control application objects that were added to your tree during your Zenworks installation. In that case, you need to associate these application objects to the users and then have the ZENworks Application launcher install these agents automatically on the workstation. For more information, see Chapter 5, Creating and Using Application Objects.

The Remote Management system will make a peer-to-peer connection between the administrator's workstation and the remote workstation. This may be done using either the IPX or the TCP/IP protocol. In this policy, you may specify the preferred protocol for the connection. This protocol is attempted first, but if the connection can't be made, then the alternate protocol will be used.

Remote controlling a workstation via ZENworks also requires rights within the Workstation Object that represent the workstation wanting to be controlled. Without these rights, the administrator will not be able to gain access to the remote control subsystem. Both the session manager and the agents validate that the user has rights to remote control the workstation. You'll assign remote control rights through the Remote Management Rights wizard or in the workstation object in the Remote Operators page.

Remote Management Page

The Remote Management page identifies the features that you want to be activated with the Remote Management system. Figures 7.4 through 7.6 show the Remote Management page and the tabbed values of the policy.

The following describes each of the options available under each tab of the Remote Management policy:

- ► General Tab — This tab has options on general system functions.

- ► Enable Chat — The chat feature is not available for Windows 3.1 so this field is disabled.

- ► Enable Diagnostics — The diagnostics are not available for Windows 3.1 so this field is grayed-out.

- ► Display Remote Management Agent icon to user — With this flag set, an icon will be displayed on the system tray/task bar.

► · ◄

FIGURE 7.4 Remote Management Policy page, General tab

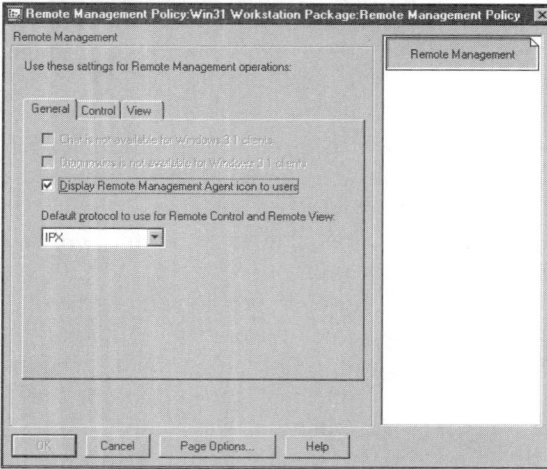

FIGURE 7.5 Remote Management Policy page, Control tab

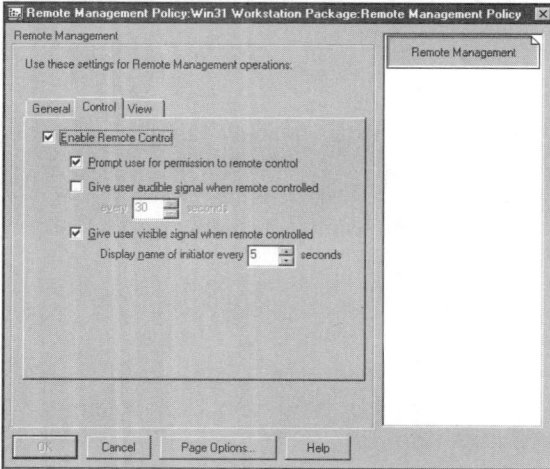

FIGURE 7.6 *Remote Management Policy page, View tab*

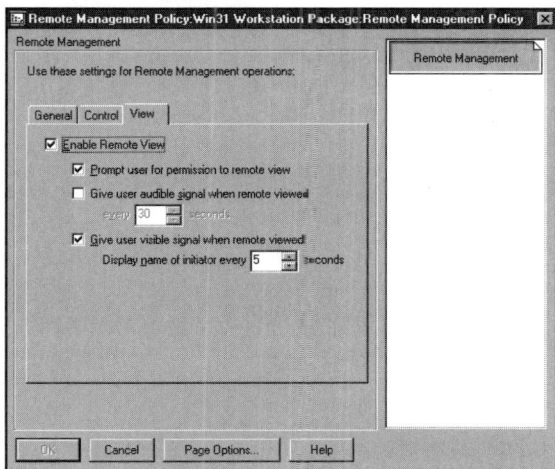

- Default protocol to use for Remote Control and Remote View — This field allows you to choose whether the remote control uses IP or IPX protocol for default.

- Control Tab — This tab describes the feature enabling of remote control functions.

- Enable Remote Control — When this option is enabled, you can activate the remote control subsystem. Without this setting, the policy associated with this user object does not allow anyone to control a workstation (where a user is currently logged in) remotely.

- Prompt user for permission to remote control — This option will cause a dialog box to be displayed on the end-user's machine when a remote control session is started. The end-user has the option of accepting or denying the remote control request. Within this dialog box the user is told who wants to remote control their machine and asks if this is approved. If the user denies the remote control session, then the session is terminated and the administrator cannot remote control the workstation.

- Give user audible system when remote controlled — This option will provide the end user a tone periodically while the remote control session is active. You can also set the number of seconds between each beep.

- Give user visible signal when remote controlled — This option will display a dialog box on the end user's desktop while the remote control session is active. The dialog box shows that the workstation is being remote controlled and also displays the NDS name of the user that is remote controlling the workstation. You can set the number of seconds that you want to have between flashing the name of the user initiating the remote control session.

- View Tab — This tab describes the feature enabling of the remote view functions. Remote view is the ability for the administrator to view the remote windows screen of the target machine but not be able to control the mouse or keyboard of the machine.

- Enable Remote View — When this option is enabled, then the remote view subsystem can be activated. Without this setting on, no one may remote view the workstations where the currently logged in user has this policy associated with their user object.

- Prompt user for permission to remote view — This option will cause a dialog box to be displayed on the end-user's machine when a remote view session is started. The end-user has the option of accepting or denying the remote view request. Within this dialog box the user is told who wants to remote view their machine and asks if this is approved. If the user denies the remote view session, then the session is terminated and the administrator cannot remote view the workstation.

- Give user audible system when remote viewed — This option will provide the end user a tone periodically while the remote view session is active. You can also set the number of seconds between each beep.

- Give user visible signal when remote viewed — This option will display a dialog box on the end user's desktop while the remote view session is active. The dialog box displays that the workstation is being remote viewed and also displays the NDS name of the user that is remote viewing the workstation. You can set the number of seconds that you want to have between flashing the name of the user initiating the remote view session.

Creating a Windows 95/98 Computer Policy Package

If you want to have a policy that affects workstations, is connected to the tree, and runs the Windows 95 and Windows 98 operating systems, you must create a Windows 95/98 Workstation Policy Package. Although the computer policy is titled Windows 95 Computer Policy, it is effective for both the Windows 95 and Windows 98 systems. To create a Windows 95 Workstation Policy Package do the following:

1. Start NWAdmin32.

2. Browse to the container where you would like to have the policy package. Remember that you do not have to create the policy package in the container where you are doing the associations. You can associate the same policy package to many containers in your tree.

3. Create the policy package by pressing the right mouse button and choosing Create.

4. Select the Policy Package object in the list of objects that can be created in the selected container.

5. In the Create Policy Package dialog box select the type of package to be a Windows 95 Workstation Policy Package and name the object. Also, select the Define Additional Attributes checkbox so you can define policies.

6. Press OK. Next, NWAdmin32 will display a dialog box that allows you to create policies for this policy package.

7. Check and set any policies you desire for this Windows 95/98 Workstation Policy package and press OK.

Policies Page

Once you have created a Windows 95/98 Workstation Policy Package you can now activate policies that will be used for all Windows 95 and Windows 98 workstations that were associated with the policy package. By clicking on a policy within the policy package, that policy becomes active. An active policy is designated by a check in the check box. The details of any particular policy can be modified by selecting the policy and pressing the Details button, or by double-clicking on the policy itself. Figure 7.7 displays this policy screen.

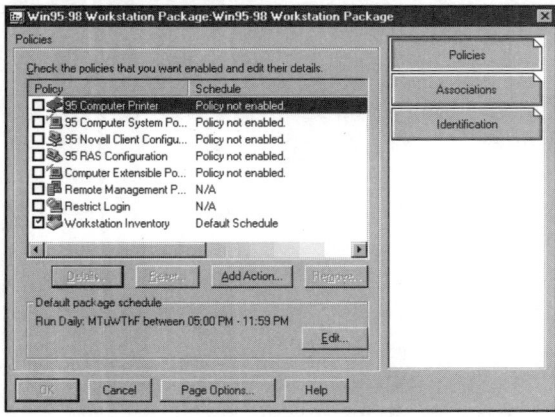

F I G U R E   7.7   *Windows 95/98 Policy Package policies page*

The Reset button on the policies page will reset the selected policy back to the system defaults for that policy.

Associations Page

The Associations page of the Windows 95/98 Workstation Policy Package displays all of the locations in the tree (containers) where the policy package has been placed. The Windows 95/98 workstations that are in or below those containers will have this policy package enforced.

Identification Page

The Identification page of the Windows 95/98 Workstation Policy Package simply allows users to enter in additional description information to help understand the purpose of the particular policy package.

Adding a 95 Computer Printer Policy

This policy, shown in Figure 7.8, allows the administrator to set up network printers onto the local Windows 95 desktop. In order to add printers to the policy you must have already set up some printers into your NetWare system and have corresponding printer and print queue objects in your Novell Directory Services tree.

FIGURE 7.8 *Windows 95 Computer Printer policy*

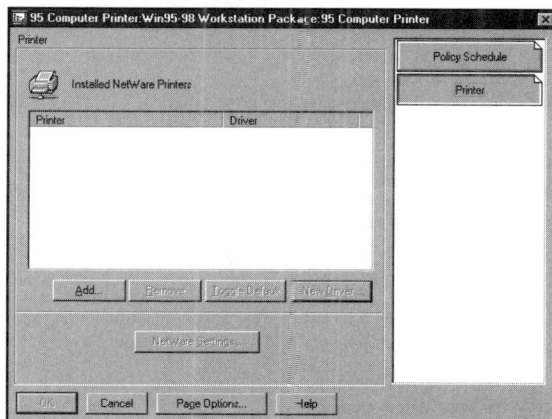

Perform the following steps to add a printer to the printer policy:

1. Press the Add button.

2. Browse through the dialog box and select the Printer or Print Queue object that you want to deliver to the users associated with the policy.

To remove a printer from the policy, simply highlight the printer from the list and then press the Remove button.

Any printers that have been added to this list will be added to the user's desktop automatically when he or she first logs into the system. When the printer is removed from this list, then the printer will be removed from the local system account the next time that the user logs into the workstation.

Adding 95 Computer System Policies

This policy allows you access to the ZAW/ZAK features that are exposed by the Microsoft Windows system. Within the ZENworks system these ZAW/ZAK policies are divided into their logical parts: Desktop Preferences, User System Policies and Workstation Policies. This policy allows the administrator to set the desktop preferences for any Windows 95/98 system. This policy will be associated with the workstation and will not follow users as he or she moves from workstation to workstation.

Microsoft provides a tool called *poledit* that allows an administrator to construct some registry setting (ZAW/ZAK) features and have those settings saved in a .POL file. This .POL file can then be applied to any workstation by having the system look for these files on the server. The problem here is that these policy files must be located on every server that any user may use as an initial connection. With ZENworks this information is stored in these policies and into Novell Directory Services, thus making it accessible to every user who connects to the system without making it necessary to place these policy files on every server. To make the system more familiar, ZENworks has mimicked the user interface of the poledit program.

95 Computer System Policies Page

The 95 Computer System Policies page allows you to specify ZAW/ZAK packages for a Windows 95 workstation. Figure 7.9 displays a copy of this page.

► • ◄

F I G U R E   7 . 9 *Windows 95/98 Computer System Policies*

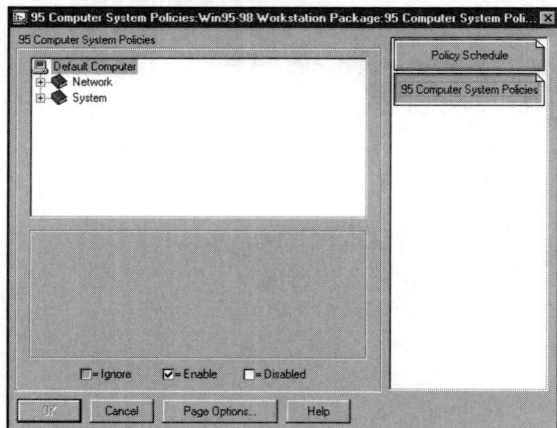

You can edit the above user system policy by simply clicking on the tree components and then clicking on the checkbox next to each item to enable, disable, or ignore the workstation setting. In some respects this can be a very confusing interface, but you need to keep in mind that you are choosing to either: 1) Enable — check the box and allow this capability to the user, 2) Disable — don't check box and turn off this capability for the user, or 3) Ignore — a grayed box meaning that you want to leave the setting as it is in the registry on the workstation (for example, if the feature is turned off it will be left off, or if it is already turned on it will be left on).

Remember that the computer policies are an accumulation of all of the workstation policies found in the tree associated with the workstation or the containers. Consequently, if there are several Workstation System policies in the tree that are associated with the workstation, then the first policy found that has a setting of Enable or Disable for the particular attribute of the policy will be used. Should the attribute be set Ignore, then a setting of Enable or Disable in another policy may be applied.

You can administer each of the settings by simply walking the expanding book folders presented in the policy page. Once the folder is expanded and the final attribute is displayed, you may cycle through the Ignore, Enable, Disable settings by single clicking with the mouse on the check box associated with each attribute.

Adding a Novell Client Configuration Policy

A Novell Client Configuration policy is activated for this policy package by either double clicking the Novell Client Configuration or selecting the check box on the Novell Client Configuration policy. Once this is selected and a check is displayed in the check-box, then this Novell Client Configuration policy is activated for all Windows 95 and Windows 98 workstations that are associated with this policy package.

This policy allows you the administrator, to control the client configurations for all of these workstations from a single policy. Previously one had to visit each individual workstation to make all of these settings. From this one policy all client configurations may be administered and made effective the next time that a user logs into the system.

Settings Page

From the settings page shown in Figure 7.10, you may administer all of the aspects of the client that are installed on the associated Windows 95 and Windows 98 workstations.

If you select the Summary view, you will be presented with a list of the parameters currently set by this policy. If, on the other hand, you select the All View Radio button, it will display the list of parameters that an administrator can configure.

In order to configure a particular parameter, you must first select a specific parameter to change. Once you have selected the parameter then clicking the Configure button will bring up the appropriate dialogs to set that parameter. This button will bring up a dialog box that is similar to the standard dialogs that are used on the client to configure these parameters. These parameters are specific to the client and additional information about these parameters may be found in client documentation.

FIGURE 7.10 *Settings page of the Novell Client Configuration policy*

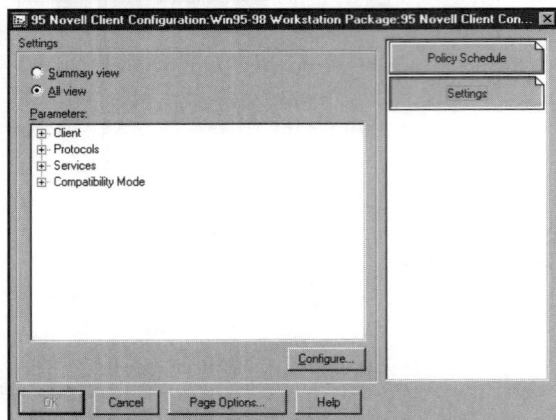

Adding a 95 RAS Configuration Policy

The RAS Configuration Policy allows a workstation to dial into a network and establish a connection before any action is executed. The workstation itself may have some dial-up numbers that have already been defined with the local Windows Dial-Up Networking utilities. These local numbers will not be administered with this policy. Figure 7.11 displays the Dial-Up Networking page.

This page allows the administrator to create numbers to be used in dialing up servers in the network. To create a new dial-up entry perform the following:

1. Select the New button. This will cause a dialog to come up that allows you to administer this new entry.

2. Within the Basic tab, enter an Entry name and the phone number in the appropriate fields.

3. If you wish to change the Country code and Area codes, then check the Use Telephony dialing properties checkbox. This will enable these fields so that you can select a country code and enter in the area code for the number.

4. Proceed to the Server tab and complete the administration by entering the fields for dial-up server type, protocols, and so on.

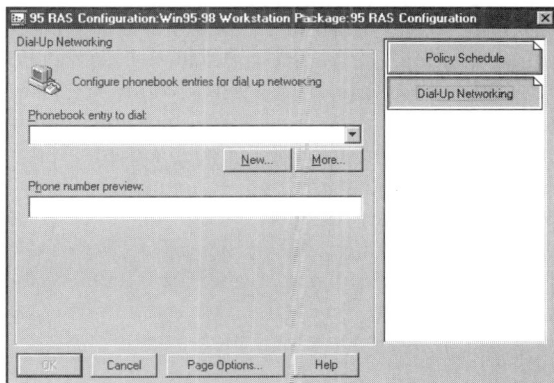

The More button provides the capability to edit or delete the specific phonebook entries that have been entered into the policy. You must first select the entry in the phonebook that you wish to modify. This can be done by selecting the drop-down list under the entry to dial. Next, select the entry to modify or delete. The number that is displayed in the preview is the number that has been administered for the current selection.

Adding a Remote Management Policy

A Remote Management Policy is activated for this policy package by either double-clicking the Remote Management Policy button or selecting the Remote Management Policy check box. Once this is selected, the Remote Management Policy is activated for all Windows 95/98 workstations that are associated with the Windows 95/98 Policy package.

The Remote Management Policy controls the features of the Remote Management subsystem that is shipped with the ZENworks package (not the one shipped with the ZENworks Starter Pack.) The Remote Management system is composed of two parts: a Remote Management Session Manager that makes the connection and is used by the administrator and the Remote Management Agents that are installed on the end-user's workstation. The remote control agents may have been installed onto the workstation at the same time that the client shipped with ZENworks was installed. The other option would be if the agents are installed on the workstation through the remote control application objects that were added to your tree during your ZENworks installation. In that case, you need to associate these application objects to the users and then have the ZENworks Application launcher install these agents automatically on the workstation. For more information, see Chapter 5.

The Remote Management system will make a peer-to-peer connection between the administrator's workstation and the remote workstation. This may be done using either the IPX or the TCP/IP protocol. In this policy you may specify the preferred protocol for the connection. This protocol is attempted first, but if the connection cannot be made, then the alternate protocol will be used.

Remote controlling a workstation via ZENworks also requires rights within the Workstation Object that represents the workstation wanting to be controlled. Without these rights the administrator will be denied access to the remote control subsystem. Both the session manager and the agents verify assign the remote control rights is through the Remote Management Rights wizard or in the workstation object in the Remote Operators page.

Remote Management Page

The Remote Management page identifies the features that you want to be activated with the Remote Management system. Figures 7.12 through 7.15 show the Remote Management page and the tabbed values of the policy.

► . . . . ◄

F I G U R E   7.12   *Remote Management Policy page, General tab*

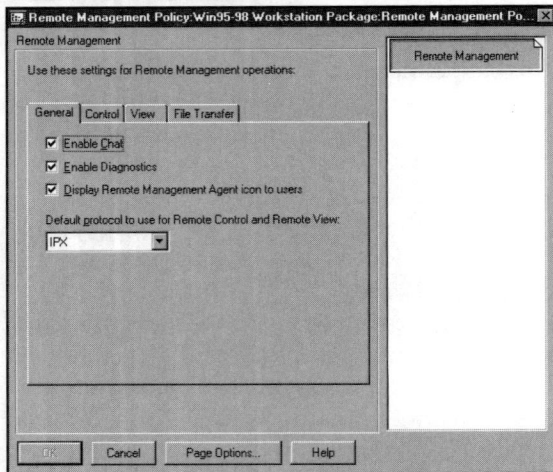

FIGURE 7.13 *Remote Management Policy page, Control tab*

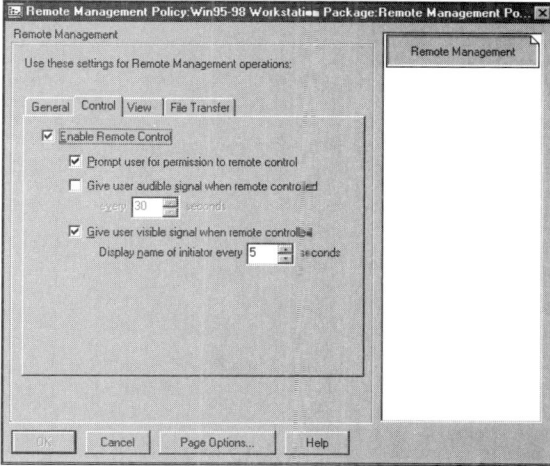

FIGURE 7.14 *Remote Management Policy page, View tab*

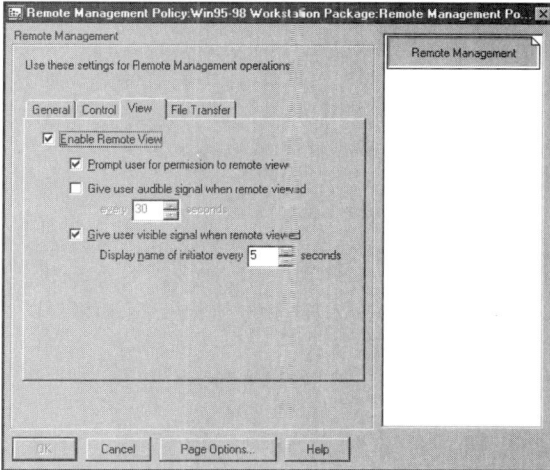

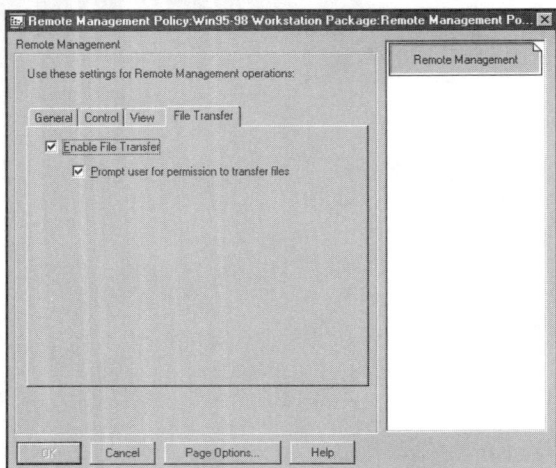

The following describes each of the options available under each tab of the Remote Management policy:

► General Tab — This tab has options on general system functions.

► Enable Chat — This enables those who have this policy associated with them to accept a chat request. Chat sets up a communication system between the initiator and the receiver and allows them to type and send messages to one another.

► Enable Diagnostics — This allows the agent on the workstations to perform a diagnostics report. This can be done from the Tools ⇨ ZENworks Remote Management menu. The Diagnostics utility will perform some basic queries on the system and return the information about the workstation. This information includes memory, environment, and processes running. Additionally, it would include NDS and Netware connection information, client information, network drives and open file lists, as well as printers, Network protocols and network services active.

► Display Remote Management Agent icon to user — With this flag set an icon will be displayed on the system tray/task bar.

► Default protocol to use for Remote Control and Remote View — This field allows you to choose whether you want the remote control to use IP or IPX protocol for default.

- ▶ Control Tab — This tab describes the feature enabling of remote control functions.

- ▶ Enable Remote Control — When this option is enabled, then the remote control subsystem can be activated. Without this setting, the policy associated with this user object does not allow anyone to control a workstation remotely.

- ▶ Prompt user for permission to remote control — This option will cause a dialog box to be displayed on the end-user's machine when a remote control session is started. The end-user has the option of accepting or denying the remote control request. Within this dialog box the user is told who wants to remote control their machine and asks if this is approved. If the user denies the remote control session, then the session is terminated and the administrator cannot remote control the workstation.

- ▶ Give user audible system when remote controlled — This option will provide the end user a tone periodically while the remote control session is active. You can also set the number of seconds between each beep.

- ▶ Give user visible signal when remote controlled — This option will display a dialog box on the end user's desktop while the remote control session is active. The dialog box displays that the workstation is being remote controlled and also displays the NDS name of the user that is remote controlling the workstation. You can set the number of seconds that you want to have between flashing the name of the user that is initiating the remote control session.

- ▶ View Tab — This tab describes the feature enabling of the remote view functions. Remote view is the ability for the administrator to view the remote windows screen of the target machine but not be able to control the mouse or keyboard of the machine.

- ▶ Enable Remote View — When this option is enabled, you can activate the remote view subsystem. Without this setting on, no one may remote view the workstations where the currently logged in user has this policy associated with their user object.

- ▶ Prompt user for permission to remote view — This option will cause a dialog box to be displayed on the end-user's machine when a remote view session is started. The end-user has the option of accepting or denying the remote view request. Within this dialog box the user is told who wants to remote view their machine and asks if this is approved. If the user denies the remote view session, then the session is terminated and the administrator cannot remote view the workstation.

▶ Give user audible system when remote viewed — This option will provide the end user a tone periodically while the remote view session is active. You can also set the number of seconds between each beep.

▶ Give user visible signal when remote viewed — This option will display a dialog box on the end user's desktop while the remote view session is active. The dialog box displays that the workstation is being remote viewed and also displays the NDS name of the user that is remote viewing the workstation. You can set the number of seconds that you want to have between flashing the name of the user that is initiating the remote view session.

▶ File Transfer Tab — This tab describes the feature enabling of the file transfer system. This will allow you, the administrator, to send files to the remote workstation.

▶ Enable File Transfer — When this option is enabled, then the file transfer subsystem can be activated. Without this setting on, no one may send files to the workstations where the currently logged in user has this policy associated with their user object.

▶ Prompt user for permission to transfer files — This option will cause a dialog box to be displayed on the end-user's machine when a file transfer session is started. The end-user has the option of accepting or denying the file transfer request. Within this dialog box the user is told who wants to perform the file transfer to or from his or her machine and asks if this is approved. If the user denies the file transfer session, then the session is terminated and the administrator cannot send the files to the workstation.

Adding a Computer Extensible Policy

Microsoft has required that all software packages which bear the Windows-approved logo be configurable through .POL files. The poledit program allows you to edit these "extensible policies" and include them in the system .POL file. ZENworks also allows the policies that are stored in NDS to accept these additional "extensible polices" and provide them to all of the users that are associated with these policies.

The User Extensible policy will allow you to import these special .ADM files into the NDS tree and have them administered and dispersed to the users associated with the policy package. These settings will be applied in the same way as the User System Policies.

Extensible Policies

When you first bring up the Computer Extensible Policies dialog you will be presented with a scheduled page as well as the Extensible Policies page. The Extensible Policies page is displayed in Figure 7.16.

FIGURE 7.16 *Extensible Policies page of the Computer Extensible Policies policy*

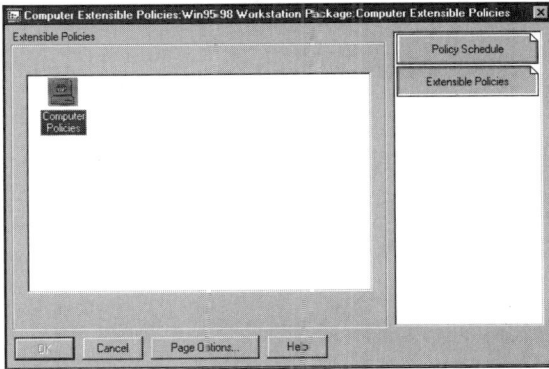

From the Extensible Policies page you can double click on the Computer Policies icon. This will launch a program to import the .ADM files. The window that is displayed from the program is displayed in Figure 7.17.

When the import program is brought up you must then specify the .ADM file that you want to import into the policy. Pressing the Add button will bring up a dialog to either specify the .ADM file or to browse to the location of the file. Once the file is specified then pressing OK will bring it into the Extensible Policies system. Figure 7.18 displays the screen after a sample Windows NT .ADM file has been brought into the system and a few folders have been opened.

The Settings for Custom Network Neighborhood area of the screen will display the key that is being modified with the checkbox setting. By browsing through the settings you can set the keys just like you do in POLEDIT.EXE.

> **NOTE** The .ADM file must be stored on a server to which users have access. The policy will reference the .ADM file and will need to retrieve it to apply it to the users and to allow the administrators to modify the settings. It would be recommended, therefore, to use a UNC path in specifying the location of the file.

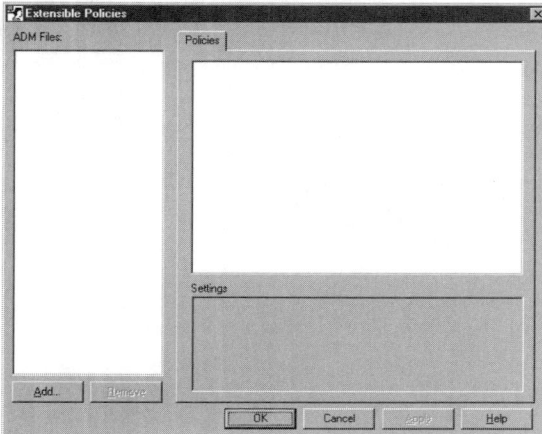

F I G U R E   7.17 Computer policies import program initial screen

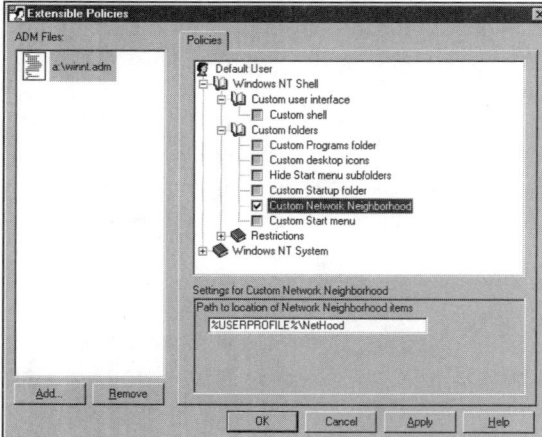

F I G U R E   7.18 Computer policies import program with an imported .ADM file

Adding a Restrict Login Policy

This policy will allow the administrator to specify the users that may or may not log into the system from the workstations that are associated with this policy. This will restrict all volatile users within the Dynamic Local User features of ZENworks from logging into the system, including the local workstation. However, if there is an account for the user already on the workstation (non-volatile) then the user may still log into the machine locally even though they cannot log into the network.

The policy will not allow duplicates in both lists and if this is attempted it will ask the administrator to choose whether the entry should be allowed to log in to the system or not (from this particular workstation policy).

You can specify within the list any user, group, or container to which you want to grant or deny login privileges. If you specify a container, then the agent will only restrict users that are directly in that container and won't go down into the sub-containers. For example, if you specify the Provo.Novell container in the Deny login from field, then all users with the context of Provo.Novell will be denied access. If a user has the context of North.Provo.Novell then they will be allowed to log into the system. Figure 7.19 displays the login restriction.

FIGURE 7.19   Login Restrictions policy

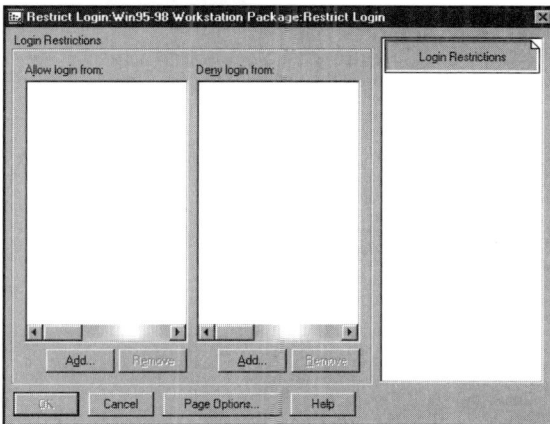

Do the following to add a user, group, or container to either of the Allow login from or Deny login from fields:

1. Press the appropriate Add button for the field. This will bring up a NWAdmin32 browse dialog.

2. Browse within the tree to select the Novell Directory Services user, group, or container. Select the desired user, group, or container and press the OK button. This object will be added to the list.

To remove an entry, simply select the object in the appropriate list and press the Remove button.

Adding a Workstation Inventory Policy

ZENworks has introduced full hardware and software scanning into the system. When ZENworks is installed into the system, the administrator has the option of installing an inventory database. This inventory database is then placed on a volume in a server in the tree. Inventory information, through this policy, can then be placed within that database. Additionally, the selected subset of the inventory information will be placed in the Workstation Object.

Figure 7.20 displays the Scanner Configuration page of the Inventory Policy.

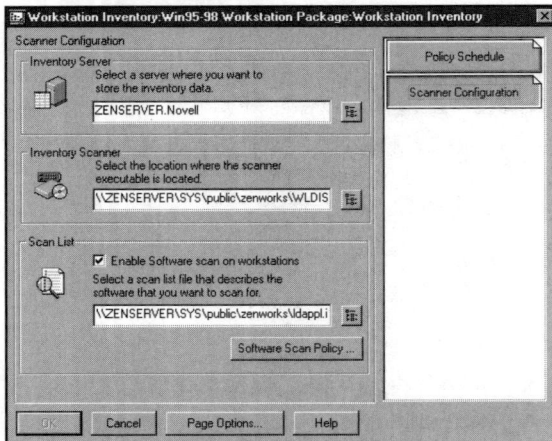

► • ◄

F I G U R E   7.20   *Workstation Inventory policy*

Within the inventory policy the administrator has the ability to administer three things about the hardware and software scanning that occurs on the workstation. The following describes the three parameters and the workings of the inventory system.

- Inventory Server — This field represents the server object that holds the ZENworks database. This database should have been placed on the server when ZENworks was originally installed. You can have multiple databases within a single tree, but each database is managed independently and the information in one database is not transmitted to another. All workstations that have this policy associated with them will send their scanned information to the specified server.

- Inventory Scanner — This field represents the executable program location of the scanner. This scanner is executed on the workstation based on the specified inventory schedule. When the scanner is executed it creates a file on the local workstation called scan.txt. Portions of this file are then transmitted and stored in the workstation object of the workstation and the full contents of the scan is transmitted and stored in the ZENworks database. The hardware is probed for discovery; in addition to probing, ZENworks scanning supports DMI 2.0 library interfaces and will include the DMI information in the hardware reports.

- Scan List — This field hold two separate data values: Enable Software scan on workstation and the location of the software scan list. When the Enable Software scan on workstations option is checked, a software scan will be done on the workstation in addition to the standard hardware probe. The software scan list is an .INI file that lists the names and files of the software that is to be scanned and recognized. ZENworks will provide ways to update this list with new database entries as well as entries of personal files.

At the scheduled time the scanner executable specified by the policy is launched on the workstation. This scanner will attempt to make DMI 2.0 calls to get DMI information. It will also make hardware probes in an effort to discover the hardware in the workstation. Following the hardware scanning, the software will then make a scan of the local drives to locate the software on the drives. The software is recognized by whether or not it matches any of the files specified in the software scan list. This list of software packages is also stored with the hardware information. The scanner will generate a file called scan.txt on the local workstation drive.

Once the scan is completed, then the scanner will make a connection (IP or IPX) to the Inventory Server and attempt to communicate with the database service that was placed there with the ZENworks install. This service will collect the information and then place it in the database on that inventory server. Additionally, the scanner will return a "sweet spot" of information and have that placed in the workstation object in NDS. Both the "sweet spot" of information and the data in the database may be viewed through NWAdmin by going to the workstation object and looking at the inventory page.

If you are having the system perform a software scan of the local hardware drives then you need to take into consideration the intensity of the scan. The scan does happen in the background, but it will always increase the usage on the workstation. Each location will need to determine how often you need to scan, but it probably does not need to be more often than once a week.

▶ . . . . ◀

Creating a Windows NT Computer Policy Package

If you want to have a policy that affects workstations, is connected to the tree, and runs the Windows NT operating systems, you must create a Windows NT Workstation Policy Package. To create a Windows NT Workstation Policy Package, do the following:

1. Start NWAdmin32.

2. Browse to the container where you would like to have the policy package. Remember that you do not have to create the policy package in the container where you are doing the associations. You can associate the same policy package to many containers in your tree.

3. Create the policy package by pressing the right mouse button and choosing Create.

4. Select the Policy Package object in the list of objects that can be created in the selected container.

5. In the Create Policy Package wizard dialog select the type of package to be a Windows NT Workstation Policy Package and name the object. Also select the "Define Additional Attributes" checkbox so that we can define policies.

6. Press OK. Next NWAdmin32 will display a dialog that allows you to create policies for this policy package.

7. Check and set any policies you desire for this Windows NT Workstation Policy package and press OK.

Policies Page

Once you have created a Windows NT Workstation Policy Package you can now activate policies that will be used for all Windows NT workstations that were associated with the policy package. By clicking on a policy within the policy package, that policy becomes active. You designate an active policy by checking a check box. The details of any particular policy can be modified by selecting the policy and pressing the Details button, or by double-clicking on the policy itself. Figure 7.21 displays this policy screen.

F I G U R E   7.21   Windows NT Policy Package policies page

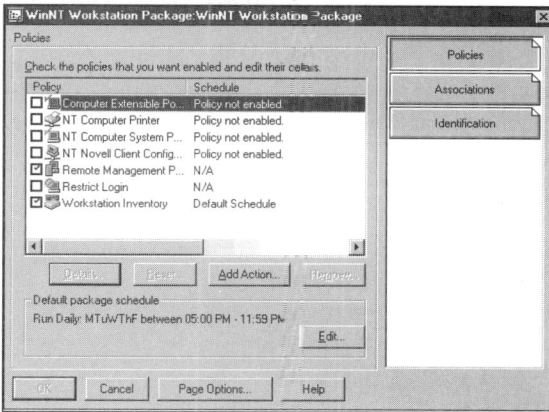

The Reset button on the policies page will reset the selected policy back to the system defaults for that policy.

Associations Page

The Associations page of the Windows NT Workstation Policy Package displays all of the locations in the tree (containers) where the policy package has been placed. The Windows NT workstations that are in or below those containers will have this policy package enforced.

Identification Page

The Identification page of the Windows NT Workstation Policy Package simply allows users to enter in additional description information to help understand the purpose of the particular policy package.

Adding a Computer Extensible Policy

Microsoft has required that software packages that bear the Windows approved logo provide abilities to be configured through .POL files. The poledit program allows you to edit these "extensible policies" and include them in the system .POL file. ZENworks also allows the policies that are stored in NDS to accept these additional "extensible polices" and provide them to all of the users that are associated with these policies.

The Computer Extensible policy will allow you to import these special .ADM files into the NDS tree and have them administered and dispersed to the users associated with the policy package. Once these .ADM files have been imported into the tree they can be administered and associated to users in the NDS tree. These settings will be applied like the Computer System Policies.

Extensible Policies

When you first bring up the Computer Extensible Policies dialog you will be presented with a scheduled page as well as the Extensible Policies page. This page is displayed in Figure 7.22.

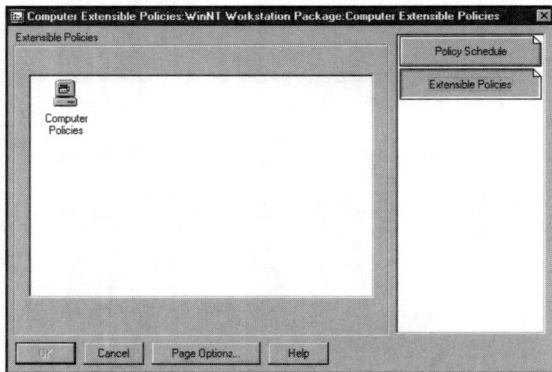

FIGURE 7.22 *Extensible Policies page of the Computer Extensible Policies policy*

From the Extensible Policies page you can double click on the Computer Policies icon. This will launch a program to import the .ADM files. The window that is displayed from the program is displayed in Figure 7.23.

Computer policies import program initial screen

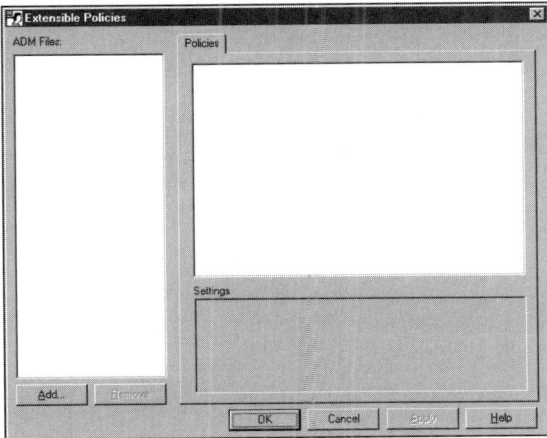

When the import program is brought up you must then specify the .ADM file that you want to import into the policy. Pressing the Add button will bring up a dialog to either specify the .ADM file or to browse to the location of the file. Once the file is specified, then pressing OK will bring it into the Extensible Policies system. Figure 7.24 displays the screen after a sample Windows NT .ADM file has been brought into the system and a few folders have been opened.

The Settings for Custom Network Neighborhood area of the screen will display the key that is being modified with the check box setting. By browsing through the settings you can set the keys just as you do in poledit.exe.

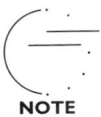

> **NOTE**
> The .ADM file must be stored on a server to which users have access. The policy will reference the .ADM file and will need to retrieve it to apply it to the users and to allow the administrators to modify the settings. It would be recommended, therefore, to use a UNC path in specifying the location of the file.

Computer policies import program with an imported .ADM file

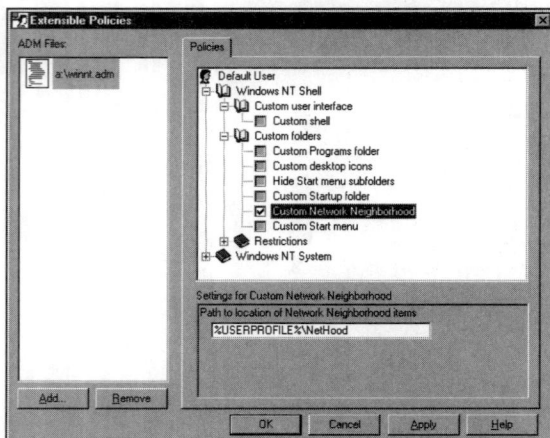

Adding a NT Computer Printer Policy

This policy allows the administrator to set up network printers on the local Windows NT desktop. In order to add printers to the policy you must have already set up some printers in your NetWare system and have corresponding printer and print queue objects in your Novell Directory Services tree. Figure 7.25 displays the printer policy screen.

Perform the following steps to add a printer to the printer policy:

I. Press the Add button.

2. Browse through the dialog box and select the Printer or Print Queue object that you want to deliver to the users associated with the policy.

To remove a printer from the policy, simply highlight the printer from the list and then press the Remove button.

Any printers that have been added to this list will be added to the user's desktop automatically when they first log into the system. When the printer is removed from this list, then the printer will be removed from the local system account the next time that the user logs into the workstation.

FIGURE 7.25 Windows NT Computer Printer policy

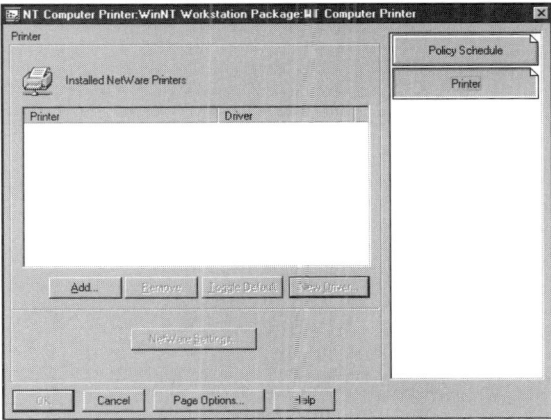

Adding NT Computer System Policies

This policy allows you access to the ZAW/ZAK features that are exposed by the Microsoft Windows system. Within the ZENworks system these ZAW/ZAK policies are divided into their logical parts: Desktop Preferences, User System Policies, and Workstation Policies. This policy allows the administrator to set the desktop preferences for any Windows NT system. This policy will be associated with the workstation and will not follow the user as they move from workstation to workstation.

Microsoft provides a tool called poledit that allows an administrator to construct some registry setting (ZAW/ZAK features) and have those settings saved in a .POL file. This .POL file can then be applied to any workstation by having the system look for these files on the server. The problem here is that these policy files must be located on every server that any user may use as an initial connection. With ZENworks this information is stored in these policies and in Novell Directory Services, thus making it always accessible to every user that connects to the system without your having to place these policy files on every server. To make the system more familiar, ZENworks has mimicked the user interface of the poledit program.

NT Computer System Policies Page

This page allows you to specify the registry settings for the Computer System ZAW/ZAK policies. Figure 7.26 shows this page.

FIGURE 7.26 *Windows NT Computer System Policies*

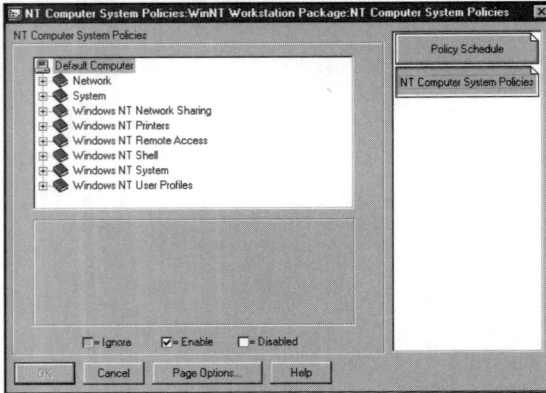

You would edit the user system policy simply by clicking on the tree components and then clicking on the check box next to each item to enable, disable, or ignore the workstation setting. In some respects this can be a very confusing interface, but you need to keep in mind that you are choosing to either: 1) Enable—a check is present, allowing this capability to the user, 2) Disable—a check is not present, turning off this capability for the user, or 3) Ignore—a grayed box, meaning that you want to leave the setting as it already is in the registry on the workstation (for example, if the feature is turned off it will be left off or if it is already turned on it will be left on).

Remember that the computer policies are an accumulation of all of the workstation policies found in the tree associated with the workstation or the containers, walking up the tree until the root is found or a search policy restricts the searching. Consequently, if there are several Workstation System policies in the tree that are associated with the workstation, then the first policy found that has a setting of Enable or Disable for the particular attribute of the policy will be used. Should the attribute be set to Ignore, then a setting of Enable or Disabled in another policy may be applied.

You can administer each of the settings by simply walking the expanding book folders presented in the policy page. Once the folder is expanded, and the final attribute is displayed you may cycle through the Ignore, Enable, Disabled settings by single clicking with the mouse on the check box associated with each attribute.

Adding a Novell Client Configuration Policy

A Novell Client Configuration Policy is activated for this policy package by either double clicking the Novell Client Configuration or selecting the check box on the Novell Client Configuration Policy. Once this is selected and a check is displayed in the check box, then this Novell Client Configuration Policy is activated for all Windows NT workstations that are associated with this policy package.

This policy allows you, the administrator, to control the client configurations for all of these workstations from a single policy. Previously one had to visit each individual workstation to make all of these settings. From this one policy all client configurations may be administered and made effective the next time that a user logs into the system.

Settings Page

From the settings page you may administer all of the aspects of the client that are installed on the associated Windows NT workstations. You can additionally administer the features of the ZENworks Workstation Manager agent. Figure 7.27 shows the Settings Page.

FIGURE 7.27 *Settings page of the Novell Client Configuration*

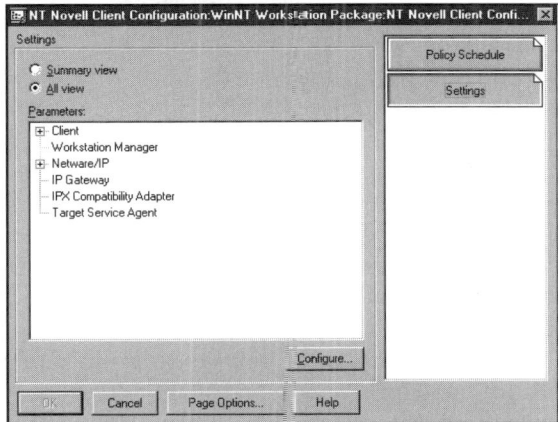

By selecting the Summary view you will be presented with a list of the parameters currently set by this policy, whereas selecting the All view radio button will display the list of all of the parameters that an administrator can configure.

In order to configure a particular parameter, you must first select a specific parameter to change. Once you have selected the parameter, then clicking the Configure button will bring up the appropriate dialogs to set that parameter. This button will bring up a dialog box that is similar to the standard dialogs that are used on the client to configure these parameters. These parameters are specific to the client and additional information about these parameters may be found in client documentation.

Adding a Remote Management Policy

A Remote Management Policy is activated for this policy package by either double clicking the Remote Management Policy or selecting the check box on the Remote Management Policy. Once this is selected and a check is displayed in the check box, then this Remote Management Policy is activated for all Windows NT workstations that are associated with the Windows NT Policy package.

The Remote Management Policy controls the features of the Remote Management subsystem that is shipped with the ZENworks package but is not shipped with the ZENworks Starter Pack. The Remote Management system is composed of two parts: Remote Management Session Manager, which makes the connection and is used by the administrator, and the Remote Management Agents that are installed on the end-user's workstation. The remote control agents may be installed onto the workstation when the client that is shipped with ZENworks is installed, or the agents may be installed on the workstation through the remote control application objects that were added to your tree when you installed ZENworks. You would simply need to associate these application objects to the users and then have the ZENworks Application launcher install these agents automatically on the workstation. For more information, see Chapter 5, Creating and Using Application Objects.

The Remote Management system will make a peer-to-peer connection between the administrator's workstation and the remote workstation. This may be done using either the IPX or the TCP/IP protocol. In this policy you may specify the preferred protocol for the connection. That protocol is attempted first, but if the connection cannot be made, then the alternate protocol will be used.

Remote controlling a workstation via ZENworks also requires rights within the Workstation Object that represents the workstation wanting to be controlled. Without these rights the administrator will be denied access to the remote control subsystem. Both the session manager and the agents validate that the user has rights to remote control the workstation. The way that you assign the remote control rights is through the Remote Management Rights wizard or in the workstation object in the Remote Operators page.

Remote Management Page

The Remote Management page identifies the features that you want to be activated with the Remote Management system. Figures 7.28 through 7.31 below show the Remote Management page and the tabbed values of the policy.

FIGURE 7.28 *Remote Management Policy page, General tab*

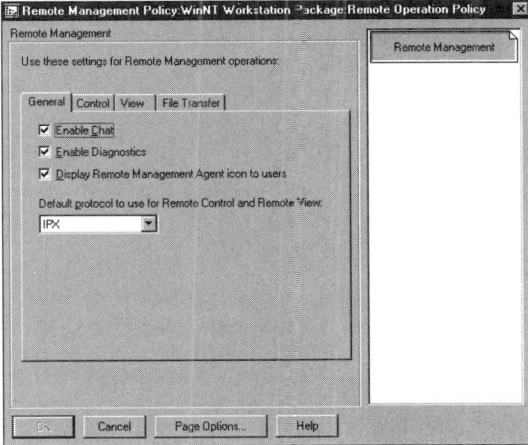

FIGURE 7.29 *Remote Management Policy page, Control tab*

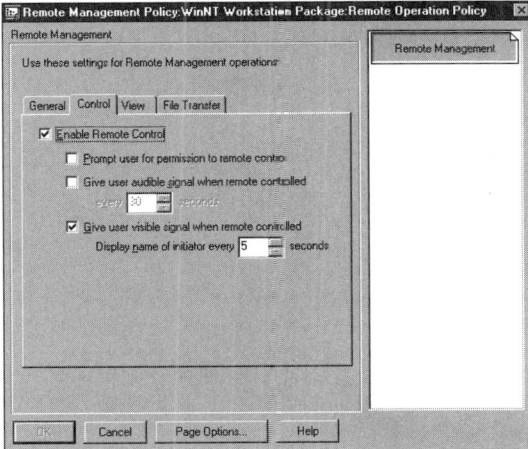

FIGURE 7.30 *Remote Management Policy page, View tab*

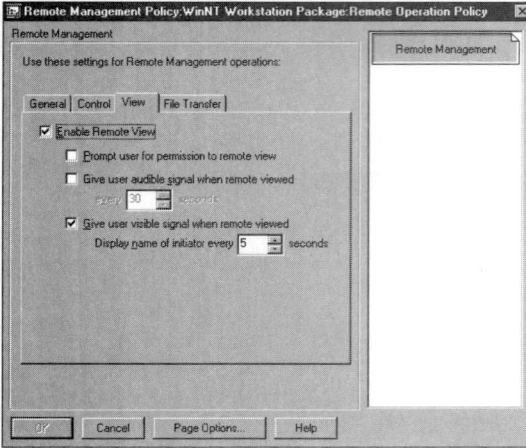

FIGURE 7.31 *Remote Management Policy page, File Transfer*

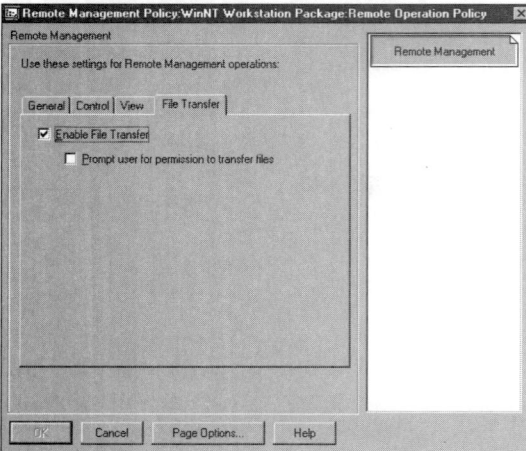

The following describes each of the options available under each tab of the Remote Management policy:

- ▶ General Tab — This tab has options on general system functions.

- ▶ Enable Chat — This enables those who have this policy associated with them to accept a chat request. Chat sets up a communication system between the initiator and the receiver and allows them to type and send messages to one another.

- ▶ Enable Diagnostics — This allows the agent on the workstations to perform a diagnostics report. This can be done from the Tools ⇨ ZENworks Remote Management menu. The Diagnostics utility will perform some basic queries on the system and return the information about the workstation. This information includes memory, environment, and processes running. Additionally, it would include NDS and Netware connection information, client information, network drives, and open file lists as well as printers, Network protocols, and network services active.

- ▶ Display Remote Management Agent icon to user — With this flag set an icon will be displayed on the system tray/task bar.

- ▶ Default protocol to use for Remote Control and Remote View — This field has the ability for you to choose whether you want the remote control to use IP or IPX protocol for default.

- ▶ Control Tab — This tab describes the feature enabling of remote control functions.

- ▶ Enable Remote Control — When this option is enabled, then the remote control subsystem can be activated. Without this setting on, no one may remote control the workstations where the currently logged in user has this policy associated with their user object.

- ▶ Prompt user for permission to remote control — This option will cause a dialog box to be displayed on the end-user's machine when a remote control session is started. The end-user has the option of accepting or denying the remote control request. Within this dialog box the user is told who wants to remote control their machine and asks if this is approved. If the user denies the remote control session, then the session is terminated and the administrator cannot remote control the workstation.

- ▶ Give user audible system when remote controlled — This option will provide the end user a tone periodically while the remote control session is active. You can also set the number of seconds between each beep.

▶ Give user visible signal when remote controlled — This option will display a dialog box on the end user's desktop while the remote control session is active. The dialog box displays that the workstation is being remote controlled and also displays the NDS name of the user that is remote controlling the workstation. You can set the number of seconds that you want to have between flashes of the name of the user that is initiating the remote control session.

▶ View Tab — This tab describes the feature enabling of the remote view functions. Remote view is the ability for the administrator to view the remote windows screen of the target machine but not be able to control the mouse or keyboard of the machine.

▶ Enable Remote View — With this option enabled, then the remote view subsystem can be activated. Without this setting on, no one may remote view the workstations where the currently logged in user has this policy associated with their user object.

▶ Prompt user for permission to remote view — This option will cause a dialog box to be displayed on the end-user's machine when a remote view session is started. The end-user has the option of accepting or denying the remote view request. Within this dialog box the user is told who wants to remote view their machine and asks if this is approved. If the user denies the remote view session, then the session is terminated and the administrator cannot remote view the workstation.

▶ Give user audible system when remote viewed — This option will provide the end user a tone periodically while the remote view session is active. You can also set the number of seconds between each beep.

▶ Give user visible signal when remote viewed — This option will display a dialog box on the end user's desktop while the remote view session is active. The dialog box displays that the workstation is being remote viewed and also displays the NDS name of the user that is remote viewing the workstation. You can set the number of seconds that you want to have between flashes of the name of the user that is initiating the remote view session.

▶ File Transfer Tab — This tab describes the feature enabling of the file transfer system. This will allow you, the administrator, to send files to the remote workstation.

▶ Enable File Transfer — With this option enabled, the file transfer subsystem can be activated. Until it is enabled, no one may send files to the workstations where the currently logged in user has this policy associated with their user object.

▶ Prompt user for permission to transfer files — This option will cause a dialog box to be displayed on the end-user's machine when a file transfer session is started. The end-user has the option of accepting or denying the file transfer request. Within this dialog box the user is told who wants to perform the file transfer to or from his or her machine and asks if this is approved. If the user denies the file transfer session, then the session is terminated and the administrator cannot send the files to the workstation.

Adding a Restrict Login Policy

This policy will allow the administrator to specify the users that may or may not log into the system from the workstations that are associated with this policy. This will restrict all volatile users within the Dynamic Local User features of ZENworks from logging into the system, including the local workstation. However, if there is an account for the user already on the workstation (nonvolatile) then the user may still log into the machine locally even though he or she cannot log into the network.

The policy will not allow duplicates in both lists and if a duplicate entry is attempted will ask the administrator to choose whether the entry should be allowed to login to the system or not from this workstation policy.

You can specify within the list any user, group, or container to which you want to grant or deny login privileges. If you specify a container, the agent will only restrict users that are directly in that container and will not walk down into sub-containers. For example, should you specify the Provo.Novell container in the Deny login from field then all users with the context of Provo.Novell will be denied access, if a user has the context of North.Provo.Novell then they will be allowed to log into the system.

Figure 7.32 displays the Login Restrictions page.

FIGURE 7.32 *Login Restrictions Policy page*

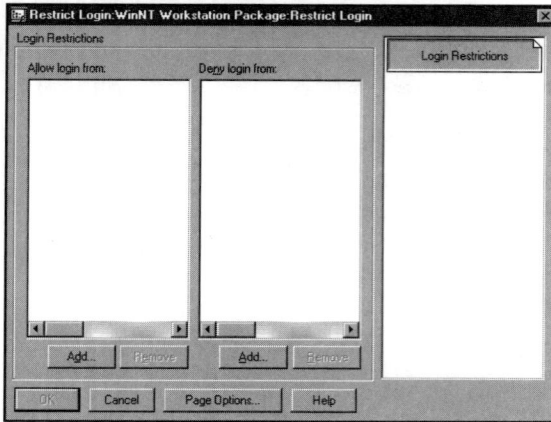

Do the following to add a user, group, or container to either of the Allow login from or Deny login from fields:

1. Press the appropriate Add button for the field. This will bring up a NWAdmin32 browse dialog.

2. Browse within the tree to select the Novell Directory Services user, group, or container. Select the desired user, group, or container and press the OK button. This object will be added to the list.

To remove an entry, simply select the object in the appropriate list and press the Remove button.

Adding a Workstation Inventory Policy

ZENworks has introduced full hardware and software scanning feature into the system. When ZENworks is installed into the system, the administrator has the option of installing an inventory database at the same time. This inventory database is then placed on a volume in a server in the tree. Through this policy, inventory information can then be placed within that database. Additionally, this selected subset of the inventory information will be placed in the Workstation Object.

Figure 7.33 displays the Scanner Configuration page of the Inventory Policy.

Workstation Inventory Policy

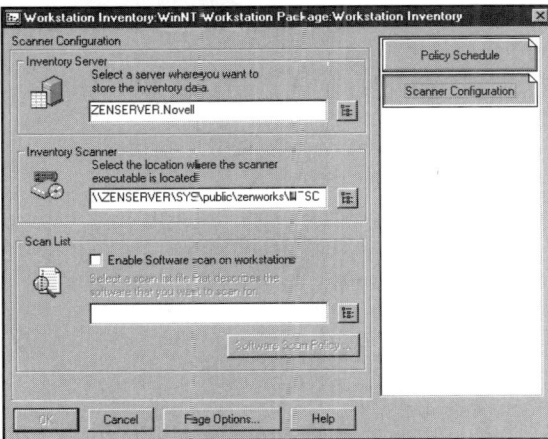

Within the inventory policy the administrator has the ability to administer three things about the hardware and software scanning that occurs on the workstation. The following describes the three parameters and the workings of the inventory system.

▶ Inventory Server — This field represents the server object that holds the ZENworks database. This database should have been placed on the server when ZENworks was originally installed. You can have multiple databases within a single tree, but each database is managed independently and the information in one database is not transmitted to another. All workstations that have this policy associated with them will send their scanned information to the specified server.

▶ Inventory Scanner — This field represents the executable program location of the scanner. This scanner is executed on the workstation based on the specified inventory schedule. When the scanner is executed it creates a file on the local workstation called scan.txt. Portions of this file are then transmitted and stored in the workstation object of the workstation and the full contents of the scan are transmitted and stored in the ZENworks database. The hardware is probed for discovery. In addition to probing, ZENworks scanning supports DMI 2.0 library interfaces and will include the DMI information in the hardware reports.

▶ Scan List — This field holds two separate data values: Enable Software scan on workstations, and the location of the software scan list. When the "Enable Software scan on workstations" is checked then a software scan will be done on the workstation in addition to the standard hardware probe. The software scan list is an .INI file that lists the names and files of the software that are to be scanned and recognized. ZENworks will provide ways to update this list with new database entries as well as entries of personal files.

▶ At the scheduled time the scanner executable specified by the policy is launched on the workstation. This scanner will attempt to make DMI 2.0 calls to get DMI information, and it will also make hardware probes in an effort to discover the hardware in the workstation. Following the hardware scanning, the software will then make a scan of the local drives to locate the software that is on the drives. The software is recognized when it matches any of the files specified in the software scan list. This list of software packages is also stored with the hardware information. The scanner will generate a file called scan.txt on the local workstation drive.

Once the scan is completed, then the scanner will make a connection (IP or IPX) to the Inventory Server and attempt to communicate with the database service that was placed there with the ZENworks install. This service will collect the information and then place it in the database on that inventory server. Additionally, the scanner will return a "sweet spot" of information and have that placed in the workstation object in NDS. Both the "sweet spot" of information and the data in the database may be viewed through NWAdmin by going to the workstation object and looking at the inventory page.

If you are having the system perform a software scan of the local hardware drives you need to take into consideration the intensity of the scan. The scan does happen in the background, but it will always increase the usage on the workstation. Each location will need to determine how often you need to scan, but it probably does not need to be more often than once a week.

CHAPTER 8

Creating a Container Policy Package

In addition to user and workstation policies, ZENworks also features a container policy package, which this chapter discusses. This package is associated with a container and affects the understanding of policies below the container level.

► · ◄

Relationship of a Container Policy Package to Other Policies

A container policy package contains a set of policies that are associated with containers. These policies are expected to affect the behavior of other ZENworks users and workstation policies, and are therefore associated only with containers.

ZENworks agents work in a standard way to search out policies within a tree, starting at either the user or the workstation object, depending on the application of the policy. Once the user or workstation object is located, the ZENworks agents next seek out a container policy package. The first container policy package that is found while the agent is walking up the tree is used to modify the behavior of the searching out of all other policies.

Once the container policy package is discovered, the agents use the information in the package to seek other users or workstation policy packages.

► · ◄

Setting up a Container Policy Package

To have a container policy package that affects the policies, you must first create the policy package. To create a container policy package follow these steps:

I. Start NWAdmin32.

2. Browse to the container where you would like to have the policy package. Remember that you do not have to create the policy package in the container where you are doing the associations. You can associate the same policy package to many containers in your tree.

3. Create the policy package by clicking the right mouse button and choosing Create.

4. Select the policy package object in the list of objects that can be created in the selected container.

5. In the Create Policy Package Wizard dialog box, select the type of package you want to be a container package and name the object. Continue through the wizard to create all the desired policies and associations.

6. Press the Finish button to conclude the creation of the policy package.

Policies Page

The policies page lists the set of available policies and indicates which of those are active. Figure 8.1 shows this policies page.

FIGURE 8.1 *Container package policies page*

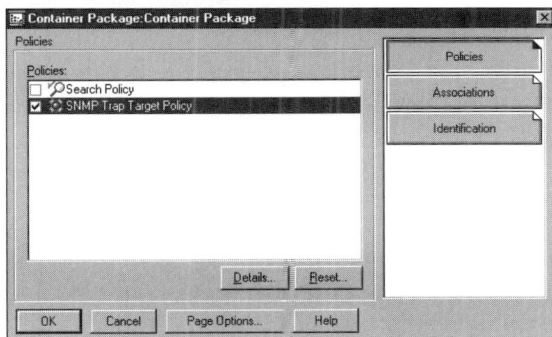

Once you have created a container package, you can now activate policies. If you click a policy within the policy package, that policy becomes active. An active policy is designated by a check in the checkbox. The details of any particular policy can be modified by selecting the policy and pressing the Details button, or by double-clicking the policy itself.

The Reset button on the policies page will reset the selected policy back to the system defaults for that policy.

Associations Page

The associations page of the container package displays all the locations in the tree (containers) where the policy package has been placed. The user and workstation policy packages that are in or below those containers will have this policy package enforced.

Identification Page

The identification page of the container package simply allows users to enter additional description information to help understand the purpose of the particular policy package.

Adding a Search Policy

A search policy governs the behavior of the ZENworks agents as they search for user and workstation policies. With all the ZENworks agents, there could be some significant walking of the tree as it searches for the policies for the identified user and workstations, especially if the tree is of a significant depth. This is the reason why ZENworks has added this search policy. Often, the performance of your network searching with ZENworks will not be significant until you cross a partition boundary. When you cross a partition boundary, the system must make a connection and authenticate to another server. This is particularly time-consuming should the system need to cross a WAN link.

The search policy tells the ZENworks agents how far up the tree they should search, and what order (object, group, container) they should follow to find the policies. Remember that the order is significant because often the first policy found will govern the behavior of the system.

Search Level Page

This page enables the administrator to identify how far up the tree the ZENworks agents should traverse in their search for policies. Figure 8.2 shows this page.

F I G U R E   8.2 *Search level page of a search policy*

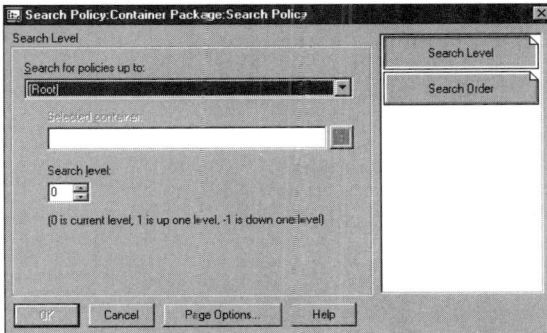

The following fields may be administered in the search level features of the search order policy:

- Search for policies up to: — This field enables you to specify the container in the tree that the searching will complete. The choices that can be made through the drop-down list include any of the following:

  - [Root] — Search up to the root of the tree.

  - Object Container — Search up to the container that holds the object that is associated with the policy. For example, if you are searching for a user policy package, the object container would be the context of the user object.

  - Partition — Search up the tree to a partition boundary. Crossing a partition boundary will cause connections to other systems in the tree. This option is available for performance considerations.

  - Selected Container — This will search up to the specified container. When this option is chosen, the Selected container field is activated and you can then browse in this field to the desired container.

- Search level: — This field will enable you to specify an additional level of container beyond that given in the Search for policies up to: field. A search level value of 0 causes searches to be limited to the specified container. A search level of a positive numerical value allows searching the number of containers specified. Should the search level be a negative number, the search will proceed at the specified level minus the number specified. For example, if the value of Object Container were selected and the object is in the Provo.Utah.Novell container, and the search level is 0, then the searching will stop at the Provo.Utah.Novell container. If the search level is 2, then the searching will continue to the Novell container. If the search level is –1, no policy will be found because the object container is already above the search level.

At first look you may think that there is no reason for having a negative search level, but there is some importance in having this value. Suppose your tree is set up as Organization.Region.Company, where Organization is the container that is given to each organization in the company and Region represents the area of the company. Now suppose you want policies to be effective only for each organization; then, you could set up a single search policy at the Region.Company level with a selected container as Region.Company and a search level of –1. This would allow each organization to have a customized policy and ensure that no organization's policies would impact each other, because the searching would stop at the Organization level.

Search Order Page

This page enables the administrator to identify the order in which the agents should go looking for policies. The default is always object, group, and then container. This policy allows the administer to change this order. Figure 8.3 shows the search order page.

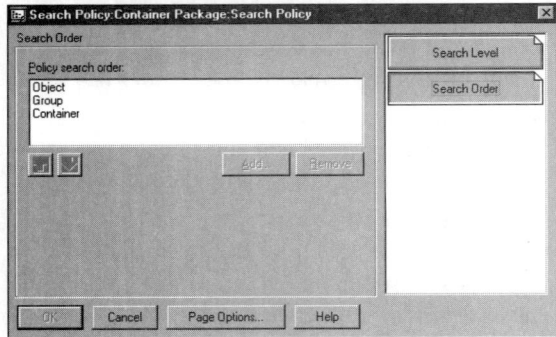

F I G U R E   8.3   *Search order page of a search policy*

You can modify the search order by selecting the item in the search order list and then clicking the up or down arrows to rearrange the list. Clicking the Remove button will remove the selected order. Clicking the Add button will add that search order item, if there are any that have been previously deleted.

Because the first policy that is found has the greatest significance in the behavior of the system, you should be sure that you have the order set (from top to bottom) in the way that you want, to find that first policy.

You should be aware of when it is a good idea to use the search order policy. Because many ZENworks features will stop walking up the tree when a policy is found, it would be wise to make policies search on objects, containers, and then groups. This is because the proximity of these objects in the tree are always going to be closer to the partition on the server. Obviously, the object will always be the closest in the tree to the workstation or user object. Then the container will be the closest in the tree-walking scenario, because the container must be known in order for the object to be found in the tree. Consequently, the container will be very close in the local replica to the object. Groups, however, can be stored in any container and they could be in a completely different part of the tree than the object. Therefore, the amount of potential walking of the tree with a group is significant. With any significant walking of the tree, there is a corresponding performance cost that should be considered as you manage your tree and search policies.

Adding an SNMP Trap Target Policy

In ZENworks, the Application Launcher has been enhanced to send an SNMP message to a central server that will store these messages and enable you to print reports on the traps. These traps can identify whether an application was successfully distributed or not, and if not it will identify the problem with the distribution.

The SNMP trap target policy is used to identify the location of the service that is accepting and recording the SNMP messages from the Application Launcher. This service is associated with the database that was installed with ZENworks. Figure 8.4 displays the trap target policy page. The service on the workstation walks the tree to find this policy and uses the service location stored in this policy as the destination of the SNMP messages.

► · ◄

FIGURE 8.4 *SNMP trap target policy page of the container package*

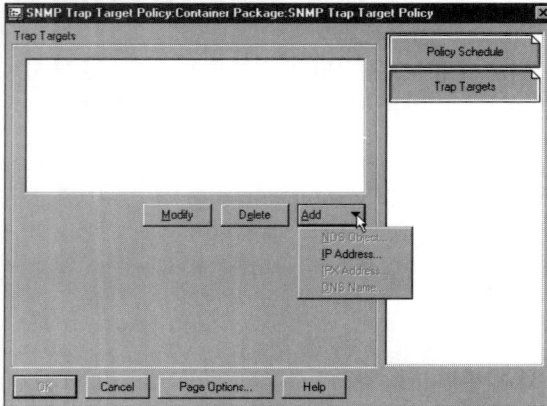

Once you've brought up the policy page, you need to add as many trap targets as you desire. The service on the workstation will send the SNMP message to all of the specified trap targets. Click the Add button and specify whether the destination can be achieved with an IP Address, an IPX Address, or a DNS name. After selecting the type, a dialog box enables to enter either the address or the DNS name of the target service.

CHAPTER 9

Maintaining a Workstation

Once the ZENworks system has been deployed across the network, the workstations have had the proper client installed, and the workstation is registered, the workstation can then be maintained and managed by the administrator from any location in the network. This provides obvious benefits because the administrator and support technicians rarely have to visit the individual workstation. This offers a significant cost improvement in maintaining your system.

Users and the Help Request System

The Help Request System is designed to function without the need to import workstations. The purpose of the Help Request System is to provide some immediate information to end users about who to contact for problems with their workstations. In many cases, users do not know who they should contact for help in problem situations, and when they finally get to the contact they often cannot provide simple information needed to help troubleshoot their system. The Help Request System provides this information to users so they can contact the right person and provide this vital information, some of which cannot be easily discovered elsewhere. The Help Request System uses the information that is stored in the policy, along with the data on the workstation, to affect its user interface and data presented to the user.

For the Help Request System to be functional, the following must have been completed:

1. A user policy package for the operating system must have been created and associated with the users who will be using the Help Request System.

2. The Help Desk policy must be enabled within the user policy package.

3. Within the Help Desk policy, the checkbox next to the Allow user to launch the Help Requester option must be checked.

4. The Help Requester application object must be associated with the users who will be using the system.

5. The users who will launch the Help Requester must be running the ZENworks Application Launcher.

When the users log in to the system, and as part of their login script they start up the ZENworks Application Launcher, they are presented with the icon for the Help Requester for their operating system. The user can then double-click this icon in order to launch the Help Requester system. Figure 9.1 displays the initial screen of the Help Requester application.

F I G U R E   9 . 1
Novell Help Requester application

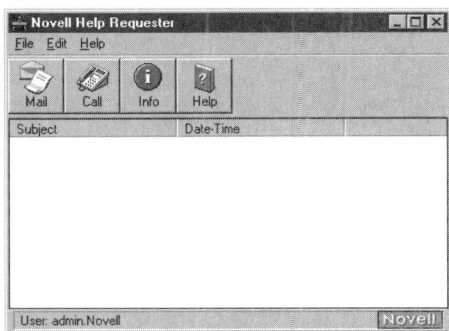

Based on the Help Desk policy associated with the user, a user may be presented with several task buttons within the Help Requester application. The user will not be given the Mail taskbar button if the Allow user to send trouble tickets from the Help Requester feature is not enabled in the Help Desk policy. A user will always be presented with the Call, Info, and Help taskbar buttons.

Mail Help Request Task

The Mail button on the Help Requester enables the user to send mail to the e-mail address specified in the Help Desk policy associated with that user. Figures 9.2 through 9.4 show the windows displayed when the Mail button is pressed.

F I G U R E   9 . 2   *Novell Help Requester Mail for Help dialog box, Message tab selected*

Novell Help Requester Mail for Help dialog box, User tab selected

Novell Help Requester Mail for Help dialog box, Workstation tab selected

The Message tab enables the end user to enter a message to be sent to the e-mail specified in the policy. The User tab displays the DN and information of the user currently logged in to the workstation. The information in the User tab is gathered from the user object in the NDS tree. The Workstation tab displays the DN and tree of the workstation, along with the NDS hardware inventory information. All of this information may or may not be sent in the trouble ticket, based on the options specified in the policy.

Call Button

When the user presses the Call taskbar button, the Call for Help dialog box appears (see Figure 9.5). This displays the Help Desk data that was entered in the information page of the Help Desk policy. It also contains the contact name and number, along with basic information about the user and workstation object and tree. The information in the tabs is the same information displayed in the Mail dialog box, as discussed previously.

FIGURE 9.5 *Novell Help Requester Call for Help dialog box, User tab selected*

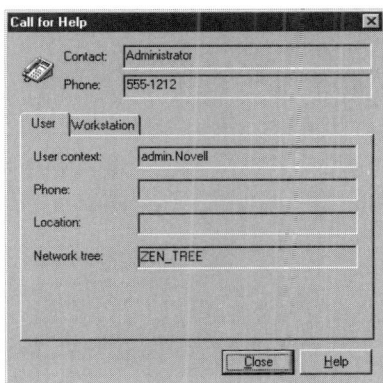

Info Button

The Info button presents the same information in the User and Workstation tabs as discussed previously with the Call and Mail buttons. Figure 9.6 displays the initial dialog box presented by clicking the Info button. This additional information includes the Help Desk e-mail and the policy package that the Help Requester application is using.

FIGURE 9.6 *Novell Help Requester Information*

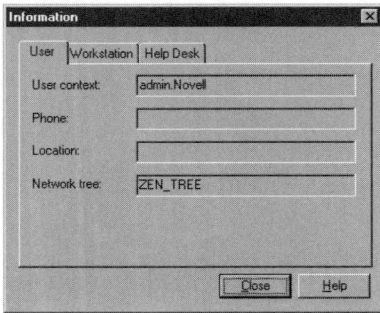

The Help Desk tab shown in Figure 9.7 displays additional information about the Help Desk policy that is being used by the Help Requester program. This indicates the contact information and the policy object that is being used.

FIGURE 9.7 *Novell Help Requester Information dialog box with the Help Desk tab selected*

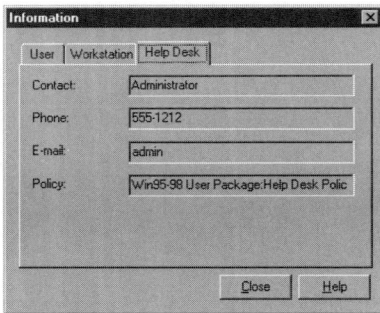

Workstation Inventory

The purpose of the workstation inventory in the first release of the ZENworks product is to provide some basic information about the workstation for diagnostic purposes and some basic asset management. Versions shipped after 1.0 increased the scope and use of the inventory data by adding a software scanner, support for DMI 2.0, and a database.

The data in the workstation object within the Novell Directory Services is designed to be sufficient to inform you of what type of system you are dealing with when you need to provide support for the user on that system. This support could be over a phone or via the remote control features of ZENworks. The reason more information is not stored in the workstation object is that ZENworks must have a balance between the information in the directory and the space required to store that information. Once the information is within Novell Directory Services, this basic information for any workstation in the tree can be retrieved by any administrator, anywhere in the system.

In order to get workstation inventory into the tree, the following must be completed:

1. The workstation must have been imported into the tree.

2. A workstation policy package must have been created and associated with the workstation, by direct association with either the workstation, workstation group, or container.

3. The workstation inventory policy must be enabled within the policy package.

4. The schedule for the inventory must have passed so that the scanner has had an opportunity to retrieve the information and place it in the tree and in the inventory database. The default scheduled time is daily.

To view the data, you simply need to browse within NWAdmin32 to the workstation object and then click on the workstation inventory page. From there, you can view the basic and advanced information about this physical workstation. Figure 9.8 shows the screen that is displayed as part of the workstation object.

The workstation inventory page provides some basic information about the workstation. The intention is to help the administrator obtain the correct context for how to work with the workstation.

The administrator may view additional information by pressing the More Workstation Information button. This button brings up the dialog box shown in Figure 9.9.

F I G U R E   9 . 8   *Workstation inventory summary page within a Windows 95 workstation object*

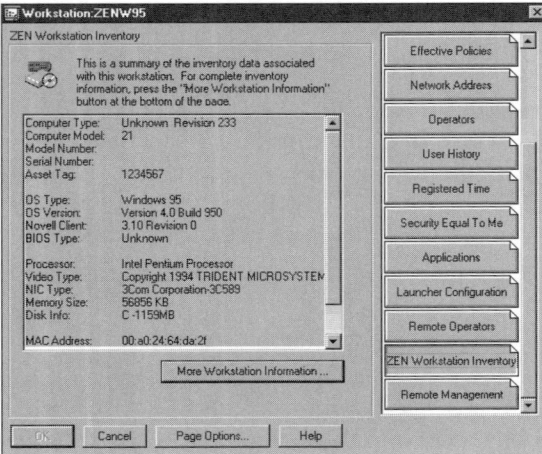

F I G U R E   9 . 9   *Workstation Inventory advanced dialog box within details of a container*

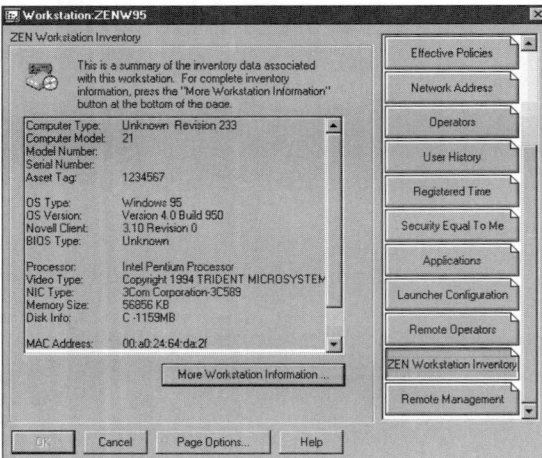

This dialog box retrieves information from the database scan and has folders that describe the discovered software, hardware (probed), network information, server connections, miscellaneous, and DMI components. Following is a brief listing of the information on these screens:

- Software — A list of all of the drivers, software packages, operating system and scanner information. The list would include those scanned for in the workstation inventory policy.

- Hardware — This lists probed information that has been discovered about the workstation. This includes the mouse, keyboard, display, BIOS, processor, memory, and disks (including floppies, hard drives, mapped drives, and CD-ROM). Additionally, this field includes the serial and parallel ports and the bus information on the workstation.

- Network — This includes networking information such as the connections and the client version number.

- Server Connection — This can include the connections to the various servers at the time of the scan.

- Miscellaneous — This folder includes various information including configuration files, environment information, and any NT services that are active.

- DMI Components — This folder holds all of the information that was discovered by attempting to make DMI 2.0 calls on the workstation.

Remote Controlling a Workstation

On occasion, it may be necessary to remote control a workstation from any other workstation in the tree. You may remote control a workstation via IP or IPX protocol, and from any workstation in the network; however, you must have Novell Directory Services rights to control the workstation. Before you can remote control a workstation, the following must be completed:

1. The proper remote control agents must be present on the workstation. This can be accomplished by installing the ZENworks client that ships with the product. The client that comes with ZENworks will always have the latest agents that are available.

   You can also deliver the agents to the workstation via the ZENworks Application Launcher. When ZENworks is installed into the tree, several application objects are created for the remote control agents for Windows NT, Windows 95/98, and Windows 3.1. If you have the Application Launcher launched from the login scripts of your users, you can force-run the deployment of these agents to ensure that all workstations have the proper agent.

2. The workstation must be registered with Novell Directory Services and have a workstation object imported and associated with the workstation.

A good way to test that you have a good association is to modify some of the policies associated with the workstation and see if the changes take effect. One thing to try is to change the remote control policy so that the icon shows on the taskbar or the desktop, and then see if this takes effect on the workstation. By accomplishing this, you know that the workstation is associated with the object and that the system is communicating properly with Novell Directory Services.

3. You must have rights to perform the remote control. When the remote control session starts, the session manager (the program that runs from NWAdmin32) checks to see if you have rights to remote control the workstation. Additionally, the agent will verify that you have rights to control the workstation.

The rights to remote control a workstation can be given in several ways. One way is through the ZENworks Manage Remote Operators Wizard launched from the Tools menu. This wizard will walk the tree starting at the specified container and make sure that the users specified gain rights to remote control the workstations. Additionally, you can go to the workstation object itself and add users to the remote operators page. When the users are added to this page, they are given rights to remote control this workstation.

Once the system is set up with the workstation, you may remote control any workstation that has registered, and you have rights to remote control. To remote control a workstation, you need to do the following:

I. Start NWAdmin32.

2. Browse in the tree to the particular workstation you want to remote control. Highlight the workstation object. You may start remote controlling the workstation by selecting Tools ⇨ Remote Control on the menu, or you may go into the details of the workstation and launch remote control from the Remote Control page.

3. The remote control session manager will launch and verify that you have rights, and then attempt to connect to the remote control agents on the workstation that is associated with the object. The agent will then respond and begin the remote controlling of the workstation, and you will be presented with a window on your machine that represents the desktop of the remote machine. You now have control of the remote workstation, and will continue to have control until you exit the remote control session.

Workstation Diagnostics

On occasion, it may be beneficial to perform some immediate diagnostics on a particular workstation. From the NWAdmin32 utility, you can perform immediate diagnostics on the workstation. These diagnostics will perform an immediate connection to the agent on the workstation, and then will deliver to the administrator information about the workstation. Figure 9.10 shows the output screen from the diagnostics.

FIGURE 9.10 *Workstation diagnostics of a Windows 95 workstation*

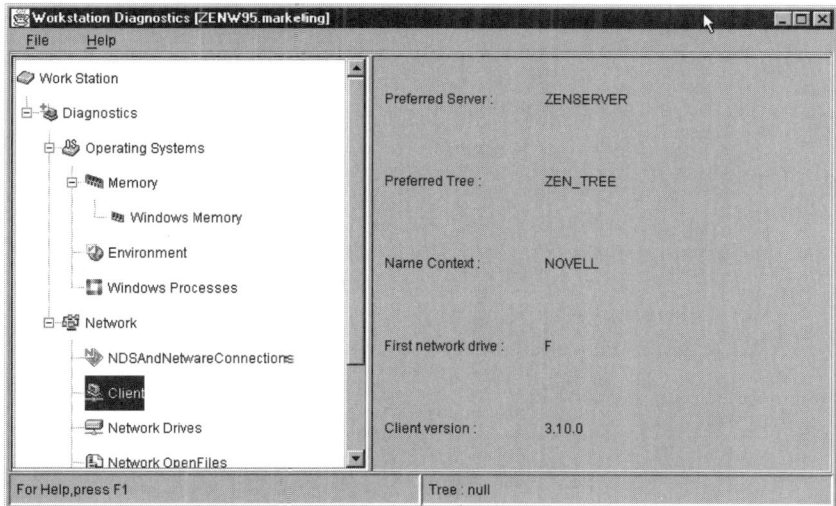

The diagnostics information include the amount of memory available and used, the environment information, and the Windows processes that are active. In addition, it will display the network connections, drives, and open files. It will also show client information, printers, network protocols, and services.

This tool can provide you with some real-time information about the workstation as you debug the system and repair your users' problems.

Un-registering a Workstation

The first user to log in to a tree from a clean workstation will register that workstation to his or her primary tree. Some support organizations will set up a workstation with all the appropriate hardware, installing the client and standard software before sending the workstation to the final end user. During this setup process, it is very likely that the support personnel will log in to the tree and consequently will register the workstation with the support person as the primary user. In this case, you should un-register the workstation before shipping it to the final end user, so that when the end user logs into the system it will register at that time with the final end user as the primary user. At times it may also be useful to reset the whole workstation importing process and re-register the workstation with the tree to get the entire process running from scratch. Fortunately, ZENworks provides a tool to assist you in un-registering your workstation, so you can have it re-register with the tree the next time a user logs in to the tree from that workstation.

The following steps must be taken to un-register your workstation from the Novell Directory Services tree:

1. If a workstation object has already been imported for the workstation, make sure the workstation object is deleted from the tree. This is done by launching NWAdmin32 and browsing to the container with the workstation object, highlighting the object, and then pressing the Delete key or choosing Object ⇨ Delete.

2. Log in to the workstation with local workstation administrator privileges. You do not need to be the administrator for the tree.

3. Execute the program SYS:\PUBLIC\UNREG32.EXE. This removes the registry keys that the ZENworks agents use to keep track of the workstation object.

4. The next user to log in to the system will start the registration process again.

CHAPTER 10

Using ZENworks Software Metering

A major advantage included in ZENworks is software metering. ZENworks software metering gives organizations the capability to manage software licenses and track software usage through using ZENworks application management and Novell's Licensing Services (NLS).

Once software metering is configured for an Application Launcher application, a license is used each time a user launches the application. In other words, every time a user runs the application, one of the licenses is also in use.

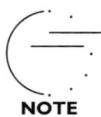

> **NOTE**
> Applications must be delivered to the user through Application Launcher Explorer or Application Launcher in order to take advantage of software metering. Application objects must also be associated with license containers.

To set up and use ZENworks software metering, you need to become familiar with the following procedures.

Using NLS Manager

The first piece of software metering you should be familiar with using is the NLS Manager. The NLS Manager is a utility provided with software metering, and is found in the following location:

```
SYS:\PUBLIC\WIN32\NLSMAN32.EXE
```

You should use the NLS Manager utility to create metered certificates and to add new certificates to existing license containers. You can also use the NLS Manager utility to generate reports and view information about software metering.

Once the NLS Manager is started, a window similar to the one in Figure 10.1 is displayed. The following sections describe the most important procedures you should be aware of when using the NLS Manager window.

Installing a License Certificate Using NLS Manager

The first procedure in NLS Manager you should know is how to install a license certificate. License Certificate objects contain information about the product, such as the publisher, product name, version, and how many licenses (units) the certificate has. Installing a certificate for an NLS-aware application adds a license container object to the NDS database, as well as a license certificate object inside that container object.

FIGURE 10.1 *The main window in NLS Manager*

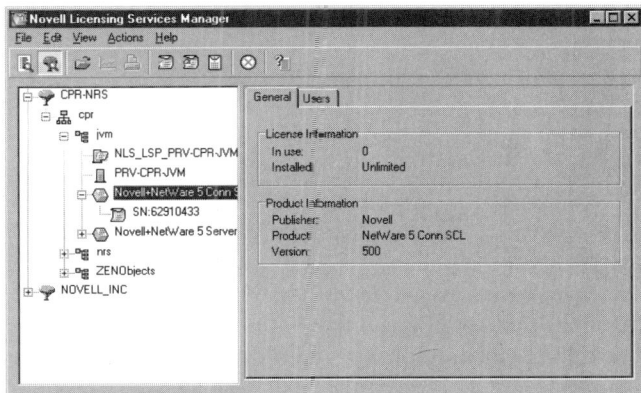

To install a license certificate in NLS Manager, perform the following steps:

1. From NLS Manager's main browser window, select View ⇨ Tree View.

2. Select Actions ⇨ Install License Certificate; a screen similar to the one in Figure 10.2 appears.

3. From that screen, enter the path and filename of the certificate you wish to install.

4. Select the NDS context where the certificate object should be installed.

5. Once both fields are entered, click OK to install the license certificate.

> A license certificate requires an activation key. If NLS Manager can't find one while you are installing a certificate, an Activation Key window enables you to enter one.
>
> **NOTE**

► • ◄

F I G U R E   10.2   *The Install a License Certificate window*

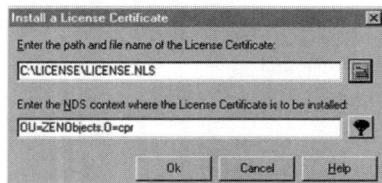

Creating a Metered Certificate Using NLS Manager

The next procedure in NLS Manager you should know is creating a metered certificate. Metered certificates let you monitor usage of applications, whereas license certificates enable you to limit the usage of applications. Using metered certificates lets you track and manage the licenses for user applications even if they are not NLS-aware.

To create a metered certificate using NLS Manager, follow these steps from NLS Manager:

1. Select View2 ⇨ Tree View.

2. Next Select Actions ⇨ Create Metered Certificate; a screen similar to the one in Figure 10.3 appears.

3. From that screen, enter the name of the software publisher.

4. Enter the product name.

5. Enter the version.

6. Set the NDS context for the license certificate.

7. Set the number of licenses for the certificate.

8. Enter or select the number of grace licenses you will allow.

9. Indicate whether or not users will use a single license when launching an application multiple times from one workstation.

10. Click OK to finish.

NOTE

The grace licenses option enables additional users to run. If you do not enter a number of grace licenses, users will not be allowed to open additional applications beyond the number specified in Number of Licenses.

• • • •

FIGURE 10.3 *The Create Metered Certificate window*

Create Metered Certificate

Publisher name:	Netscape
Product name:	Communicator
Version:	4.06
Create in context:	O=cpr
Number of license units:	50

Options
Grace license units:	4
Update Interval (Min)	15

☐ Multiple launches at a workstation use just 1 license

☐ Create another Certificate

[OK]   [Cancel]   [Help]

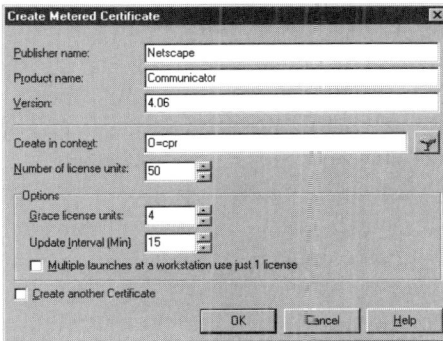

Assigning Licenses to Users Using NLS Manager

Once you know how to install license certificates and create metering certificates, you need to know how to assign licenses to users using NLS Manager.

The NDS user who installs the license certificate is the owner. An owner can give the following objects access to the licenses:

- User
- Group
- Organization
- Organizational unit
- Server

For example, if an owner assigns a container object to use a certificate, all users in and below that container will be able to use the certificate. Once the license assignments are made, only the objects that have been assigned to the license certificates can use the license.

To assign and delete access to licenses using NLS Manager, perform the following procedures through an assignments property page.

Here are the steps for assigning objects to a license certificate:

1. Select View ⇨ Tree View.
2. Select the license certificate you want users to access.
3. Select the Assignments property page.
4. Click Add to add objects.
5. Locate and select the object that allows the correct users to access the certificate's licenses

Here are the steps for deleting assignments to a license certificate:

1. Navigate to the assignments property page of the license certificate object you wish to delete assignments on.

2. Select the object and click Remove.

Assigning a New Owner to a License Certificate Using NLS Manager

The next procedure in NLS Manager you should know is assigning a new owner to a license certificate. Because the user who installs a certificate automatically becomes the owner of that certificate, you may want to reassign ownership at a later date.

NLS Manager enables you to assign a new owner to a license certificate at any time using the following steps:

1. Select View ⮕ Tree View.

2. Select the license certificate.

3. Select the Owner property page.

4. Click on the tree icon next to the License Owner field.

5. Finally, locate and select the object you want to assign as owner of this certificate.

> Only a certificate's owner can reassign ownership of the certificate.
>
> **NOTE**

Working with Reports in NLS Manager

The final procedure you should know in NLS Manager is its capability to create reports about licensed and metered products. Because NLS Manager tracks data about licenses and metered products, you can create reports that help you assess and monitor usage and compliance concerning these products for the past 15 months.

These reports can range from information about a single license certificate to information about all license certificates currently being used for a given product.

Creating a Report in NLS Manager

The first step in working with reports in NLS Manager is to create one of the following reports.

To create a report for a specific license certificate, perform the following steps:

1. Select View ➪ Quick View.

2. Select a license container object's context.

3. Access the Usage Report Wizard by double-clicking the license container's context.

4. Follow the prompts.

To create a report for a product, perform the following steps:

1. Select View ➪ Quick View.

2. Select the product you wish to create a report of.

3. Access the Usage Report Wizard by double-clicking the product.

4. Follow the prompts.

Viewing a Report

When you have created a report using NLS Manager, you can toggle between a graphical view of the report and that report's text.

To use the graphical view, click Graph, and a graphical representation of the data in the report is displayed on the screen. This view displays the number of license units installed and the number used. The dates along the bottom of the graph show the start and end dates that the report covers. You can change these dates to make the data more informational.

To use the textual view, click Summary, and a textual representation of the data in the report is displayed on the screen.

The textual view provides the following information:

- ▸ The date and time you created the report
- ▸ The product
- ▸ The location or NDS context of the object
- ▸ Current number of licenses being used and installed
- ▸ The range of dates being reported
- ▸ Peak usage of licenses including date the peak occurred
- ▸ The number of units used and installed during peak usage
- ▸ A list of possible dates out of compliance

► · · · · · · · · · · · · · · · · · · · ◄

Setting Up Software Metering

Now that you're familiar with using the NLS Manager utility, you need to understand how to set up software metering. To set up software metering, you need to perform the following procedures to verify the metering requirements, and then set up metering certificates.

Verify Setup Requirements

The first step in setting up software metering is to make sure you meet the correct system requirements. The following are the current requirements for setting up software metering:

► You should have supervisor rights to the [ROOT] of the NDS tree in which you will install the Application Management portion of ZENworks.

► Users must have read and file scan rights to the directory in which you will install NAL.

► Users must have sufficient rights to the directories in which you will install the applications they can access.

Installed Locally or on the Network?

Once the system requirements are met, you must make sure the application is delivered to the user through the Application Launcher via the Application Launcher Window or the Application Explorer. Although software metering does not care where an application's executable file is located, it must be delivered to the user through the Application Launcher.

Ensure that Users Have Access to NLS

The next step in setting up software metering is to ensure that users have access to NLS. Users must always be attached to a NetWare server that provides licensing services.

> **TIP**
> By loading NLS on more than one server in your tree, and making sure users have a connection to one or more servers with NLS loaded, you can ensure that users have access to NLS. If a server running NLS goes down, NLS will still work as long as it is running on another server and users have a connection to that server.

Assign Users to a License Certificate Object

When you have verified that the system and setup requirements for software metering have been met, you need to assign users to a license.

If no object is specifically assigned to a license certificate object, anyone can use it. However, after assigning at least one user to a license certificate object, only the users, groups, or containers who are assigned to that license can use it. This limits access to the licenses.

To assign users to a license certificate object, use NLS Manager or the following steps in the NWAdmin utility:

1. Double-click a product license container.

2. Select a license certificate object.

3. Right-click and select Details to add users.

Create a License Container and Metered Certificate Object

The next step in setting up software metering is to create a license container and metered certificate object. These objects enable ZENworks to track and control access to license objects.

The license container is a special container object in NDS that stores metered certificate objects.

The metered certificate object contains the information you enter. License containers can contain multiple metered certificate objects.

To create a metered certificate object and a license container, use NLS Manager or the following steps in the NWAdmin utility:

1. Highlight the container where you want to create a metered certificate.

2. Select Tools ⇨ Install License ⇨ Create Metered Certificate; a screen similar to the one in Figure 10.4 appears.

3. From that screen, enter information about the application that you want to meter, such as software publisher name, software product name, and version or revision.

4. Click OK.

▶ • ◀

F I G U R E   1 0 . 4 *The Create Metered Certificate window in NWAdmin*

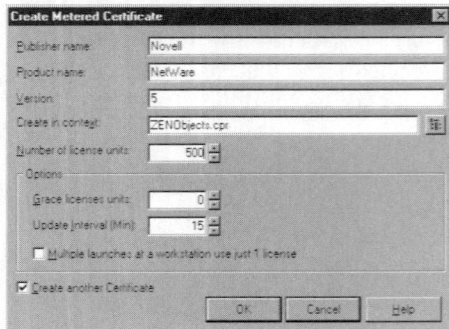

Add Additional Licenses (Metered Certificates)

The last procedure you need to be aware of when setting up software metering is adding additional licenses — for example, if you originally installed a 50-user license of an application and want to extend this to a 75-user license. To extend the license of the application, you need to create another metered certificate object.

The license container is a container class object in NDS and cannot be renamed. The metered certificate is a leaf object of the license container. The metered certificate basically represents the individual license count. To get a total license count, the license container totals up all leaf metered certificates beneath it.

To add additional licenses, add additional metered certificates using NLS Manager, or perform the following steps in the NWAdmin utility:

1. Highlight the container where you want to add a license.

2. Select Tools ⇨ Install License ⇨ Create Metered Certificate.

3. From that screen, enter the same name as the original license container to which you want to add licenses.

If you enter the same software publisher name, software product name, and same version number, a new metered certificate will be created below the license container. This metered certificate will be added to those already located in the license container to form a new license total.

CHAPTER 11

Using ZENworks Check 2000 to Resolve Y2K Issues

Check 2000 is a diagnostic tool that scans workstation hardware, software, and data for year 2000 issues. This enables companies to prepare their networks for the next century by providing assistance in identifying and alerting network administrators to potential year 2000-related issues.

Once the issues are found, administrators can use ZENworks to repair problems by pushing fixes out to all clients on the network. Administrators will also be able to use the ZENworks and Check 2000 combination to maintain network stability by continually checking the status of clients and servers on the network to ensure year 2000 readiness.

The purpose of this chapter is to give you a brief description of the Check 2000 components that are included with ZENworks, and how to get started using them. For more detailed information on each of these components, you should refer the to MANUAL.PDF file that is installed with Check 2000 in the following location:

```
SYS:\PUBLIC\C2K\INSTALL
```

The Check 2000 Client Server product for ZENworks consists of the components described in the following sections. These components can be installed from the ZENworks install in the Server ⇨ Third-Party Apps page.

The Workstation Scanners

The first component of the Check 2000 product is the workstation scanners. The Workstation Scanning agent is supplied for ZENworks in the following three versions:

- ▶ C2KWC16.EXE — A 16-bit version for scanning Windows 3.*x* workstations
- ▶ C2KWC32.EXE — A 32-bit version for scanning Windows 95/98 and NT workstations
- ▶ C2KDOS.EXE — A DOS version of the scanner

> **NOTE**
> You should enable the ZENworks option in the Configuration tool, discussed later in this chapter, before running the workstation scanners.

When the client workstation scanner is loaded, a screen similar to the one in Figure 11.1 is displayed. This screen lets you know that the Check 2000 Windows client will perform the following tasks:

- ► Collect information about your installed PC software programs.

- ► Tell you whether your basic input/output system (BIOS) will roll over from 1999 to 2000.

- ► Tell you whether your BIOS knows that 2000 is a leap year.

- ► Scan your local hard drives for recognizable software programs.

- ► Scan your local hard drives for possible user data files.

- ► Scan your system for selected hardware information.

- ► Test your computer for its capability to handle date rollover into the next century.

FIGURE 11.1 *The main screen in the client workstation scanner*

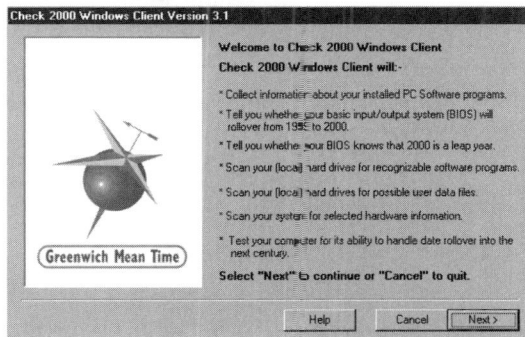

When you select Next, a screen appears and enables you to define the location to which the data file results will be output. If you have enabled the ZENworks option in the Configuration tool, then this information is filled in automatically for you by ZENworks. Otherwise, use the Browse button to select an appropriate location for the output file, as shown in Figure 11.2.

The data file location screen

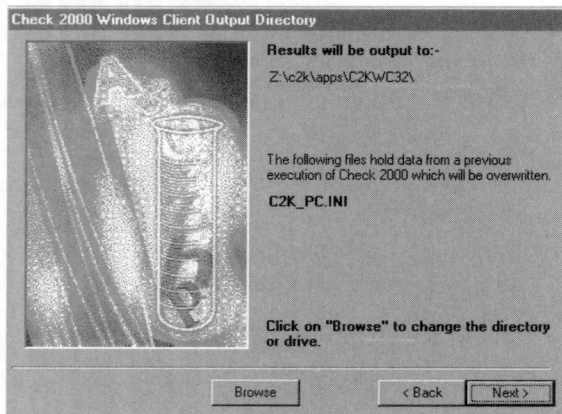

Once you have selected the location to which the output should be saved, click Next. A screen similar to the one in Figure 11.3 is displayed. If you have enabled the ZENworks option in the Configuration tool, then this information is filled in automatically for you by ZENworks. Otherwise, use this screen to input the appropriate information to record.

The recorded information selection

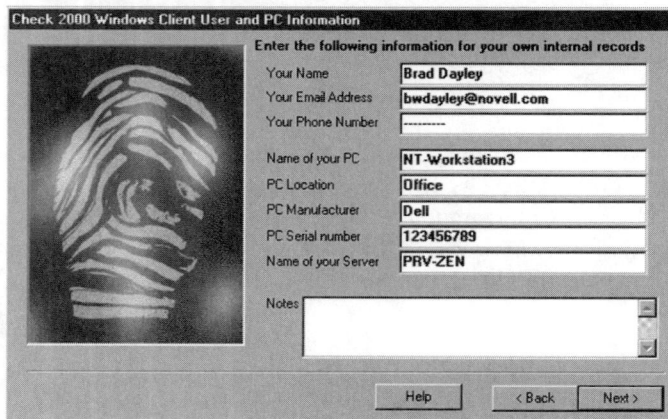

When you click Next, the Check 2000 Workstation client begins collecting data from your workstation. Figure 11.4 displays the status of Check 2000 as it sets and tests the following dates on your workstation:

- ► Set Dates
  - January 1, 1980
  - January 1, 2000
- ► Rollover Dates – The day after
  - September 8, 1999
  - December 31, 1999
  - February 28, 2000
  - December 31, 2000
  - February 28, 2001

FIGURE 11.4 *The dates scanning screen*

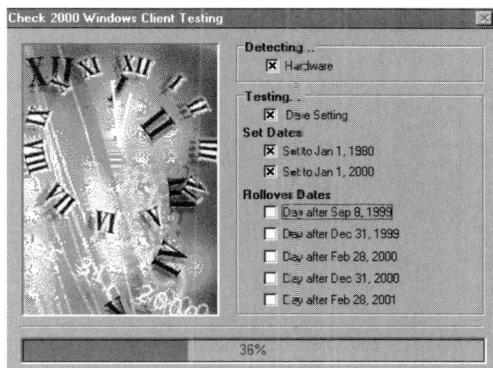

Once the dates have been tested, Check 2000 begins scanning files on your local drives to determine file compliance with the year 2000 for database files, and so on (see Figure 11.5).

▶ · ◀

F I G U R E   11.5   *The files scanning screen*

When Check 2000 has finished analyzing your workstation, a screen similar to the one in Figure 11.6 is displayed. From this window, you can click the Hardware, BIOS, or User Data Files button to view the specific results of the workstation scan that has taken place.

▶ · ◀

F I G U R E   11.6   *The view summary screen*

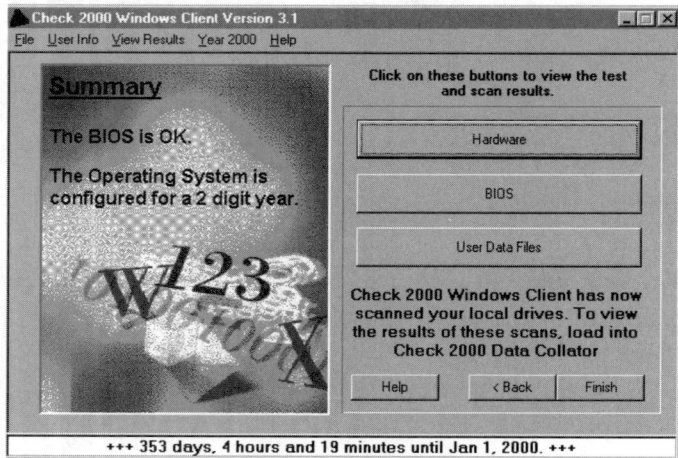

At this point, you can view the results of the hardware analysis, as shown in Figure 11.7. Notice that the Windows Date Setting failed. Clicking the information button produces a screen that gives an explanation of why the failure occurred.

▶ ◀

The hardware results summary window

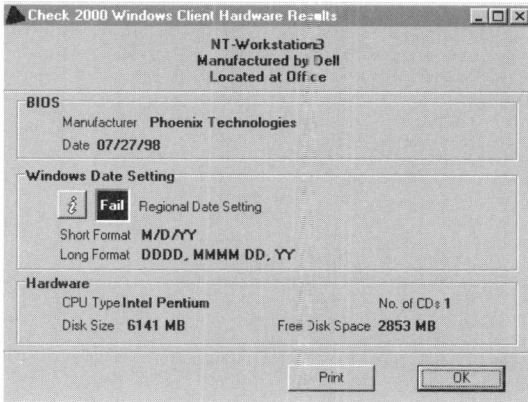

Next, you can view the results of the BIOS, as shown in Figure 11.8. Notice that Check 2000 checked the set dates and rollover dates for the important dates regarding year 2000 issues.

▶ ◀

The BIOS results summary window

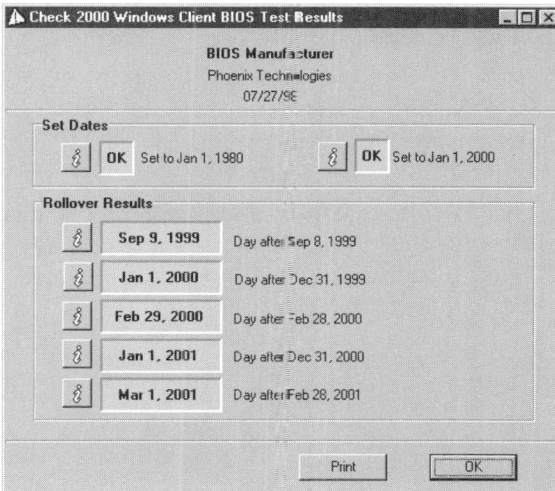

Finally, you can view a list of files detected by Check 2000, which may contain user data as shown in Figure 11.9.

► · ◄

F I G U R E   11.9   *The user files results summary window*

	Path	File Name	Ext	File Size	Time Stamp
1	C:\	BOOTLOG	TXT	27397	1998/10/30 11:04
2	C:\	SUHDLOG	DAT	10430	1998/10/30 10:27
3	C:\	FRUNLOG	TXT	1087	1998/10/30 10:30
4	C:\	SETUPLOG	TXT	104228	1998/10/30 10:39
5	C:\	NETLOG	TXT	6066	1998/10/30 10:39
6	C:\	DETLOG	TXT	72392	1998/10/30 10:32
7	C:\WINDOWS\	LICENSE	TXT	31149	1998/05/11 20:01
8	C:\WINDOWS\	SUPPORT	TXT	7166	1998/05/11 20:01
9	C:\WINDOWS\	JAUTOEXP	DAT	6550	1998/05/11 20:01
10	C:\WINDOWS\	HWINFO	DAT	172064	1998/10/30 10:39
11	C:\WINDOWS\	SYSTEM	DAT	2048032	1999/01/12 14:48
12	C:\WINDOWS\	USER	DAT	204832	1999/01/06 10:54
13	C:\WINDOWS\	CONFIG	TXT	17468	1998/05/11 20:01
14	C:\WINDOWS\	DISPLAY	TXT	20045	1998/05/11 20:01
15	C:\WINDOWS\	FAQ	TXT	12285	1998/05/11 20:01
16	C:\WINDOWS\	GENERAL	TXT	39907	1998/05/11 20:01

Check 2000 Windows Client User Data — Files that may contain user data

Double click for more details   OK

Other Data Collection Tools

In addition to the Check 2000 workstation component, the following data collection tools are provided with Check 2000 to collect, view, and manage information regarding year 2000 issues:

▸ C2KSS.EXE — The Server Scanner enables you to scan the NetWare server to collect information about user data files, much as the Check 2000 workstation component checks local drives.

▸ C2KDS.EXE — The Data Scanner searches PC databases, spreadsheets, and other file types, identifying any data that seems to contain dates that are not year 2000 ready. The Data Scanner enables the user to determine on what criteria to base year 2000 readiness.

The Data Collator

Once information has been collected using the client, server, or data scanner, it can be compiled into more useful information by the data collator. This data collator engine automatically collects, summarizes, and reports the individual workstation result files that are produced when the scanners are run. That summary can be a very useful collection to describe the entire organization.

The best way to familiarize you with the data collator is to describe the following important options available from the menu bar, as shown in Figure 11.10.

FIGURE 11.10 *The main screen in the data collator provided with ZENworks*

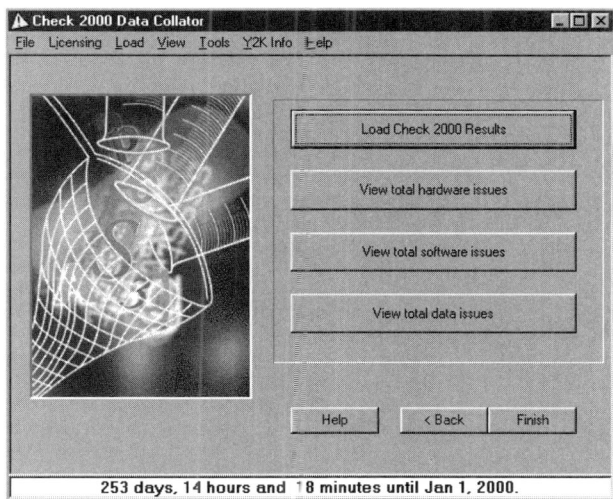

File ⇨ Export Data

The export data option under the File menu allows the export of relevant data to comma-delimited ASCII format for external use by other programs. The following items are available for export and use by other programs:

► BIOS information per PC

► Executable exceptions per PC

► All executable files per PC

▶ PC information and programs per PC

▶ Program advice

▶ Program date dependencies

▶ User data files per PC

Load Menu

The Load menu lists commands that facilitate the capability to import client output result files, from either a single machine or multiple machines, in one operation.

The following load menu options are available:

▶ Single Load

▶ Multiple Load

View Menu

The View menu lists commands that facilitate the viewing of information and results gathered from client PCs by Check 2000 Data Collator. This information is similar in nature to that reported in the Check 2000 clients. Please refer to the section of the guide entitled "Understanding the Check 2000 Client Results" for more information. The difference is that these reports represent summated and collated data sets instead of information relevant to single machines.

The following options are available under the view menu:

▶ BIOS

▶ PC

▶ Programs

▶ Workstation (changes to User if ZENworks is not enabled)

Tools Menu Description

The Tools menu provides you with access to some advanced tools and options to help you organize and control the information being collated into a more useful personalized data set.

The following options are available from the tools menu:

▶ Define User Programs — Allows you to define in-house and custom-made programs.

▶ Change Multiload Directory Levels (currently 4) — This option enables you to alter the directory depth to which Data Collator will scan for client output result files. This depth is calculated from the designated starting directory level.

▶ Reset System Totals — Useful after abnormal machine failures, such as disk full errors or power failures.

▶ Rebuild Indexes — Useful after abnormal machine failures, such as disk full errors or power failures.

▶ Empty Database — Allows the Check 2000 database to be completely cleaned out and the system refreshed to a pre-import status.

▶ Options — Enables you to specify the following advanced options in the data collator:

- Allocate all new license numbers — If this is selected, licensing information will be updated in the client data sets during the next import/load procedure.
- ZEN enabled
- Do not collect executable file information (default)
- Collect information only for executable files not in knowledgebase
- Collect information for all executable files
- Do not collect user data files (default)
- Collect user data files

Y2K Info Menu

The Y2K info menu provides some detailed background information on the year 2000 problem. Use this screen to familiarize yourself with why and how the year 2000 affects computer systems.

This information is divided into the following two main sections:

▶ Implications of the year 2000 for PC users — Describes what effects Y2K issues will have on users.

▶ A definition of year 2000 conformity — Describes what must be done to ready your network software and computers for the year 2000.

This page also offers a detailed explanation of the following typical year 2000 PC problems:

- Dates in the next century
- Ignoring century
- Limited date ranges
- Days of the week
- Losing date information
- Computation errors
- Date controlled behavior
- Abnormal program termination

The Configuration Tool

The final Check 2000 component is the Configuration tool (SCRIPTOR.EXE). The Configuration tool is used to control the behavior of the following scanning agent options when the agents are deployed to a workstation.

Screen Options

The Screen Options menu allows you to enable and disable the following screens displayed when the scanners are run, as shown in Figure 11.11:

- Select Drives (Server Scanner only)
- Allow startup to be cancelled
- Watch BIOS testing progress
- Watch program scanning progress
- Allow scanning to be cancelled
- View results
- Show warning messages

FIGURE 11.11 *The Screen Options tab window*

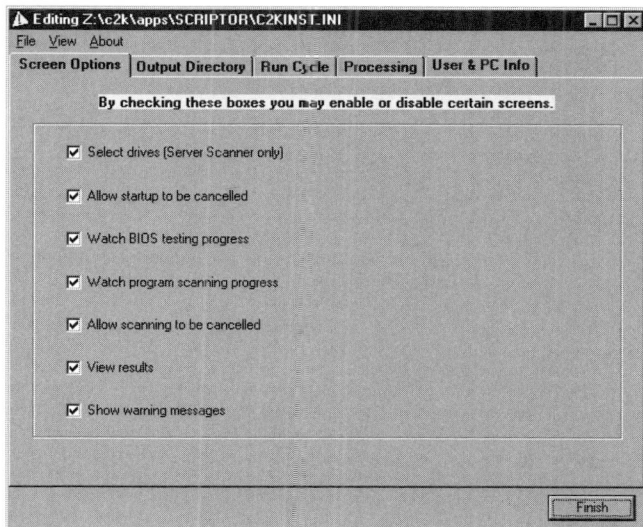

Output Directory

The Output Directory screen in the Configuration tool enables you to determine where the Check 2000 workstation client places the results. The following options are available, as shown in Figure 11.12:

- ▶ Use installation directory
- ▶ Select directory (this need not be an existing directory)
- ▶ Generate automatically as a sub-directory of a specified root directory
- ▶ User selects directory (this is the default)
- ▶ Overwrite any existing results
- ▶ Create directory at run time

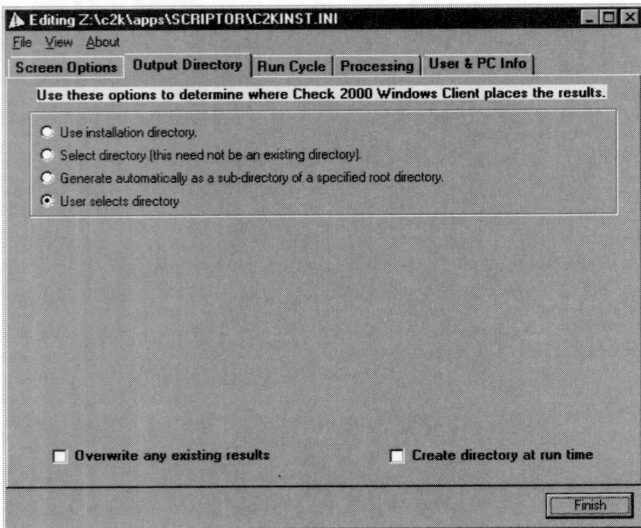

Run Cycle

The Run Cycle screen in the Configuration tool enables you set the Check 2000 workstation client to run at any time, or just in a specified period. The following options are available, as shown in Figure 11.13:

- ▶ Always (this is the default)
- ▶ Monthly
- ▶ Quarterly
- ▶ Half-Yearly
- ▶ As Specified

FIGURE 11.13 *The Run Cycle tab window*

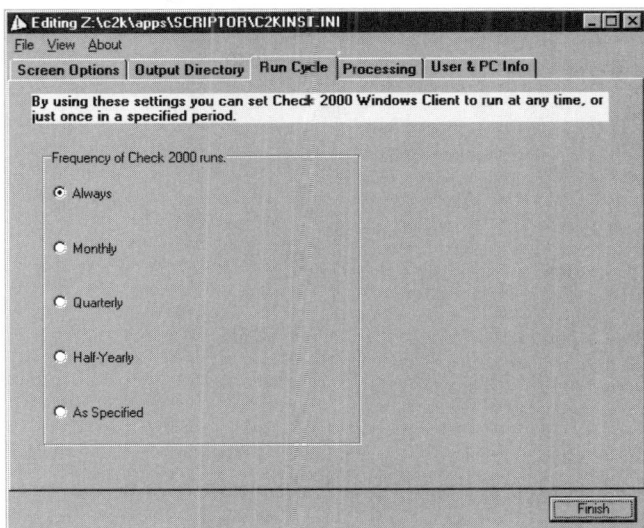

Processing

The Processing tab in the Configuration tool allows you enable or disable certain processes. The following options are available, as shown in Figure 11.14:

- ▸ Processes:
  - • Clear Previously Logged Messages
  - • Skip BIOS Tests
  - • Skip Hardware Detection
  - • Skip Application Scan
- ▸ BIOS Fix:
  - • Automate in Failed Machines
  - • Allow Manual BIOS Fix
- ▸ Automatic Start — Wait for User to Start

F I G U R E   1 1 . 1 4   *The Processing tab window*

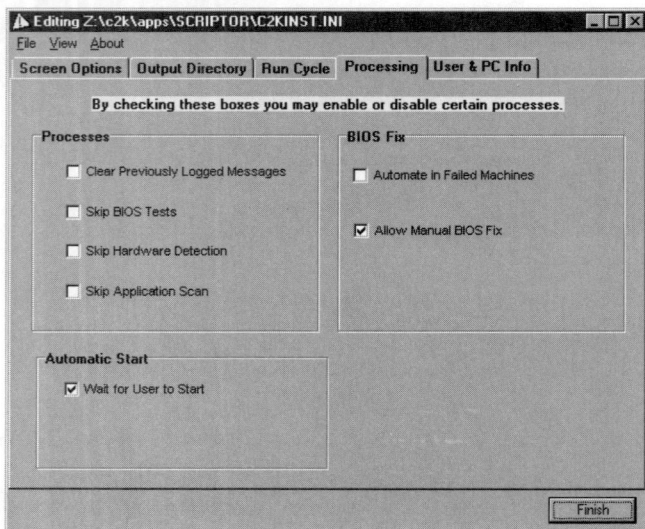

User & PC Info

The User & PC Info screen in the Configuration tool enables you to determine the source of the user and PC information. The following options are available, as shown in Figure 11.15:

- ► Enable ZENworks
- ► Use Registry Settings
- ► Use DOS Environment Variables
- ► Enter Information Manually

F I G U R E   1 1 . 1 5 The User & PC Info tab window

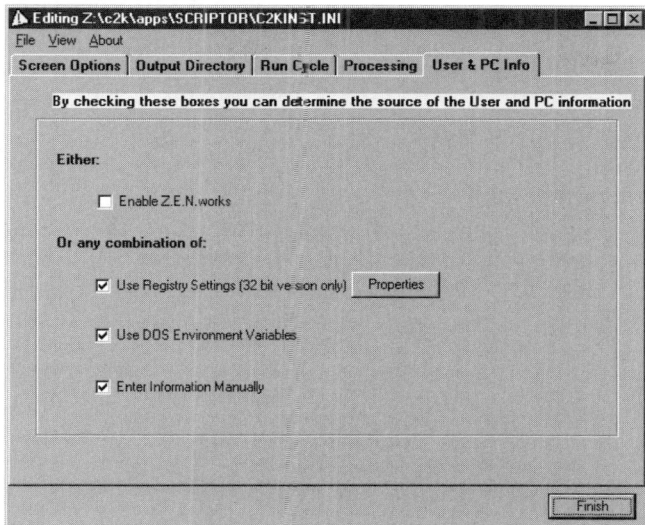

Enable ZENworks

The Enable ZENworks option tells the workstation scanners to use the automation available through ZENworks to collect data about the user and PC. The Enable ZENworks option is highly recommended, because the automation will save a lot of time and make the utilities much easier to use.

This option is exclusive; selecting this option will disable the remaining three and set the output directory selection to automatic mode. If this option is selected, then the Check 2000 client will use Novell registry settings to load the user and PC information fields and generate an output directory path.

Use Registry Settings

The Use Registry Settings option tells the Check 2000 client to load user and PC information from the Windows registry. Fields populated from the registry cannot be overwritten by subsequent input. Click Properties to specify these keys. Settings can be made for any or all of the user and PC information fields.

Use DOS Environment Variables

If the Use DOS Environment Variables option is checked, then the Check 2000 client will load user and PC information stored in designated DOS environment variables. These values may or may not be overwritten by manual input, depending on whether they have been designated as read-only; Otherwise, these values will be treated merely as default values. Fields already populated by the registry will be ignored.

Enter Information Manually

If the Enter Information Manually option is selected, the Check 2000 client will prompt the user to enter information. Fields that may have been loaded from the registry or read-only DOS environment variables will not be editable by the end user.

CHAPTER 12

Advanced Features of ZENworks

Many new features are candidates to include in future releases of ZENworks. This chapter does not discuss all of the new features, but instead focuses on just a few of the major new features for the product.

ConsoleOne

As ZENworks evolves, the administration for the objects and features will move from NWAdmin to Novell's new ConsoleOne administrator tool. Much of the interface is similar to the interfaces you have seen in NWAdmin32. This new console is written in Java and provides a unified console for all the future Novell tools.

ConsoleOne is a workstation utility designed to be executed on the administrator's workstation, much like NWAdmin runs on the workstation. Because ConsoleOne is written in Java, this allows it to move freely to other platforms that support a Java Virtual Machine. In NetWare 5, a version of ConsoleOne that was shipped with the server can be run on the console and on workstations; future versions of ConsoleOne will be more usable and much faster.

Tiered Distribution

One of the most exciting future features of ZENworks is the Multi-Tiered Distribution subsystem. This will enable you to distribute all your application files to all the application servers throughout your network. It provides a multi-tiered distribution mechanism that gives good performance in a WAN environment, because you only have to transmit the data once over the WAN to get it to all the servers across the connection. The application is written in Java and uses CORBA and TCP/IP to increase the capability to use the application on any system. With this mechanism, you can distribute to both NetWare and NT servers.

In the ZENworks Multi-Tiered Distribution architecture, you have channel objects as well as distributor, receiver, and proxy servers, each of which is administered via a corresponding object in the Novell Directory Services tree. The following is a brief description of each of the objects and systems involved in the ZENworks multi-tiered distribution:

- Software Package — This is a bundle of software files that represent the program you want to distribute through the network. This package may include files, registry settings, and Novell Directory Services objects (such as application objects) that are used in conjunction with the software package.

▶ Channel — This Novell Directory Services object represents a repository of software packages that others can receive.

▶ Distributor — This represents the software on a server that is responsible for retrieving packages from a channel and sending them to the receivers designated to receive the packages. A distributor object enables you to configure the system from Novell Directory Services. The distributor server is a collection of Java programs that perform the work and must run on the server.

▶ Receiver — This represents the software on the target server. There is a corresponding object in the tree to represent this system. The receiver server is a collection of Java programs that communicates with distributor servers to receive software packages. The receiver is responsible for unbundling the software package and putting it in the appropriate place on the target server, and for creating any required Novell Directory Services objects.

▶ Proxy — This represents a receiver/distributor that receives packages from a distributor and transmits packages to other distributors. This provides the multi-tiered distribution nature of the ZENworks application distribution feature. By placing a proxy on the far side of a WAN and hooking it to distributors on the remote location, the package will only be transmitted once across the WAN, and then the proxy will retransmit the package to all distributors on the far side.

Distributors

Before you can distribute any bundles of software, you must first determine your distributors in the network. These servers must have a distributor object in the tree, and must have the distributor server executing on the system. Once you have the distributors in the system, you need to create some receivers.

Receivers

A receiver can be any server in the network that wants to hold the final packages. Distributors and receivers can reside on the same server. You must have a corresponding receiver object in the tree to represent each receiver in the system. The receiver basically represents the target machine, and you would want one on each application server in your network. Once you have your distributors and receivers set up in the system and running, all you need is some channels to complete the system.

Channels

Channels represent a logical grouping of packages. A subscriber may subscribe to many channels, so they do not necessarily represent groups of subscribers. You can create a channel object through the ConsoleOne utility. Once a channel is created, you can associate the distributors and receivers to the set of channels you want them to monitor. When you have accomplished this, any package that is dropped into the channel will automatically be distributed via the associated distributors to the associated receivers.

Software Packages

The creation of software packages is simplified with a wizard executing in ConsoleOne. As with application object creation, this enables you to specify the files, registries, and rights associated with the application. This package will be bundled together in a compressed file and distributed through the network when placed in a channel.

Proxy

A proxy server is not necessary in order to perform a software distribution. It is necessary, however, if you require the multi-tiered features of ZENworks distribution. The proxy acts as a receiver to a channel, and as a distributor to other receivers and distributors. This allows it to receive packages from a distributor in one part of the system and then transmit it to other servers in the system. A proxy on the far side of a WAN will allow the system to transmit the package once to the proxy, and then the proxy will send it to all receivers and other distributors on the far side of the network.

CHAPTER 13

Troubleshooting ZENworks.

ZENworks is an extremely powerful tool that will save network administrators much precious time. However, because of the complexity of network environments, problems can occur that prevent ZENworks from doing its job. This chapter covers how to troubleshoot and diagnose problems in the following areas:

- Troubleshooting desktop management
- Troubleshooting distributed applications
- Troubleshooting policy packages
- Troubleshooting NetWare errors

Troubleshooting Desktop Management

The first area of troubleshooting we will cover is desktop management. Desktop management is difficult to troubleshoot because several network components are involved, such as the server, clients, NDS, and LAN.

The following sections discuss the most common areas to review when you are troubleshooting desktop management issues.

Reduce LAN Traffic

When troubleshooting desktop management issues, you may find that LAN traffic is unacceptable after you create and associate policy packages with objects; if that's the case, you may need to reduce LAN traffic. One effective way to reduce LAN traffic is by limiting how the system searches the tree for associations between the policy packages and objects we discussed in earlier chapters. Limiting the searches should reduce LAN traffic.

To reduce LAN traffic by limiting how the system searches the tree for associations between policy packages and objects, follow these steps:

1. Create a Container policy package and choose Define Additional Properties ➪ Create.

2. Enable the Search Policy.

3. Highlight the Search Policy and choose Details ➪ Search Level.

4. Set the Search For Policies Up To field to Partition, and then click OK. This limits how many directory levels are searched for associations between policy packages and objects.

5. Choose the Associations page, and associate this Container policy package to the container where you want to make the Search Policy

effective. Remember that the Search Policy affects all containers below the associated container, because the workstation manager will be looking for the container package.

Troubleshoot Help Requester

When troubleshooting desktop management issues, you may find that users are unable to run the Help Requester from a workstation; in this case, you may need to troubleshoot the following:

▶ From the User object, view the effective policies for the user and ensure you have an effective Help Desk policy. If so, highlight the policy, choose Details, and then check the settings.

▶ Ensure that you have associated a platform-specific User policy package containing a Help Desk Policy with that User object, a Group that the User object is a member of, or the container where the User object resides.

▶ Ensure that you have enabled a Help Desk policy and that the Allow Users to Send Trouble Tickets field is checked.

Troubleshoot Import

When troubleshooting desktop management issues, you may find that an attempt to import a workstation was unsuccessful; in this case, you may need to troubleshoot the import by using the following suggestions:

1. Verify that workstations were properly set up for ZENworks.

2. If the attempt to import workstations was made by choosing Tools ➪ Import Workstation, and either the Import Workstations dialog box does not appear or a Windows GPF occurred, you probably have an outdated version of comctl32.dll. A newer version of comctl32.dll ships with the OSR2 release of Windows 95, as well as with recent versions of Microsoft's Internet Explorer.

3. From the User object, view the effective policies for the user and ensure you have an effective workstation import policy. If so, highlight the policy, choose Details, and then check the settings on both the Workstation Location and Workstation Naming pages.

4. Verify that the workstation has an effective workstation import policy.

5. Verify that a container has been selected.

6. View the Error Log from the Import Results dialog box that appears when you choose Tools ➪ Import, and then continue troubleshooting from there.

7. Unregister the workstation by running UNREG32.EXE from SYS:\PUBLIC, and then reregister the workstation.

> **A workstation does not synchronize with NDS until after it has been imported and the Workstation Registration program is run again.**
>
> **NOTE**

Troubleshoot Workstation Objects

When troubleshooting desktop management issues, you may find that the Workstation object does not display in the tree after a registered workstation was imported; in this case, you should check the following:

1. From the User object, view the effective policies for the user and ensure you have an effective workstation import policy. If so, highlight the policy, choose Details, and then check the settings on both the Workstation Location and Workstation Naming pages.

2. Check the container where the User object resides to see if the Workstation object was created there.

3. Check the Workstation Registration page to see if the Workstation appears in the list.

Troubleshooting Distributed Applications

The next area of troubleshooting ZENworks we will cover is distributed applications. If users encounter problems using distributed applications, once you have created application objects and set up application distribution for them you can use the following procedures to help diagnose and debug the issues.

Troubleshoot Application Launcher and Explorer

The first place to start when troubleshooting distributed applications is the Application Launcher and Explorer. You can obtain information about Application Launcher and Application Explorer to help you troubleshoot problems your users may encounter.

Review Information About File Locations and Versions

When troubleshooting Application Launcher and Explorer, the best place to begin is to obtain information about file location and versions. This will help you determine if the correct files are being installed from the correct places.

To obtain information about file location and versions from the Application Launcher or Explorer, follow these steps:

1. From Application Launcher or the Application Explorer window, select Help ⇨ About ⇨ More.

2. Read the information about filenames, paths, and versions in use by Application Launcher. There may be later versions available from Novell's support Web site.

Review Information About State of
Currently Running Applications

The next thing to do when troubleshooting the Application Launcher is to get information about the state of currently running applications. This will help you determine if there are any resource conflicts or incompatibilities between different applications.

To get information about the state of currently running applications, follow these steps:

1. Press and hold the Shift key when opening the About box (Help ⇨ About). The Applications Running text box gives the number of currently running Application Launcher-delivered applications running for the current user. The Resources In Use text box reports the number of resources (a server connection, a drive letter, or a printer port) in use.

2. Click Applications to display debug information about the applications running. Highlight an application and click Select to see the resources for that application.

3. Click Resources to display all resource information for all applications currently running.

4. Click Environment to read information about any environment variables in use for Application Launcher-delivered applications.

Review NDS Tree Specific Information

Once you have information about files and running applications, you should look at NDS tree specific Information. For example, you may need to know the number of levels up the NDS tree the Application Launcher looks for applications.

To get the NDS tree specific information about the Application Launcher or Explorer, follow these steps:

1. From Application Launcher or the Application Explorer window, choose Help ⇨ About ⇨ More.

2. While holding down Ctrl+Alt, double-click an Application object in the Login Information list.

3. Use the information in Table 13.1.

T A B L E 1 3 . 1	*NDS-specific information about application launcher*
TEXT BOX	**ANSWERS THIS QUESTION**
Container Levels	What is the number of levels up the NDS tree that the Application Launcher looks for applications? This number is specified on the Launcher Configuration property page of the User or Container object to which the Application object is associated.
Supports Application Objects	Are Application objects supported in this tree? Does this tree have the necessary schema extensions to support Application objects?
Schema Supported	What are the version numbers of supported schemas?
Rights to Group Membership	What rights does the user have to his or her group membership attribute on his or her User object?
Monitored Connection	What is the Distinguished Name (DN) of the server that is the monitored connection? This is important to know if you have set up an application site list so that users access applications from the server that is geographically closest to them.
Save Folders	Will personal folders be saved at exit if they have been changed?
NRD Support	Is NetWare Registry Database (NRD) supported? What is the path to the NRD.DLL? If "No," NRD.DLL not found (NRDDLL16.DLL, NRDDLL95.DLL, NRDDLLNT.DLL). If "Yes, No," NRD.DLL found but tree does not have the NRD extensions or user does not have rights to the NRD attributes on their user object. If "Yes, Yes," NRD.DLL found and ready to go.

TEXT BOX	ANSWERS THIS QUESTION
E-mail Attribute	What attribute on User object is used for e-mail address in Contacts page?
Login DLL version	What is the version and path to login DLL (used for script processing)?

Enable Error Logging File

Once you have reviewed information about the files, applications, and the NDS tree, you should enable error logging. This will help you troubleshoot issues because you specify the path to a file where any errors are logged if the application fails to install or launch.

> **NOTE**
>
> No other status is tracked here except for errors. Before users can run this Application object, they must be given rights to write to this file for this option to work correctly.

View and Edit User's or Container's Application Launcher Configurations

Once you have looked at Application Launcher and Explorer, you should view and edit user or container application launcher configurations. This will help you troubleshoot issues that are caused by problems with the setup of distributed applications in the user and/or container objects. To review the Application Launcher configuration for user or container objects, use the following procedures.

Use the Launcher Configuration Property Page

The first step in reviewing the Application Launcher configuration for user or container objects is to use the Application Launcher Configuration property page in NWAdmin to do the following:

1. View the effective Application Launcher and Application Explorer configurations for a User, Organizational Unit, Organization, or Country object.

2. View the Application Launcher configuration inheritance tree (where the current object gets configurations from objects higher in the tree).

3. Set up custom Application Launcher configurations for the currently selected container object.

Review User's or Container's Effective Application Launcher Configurations

Once you have reviewed the preceding information from the main Application Launcher page in NWAdmin, you should view the effective Application Launcher configurations. Effective settings include custom configurations applied to the current object as well as configurations inherited from parent container(s). You can control how a container object inherits Application Launcher configurations by selecting the Use as Top of Inheritance Tree option.

To view the custom Application Launcher configurations from within NWAdmin, follow these steps:

1. Right-click a User, Organizational Unit, Organization, or Country object and click Details.

2. Click the Launcher Configuration button.

3. Choose View Object's Effective Settings from the Mode drop-down list.

Review Application Launcher Configuration Inheritance Tree

Once you have reviewed the custom Application Launcher configurations, you should review the Application Launcher configuration inheritance tree for the user or container object by following these steps:

1. Right-click a User, Organizational Unit, Organization, or Country object and click Details.

2. Click the Launcher Configuration button.

3. Choose View Configuration Inheritance Tree from the Mode drop-down list.

Review and Edit User's or Container's Custom Application Launcher Configurations

Once you have reviewed the Application Launcher configuration inheritance tree, you should review the container's custom Application Launcher configurations for the container object by following these steps:

1. Right-click a User, Organizational Unit, Organization, or Country object and click Details.

2. Click the Launcher Configuration button.

3. Choose View/Edit Object's Custom Configuration from the Mode drop-down list. If no settings appear in the list, no custom settings have been defined for this User or Container object.

4. Click the Edit button to customize the settings for this object.

Use Object as Top of Inheritance Tree

Another procedure that may help in troubleshooting application distribution at a container level is to set the object as the "top" of the inheritance tree.

The Application Launcher searches the NDS tree for configuration settings, starting at the lowest possible leaf object and navigating upward in the inheritance tree. It continues navigating this tree until it reaches a container object that has been designated as the "top" of the inheritance tree.

If the Application Launcher finds custom configurations in any of the objects while it is navigating the tree, they are the applied through inheritance. If it doesn't find any custom configurations, then the configuration is considered unset and the default configuration is applied. This allows control of when and where custom configurations are applied instead of the defaults.

To designate a User or container object as the "top" of the inheritance tree, select the Use Object as Top of Inheritance Tree option on the Launcher Configuration property page of that User or Container object.

Backward Compatibility

Newer versions of Application Launcher add new Launcher configuration settings above those in older versions. It's possible that at any given time while you are rolling out the new Application Launcher or Application Explorer, you'll decide you would like to preserve the old Launcher configuration settings. Make sure this option is enabled in the Application Launcher screen in NWAdmin if you wish to have backward compatibility.

Review User Object's Inheritance Applications

The next step in troubleshooting distributed application launcher problems is to look at the applications inherited by user objects. You may find that the user inherits two applications that are incompatible or that combined take up too much of the client's resources, for example.

Use the Show Inherited Applications option on the Tools ⇨ Application Launcher Tools menu to see the Application objects that have been associated with the User object, including all applications either associated with or inherited by the User object. The applications are listed by mode of delivery, such as Force Run, App Launcher, Desktop, Start Menu, and System Tray. These categories come from the Applications property page, which is available for User, Group, Organization, and Organizational Unit objects.

Use the following steps to list the applications that the user has rights to use:

1. Highlight a User object.

2. Choose Tools ⇨ Application Launcher Tools ⇨ Show Inherited Applications.

3. Expand the user object to view all associated applications.

Set Timed Refresh Frequency

A useful setting when troubleshooting distributed applications is the Set refresh frequency option, which lets you specify the refresh frequency in seconds. For example, if you set the refresh to 300 seconds, Application Launcher or Application Explorer updates applications from the network automatically every five minutes and may even run some applications, depending on how you have set them up.

Although a short timed refresh interval is very useful in situations where you want changes to refresh quickly, a short timed refresh interval will usually cause higher network traffic.

TIP
If you are having problems with network traffic when distributing applications, you should always increase the timed refresh frequency for Application Launcher and Explorer. You may need to play with the frequency value to match your specific environment.

Change Workstation Files in Use

Another useful step in troubleshooting distributed applications is to make sure the workstation was properly rebooted with the appropriate files. Occasionally, the workstation was not rebooted or a file was in use when the application was distributed, thus preventing it from being distributed properly.

When Application Launcher distributes applications, it may change workstation configuration files (for example, CONFIG.SYS, AUTOEXEC.BAT, or WIN.INI) depending on the settings in the Application object. The changes to these files do not take effect until after the workstation is rebooted. Application Launcher detects whether such changes are made, and prompts the user with a message stating that the workstation must be rebooted before the changes can take place.

Similarly, when application files are copied, the files they are replacing may be in use, and cannot be deleted or replaced. Application Launcher usually handles this situation. Generally, the new files are copied to a temporary area and then copied to their correct locations when Windows is restarted. However, if there is a problem with the temporary area or the workstation was not rebooted, then the correct files will not be properly installed.

Clean Up Network Resources

The next step in troubleshooting distributed applications in ZENworks is to make sure that network resources are being properly cleaned up.

The process of "cleaning up" means that the license for a particular network connection is removed. This prevents users from using a network connection when they don't need it. When the Clean up network resources option is selected, drive mappings and printer ports associated with Application Launcher-delivered applications are removed.

NOTE

If the resource (a connection, map, or capture) is already in use when Application Launcher or Application Explorer is started, Application Launcher or Application Explorer uses it and does not clean it up. Otherwise, the resource is created and cleaned up when all other Application Launcher or Application Explorer applications are finished using it. The connection to the server containing the resource is removed as well. If the applications that Application Launcher or Application Explorer launched are still running when either Application Launcher or Application Explorer is terminated, the allocated resources remain intact.

When an application is launched, Application Launcher or Application Explorer monitors the executable of the application. When the executable terminates, the process of cleaning up network resources begins. It's possible, however, that the executable filename is actually a "wrapper" that sets up environments, runs other executables, and then terminates. If Application Launcher or Application Explorer monitors the wrapper executable, it may prematurely start cleaning up network resources before the application has terminated.

To prevent Application Launcher and Explorer from prematurely cleaning up application resources, consult your application documentation about whether the application uses a wrapper executable. If it does, find out the name of the module that remains running. Type this name, without the extension, in the text box provided.

Write Application Administrator Notes

One of the most useful tasks you can do as a network administrator is to keep records for later use. When troubleshooting issues with distributed applications, you should use the Administrator Notes property page to create a section of notes that only you, as the administrator, can view and edit.

For example, you may want to remind yourself about some special settings for a particular application. This is true especially if your system is managed by several administrators. You could use the Administrator Notes property page to provide a history of application upgrades and file changes so that work is not duplicated.

To write administrator notes for an Application object, follow these steps:

1. Right-click the Application object and click Details.

2. Click the Administrator Notes button.

3. In the space provided, type the note, and then click OK.

Review Roll-Back Application Distribution

When troubleshooting application distribution, you should be aware that if ZENworks encounters an error during distribution, it rolls back or reverses all the changes made before the error, and resets the workstation to the state it was in before the distribution began.

When you "roll out" or distribute a complex application using Application Launcher, changes are made to the targeted workstation. These changes may include text files (such as CONFIG.SYS and AUTOEXEC.BAT), Windows registry entries, and .INI files. In addition, application files can be copied or deleted at the target workstation.

The method Application Launcher uses to roll back changes is simple. First, it creates temporary files and directories to store files and other rollback information on the workstation. If the distribution is successful, those files and directories are deleted. If the distribution encounters an error, Application Launcher uses the rollback information to restore the workstation to its original state, and then the rollback information is deleted.

Problems with rolling back can occur if, for example, a file is in use, or the application is set to overwrite an existing application when the rollback occurs. Application Launcher will be unable to roll back a file that is in use or does not exist.

Use Search and Replace Entire Application Object

A very useful tool in troubleshooting application objects is the Search and replace entire application object option in NWAdmin. You can use the Search and Replace dialog box either to search, or search and replace, the entire Application object for text strings.

For example, if a directory name was changed and the Application object no longer functioned, you could use this feature to correct the directory name every place it occurred in the application object.

To search and replace text strings in all property pages of an Application object, use the following steps:

1. Highlight the Application object that you want to search.

2. Choose Tools ⇨ Application Launcher Tools ⇨ Search and Replace.

3. Choose Options, and then choose the type of Application object settings you want to search.

4. Choose Match Case to make the search case sensitive.

5. Type the text you want to search for in the Search For text box, and then click Find Next.

6. If you want to replace that text with other text, type the new text in the Replace With text box and then click Find Next, then Replace or Replace All.

Use Search Specific Application Object Property Page

Another useful tool in troubleshooting application objects is the Search specific application object property page in NWAdmin. You can use the Find dialog box to search the current Registry Settings, .INI Settings, or Application Files property pages.

For example, if a specific registry setting was causing the application distribution to experience problems, then you could use this feature to find the registry setting in the application object.

To find specific application object settings, follow these steps:

1. Right-click the Application object and click Details.

2. Click the Registry Settings, .INI Settings, or Application Files property page.

3. Choose the Find option (in some cases this may appear on the File button).

4. Type the text that you want to find, and then click Find.

Review Application Termination

Another thing to review when troubleshooting application distribution is to make sure that the application was terminated properly. You can use the Termination property page in NWAdmin to view and modify how Application Launcher handles the termination of an application. If termination is improperly set up, users may experience problems when the application runs.

Use the following steps to view and modify termination of the application:

1. Right-click the Application object and click Details.

2. Click the Termination button.

3. Select and modify the appropriate termination behaviors (described in the following sections) from the drop-down list.

Send Message to Close Application

If users should close the application, use the Send message to close application option. For example, if you set an interval of 20 minutes, Application Launcher will send a message (if one is active) to the user every 20 minutes until the application is closed.

Send Message to Close Then Prompt to Save Data

Use the Send message to close then prompt to save data option if the application must be terminated; however, be aware that user data loss may occur. This option prompts users, for a specified period of time, to close the application on their own (this action is optional). When that period of time expires, the Application Launcher will attempt to close the application. If users have not saved data, they will be prompted to save it.

Send Message to Close, Prompt to Save, Then Force Close

Use the Send message to close, prompt to save, then force close option when the application must be terminated regardless of user data loss. This option prompts users, for a specified period of time, to close the application on their own. When that period of time expires, you can close the application after prompting users, at specified intervals, to save their work. If users have still not closed within a specified period of time, the application is forced to close.

Send Message to Close Then Force Close With Explanation

Use the Send message to close then force close with explanation option when the application must absolutely be terminated and user data loss is not a concern. This option prompts users, for a specified period of time, to close the application on their own. When that period of time expires, the application is forced to close.

Enable Dial-Up Detection

When troubleshooting distributed applications for users who use dial-up connections, make sure that dial-up detection is enabled. Application Launcher and Application Explorer automatically detect a dial-up networking session. If such a connection is detected, the user is given the option to exit Application Launcher or continue to have Application Launcher read information from NDS.

For example, suppose a network administrator puts a command in a user's login script to run NAL.EXE. The user goes home, and with a 56.6 Kbps speed modem, dials and connects to the company's network. Application Launcher recognizes the dial-up connection. Instead of waiting a long time for Application Launcher to read the NDS tree for Application object information, the user can close Application Launcher and receive any Application Launcher-delivered applications.

Troubleshooting Policy Packages

Policy packages are another area you should be familiar with when troubleshooting. There is no formal method of troubleshooting the workstation policy package; however, the following are some steps you can take to identify problems and resolutions to issues.

Review NDS Workstation Object

In the case of a workstation policy package, make sure a valid NDS Workstation Object has been created and is linked to workstations that will use the policy package. This can be checked by viewing the values shown in Table 13.2 in the workstation's registry.

TABLE 13.2	Identification key in workstation's registry
KEY	**VALUES**
HKEY_LOCAL_MACHINE\ SOFTWARE\Novell\ Registration Workstation Manager\Identification	Registered In : REG_SZ : .OU=ZEN.OU=Site.O=Company Object : REG_SZ : UserName, IPX_Network_Address, IP_Network_Address, Station_Name, etc... Workstation Object : REG_SZ : CN=StationName123456789012.OU=ZE N.OU=Site.O=Company

You are specifically looking for the Workstation Object value. It identifies which NDS Workstation Object the workstation is using when it is logged into. All Workstation Policy Packages will need to be associated with this NDS Workstation Object or to a Workstation Group that has this NDS Workstation Object as one of its members.

If a workstation policy package is not associated to the NDS Workstation Object listed in the Workstation Object registry value or a group it belongs to, then no workstation policy packages will be downloaded and applied.

Review Policy Package Type

Make sure the appropriate type of policy package has been created. For example, if the workstation is running Windows NT 4.0, make sure you have created a WINNT workstation policy package.

Review Workstation Object Associations

In the case of a workstation policy package, make sure that NDS Workstation Objects have an association to the policy package. This can be verified by looking at the details of the policy package within NWAdmin by clicking the Associations tab.

Make sure that every workstation that will use the NDS Workstation Object is listed there, is a member of a Workstation Group listed, or exists in a container listed.

> **TIP** Be sure to look for potential problems with a Container policy package if you are only using the container to associate the NDS Workstation Object. If you are not sure, it is a good idea to associate the NDS Workstation Object directly (as a troubleshooting step, not as an implementation design).

Enable Policies

Make sure that at least one policy is enabled to download. If no policies are enabled, the user will not be able to detect any change to the user/workstation environment and may question whether it is working properly.

Install Workstation Manager

Make sure that when the client for Windows 95/98 was installed, the workstation manager component was installed also. You can verify whether it has been installed by going into the Control Panel ⇨ Network Configuration tab and looking for the service called Novell Workstation Manager.

Review Trusted Trees

Make sure that workstations have the active tree listed as a Trusted Tree. The Workstation Manager component of ZENworks uses the concept of Trusted Trees, and a Windows 95 or NT Workstation will only attempt to search for a ZENworks policy package if the tree is listed as a Trusted Tree. This feature gives greater administrative flexibility as to what workstations are controlled by ZENworks.

You can set the Trusted Tree by selecting the custom installation of the Novell Client for NT or 95. If Typical Installation is selected, it will automatically set the tree you first log in to as the Trusted Tree.

To view the Trusted Tree property on a Windows NT workstation, go to the Control Panel ⇨ Network ⇨ Services ⇨ Properties of Novell Workstation Manager. Make sure that the option for Enable Workstation Manager is checked and that the Tree field has the NDS Tree name spelled correctly.

To view the Trusted Tree property on a Windows 95/98 workstation, view the registry key directly at the following location:

```
HKEY_LOCAL_MACHINE\SOFTWARE\NOVELL\Workstation
Manager\Identification
```

Troubleshooting NetWare Errors

When troubleshooting ZENworks, you should always be aware of any NetWare error messages that occur. ZENworks is heavily tied into the NetWare operating system, NDS, and file system. Therefore, any error occurring in NetWare could possibly affect ZENworks as well.

NetWare Server File System Errors

When ZENworks is having problems distributing applications, you should always look for errors in the NetWare file system. These errors will often help you narrow down the problem to a specific cause and resolution.

For example, if the ZENworks client gives the user the following error, then you would suspect a connection problem with the server and could focus troubleshooting on finding the cause and fixing that problem:

```
918: This utility was unable to get connection
information. Error code: 89FF.
```

Table 13.3 contains common file system errors.

TABLE 13.3 *Common file system errors*

CODE	TEXT	DESCRIPTION
0x8901	INSUFFICIENT SPACE	The station does not have sufficient disk space. Make sure the minimum free disk space requirements are set up for the application object being used.
0x8980	FILE IN USE	An attempt was made to open or create a file that is already open. Set the shareable attribute if you wish for multiple users to access the file at the same time.
0x8983	DISK IO ERROR	A hard disk I/O error occurred on a NetWare volume. Typically, a bad sector has been encountered and could not be migrated to the Hot Fix area. Replace the drive.
0x8999	DIR FULL	An attempt was made to write to a volume without available directory space. Make sure you are not exceeding the maximum number of directory entries for the volume.
0x899C	INSUFFICIENT RIGHTS INVALID PATH	An attempt was made to access a path with invalid rights to the path or with an invalid path name. Make sure the user has appropriate rights to the path and that the path name is correct.
0x89A8	ACCESS DENIED	Access has been denied. Make sure the user has appropriate rights to the file.
0x89BF	NAME SPACE INVALID	An invalid name space was used. Make sure the correct namespaces are loaded on the volume being used.

NDS Errors

Another area you should always review when troubleshooting ZENworks is NDS error messages. ZENworks uses NDS heavily, not only for normal authentication and access, but as a service for controlling ZENworks objects.

NDS errors can be categorized as shown in the following sections.

NDS Operating System Error Codes

Some NDS background processes require the functionality provided by the NetWare operating system. These processes, such as communication and transaction servers, can return operating system specific error codes to NDS. These error codes are then passed on to the NDS background process that initiated a request. In NetWare 4.x, versions of NDS can also generate operating system error codes.

Usually, operating system error codes that are generated by NDS have a negative numerical representation, whereas normal operating system error codes have a positive numerical representation. The numerical range for operating system error codes generated by NDS is −1 through −256; inversely, the numerical range for operating system error codes is 1 through 255.

> **NOTE**
> NDS will return the positive numerical error code rather than the negative error code normally used by NDS to prevent any incompatibility. Therefore, any occurrence of an error code within the range of 1 to 255 or −1 to −255 should be treated as the same error.

NDS Client Error Codes

The next class of NDS error codes is client error codes. Some NDS background processes require the functionality provided by other NDS servers. Use of these functions, such as bindery services, requires that an NDS server act as an NDS client to the server providing the functionality. Therefore, these functions often result in client-specific error codes being returned to the NDS background processes and operations.

NDS client error codes are generated by the NDS client that is built into NDS. The NDS client error codes fall in the range of codes numbered −301 through −399.

NDS Agent Error Codes

Another class of NDS error codes is NDS agent error codes. NDS agent error codes represent errors that originated in the NDS agent software in the server that are returned through NDS. These codes are numbered −601 through −799 (or FDA7 through F9FE).

> **NOTE**
> Temporary errors are normal, because the NDS database is designed as a loosely consistent database. You should not be alarmed if NDS error conditions exist temporarily. However, some errors may persist until the error condition is resolved.

Other NDS Error Codes

Some NDS background processes require the functionality provided by other NLM programs, such as timesync.nlm or unicode.nlm. If any of these modules encounter an error, it can be passed on to the ds.nlm. Unicode.nlm and other errors in this category range from –400 to –599.

Tools for Troubleshooting NDS Errors

To effectively troubleshoot NDS errors that affect ZENworks, you should be familiar with the tools available for troubleshooting NDS problems. The following tools are provided to monitor and repair error conditions with NDS.

The NDS Manager Utility The NDS manager utility provides partitioning and replication services for the NDS database on a NetWare server. It also provides capabilities for repairing the database from a client workstation, which alleviates the network administrator's total dependence on working from the server console.

The DSREPAIR Utility The DSrepair utility enables you to work from the server console to monitor and repair problems with the NDS database on a single-server basis. It does not correct problems on other servers from a single, centralized location. It must be run on each server that you want to correct NDS database errors on.

The DSTRACE Utility The DStrace utility enables you to work from the server console to diagnose NDS errors. These errors may appear when you are manipulating NDS objects with the administration utilities. NDS errors also show up on the DSTRACE screen.

Table 13.4 contains common NDS errors.

T A B L E 13.4	*Common NDS errors*	
CODE	TEXT	DESCRIPTION
–601 FDA7	NO SUCH ENTRY	The specified NDS object could not be found on the NDS server that is responding to a request.
–603 FDA5	NO SUCH ATTRIBUTE	The requested attribute could not be found. In NDS, if an attribute does not contain a value, then the attribute does not exist for the specific object.

CODE	TEXT	DESCRIPTION
–625 FD8F	TRANSPORT FAILURE	The source server is unable to communicate with the target server. This error is almost always LAN-related.
–626 FD8E	ALL REFERRALS FAILED	The object could not be found; however, it is still possible that the object does exist. It is likely that the server could not communicate with another server that is holding a copy of the object.
–634 FD86	NO REFERRALS	The source server has no objects that match the request and has no referrals on which to search for the object. This is not a serious error, just a response. This error will usually resolve itself.

Understanding Changes to NDS Objects

The ZENworks product adds a powerful administration and management system to NDS by extending existing objects and creating some new ones. These additions to the NDS schema give administrators considerably more flexiblity and control over applications, workstations, and users. This appendix discusses the most important changes made to NDS by ZENworks, including:

► Changes to the container object

► Changes to the user object

► Understanding the new workstation object

Changes to the Container Object

The first major change ZENworks has implemented in NDS is to the container object. The container object has been part of NDS from the beginning; however, ZENworks has added several properties pages with extended attributes given to the container object that are very useful in managing policies associated with that container.

To access the new properties pages for container objects, simply right-click a container in NWAdmin and select Details. The following property page tabs will be available on the right.

Administration of Associated Policy Packages Page

The first property page we will look at is the Associated Policy Package page. The Associated Policy Package page lists all policy packages associated with the container object. You will be able to use this page to add, view, or modify policy packages associated with the selected container object.

When you click Associated Policy Package button, a page similar to the one in Figure A.1 is displayed. The following four options are available:

► Details — Clicking the Details button enables you to edit the settings for the selected policy package.

► Add — Clicking the Add button enables you to navigate the NDS tree and add additional policy packages.

► Remove — Clicking the Remove button removes the selected policy package from the container object.

► Remove All — Clicking the Remove All button removes all policy packages from the container object.

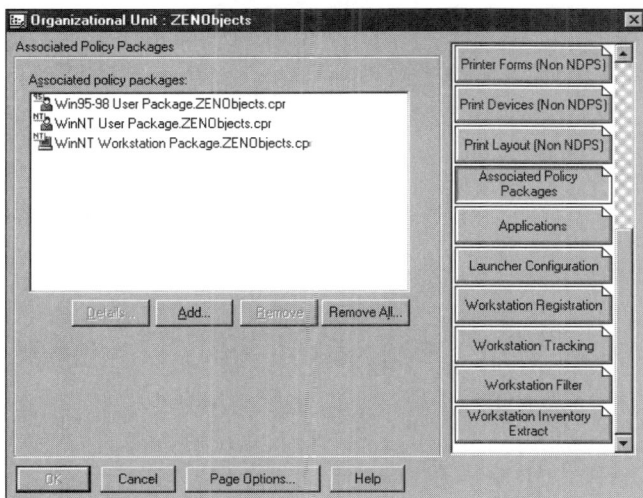

Use of the Workstation Registration Page

The next property page we will look at is the Workstation Registration page. The Workstation Registration page is primarily used to specify which registered workstation to import. When all workstations are imported, this screen is empty and the workstations are then created in the NDS tree.

When you click the Workstation Registration button, a page similar to the one in Figure A.2 is displayed. From this page, you have the option to import or remove workstations from the registered "to be imported" list.

> **NOTE** Workstation registration options can also be performed from the Tools ⇨ Workstation Utilities and Tools ⇨ Import Workstations menu options in the NWAdmin utility, and from the command line using the WSRIGHTS.EXE and WSIMPORT.EXE utilities.

Purpose of the Workstation Tracking Page

The next property page we will look at is the Workstation Tracking page. The Workstation Tracking page keeps a list of all moved or renamed workstations. This enables you to maintain a log of moved or renamed workstations.

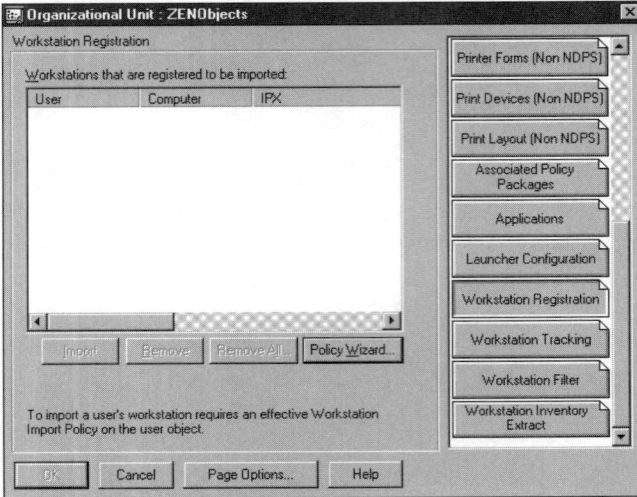

When you click the Workstation Tracking button, a page similar to the one in Figure A.3 is displayed. From this page, you have the option to view or remove workstations that have changed. You should only remove a workstation from the list when you know the workstation is no longer active in the tree.

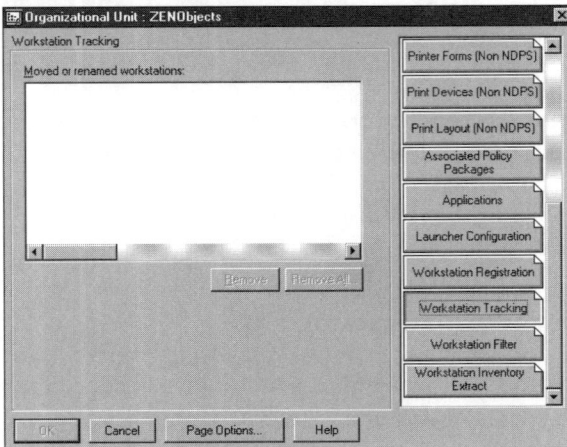

Administering the Workstation Filter Page

The next property page we will look at is the Workstation Filter page. The Workstation Filter page enables you to view the valid network addresses being imported into this container.

When you click the Workstation Filter button, a page similar to the one in Figure A.4 is displayed. From this page, you have the following options:

- ▶ Allow All Workstations to be Imported — Check this box if you don't need to limit which workstations are imported.

- ▶ Valid Network Address — This is a list of the criteria for a valid network address in this container. These will include partial network addresses with wildcard characters.

- ▶ Add — Clicking the Add button displays a window similar to the one in Figure A.5, which enables you to add a partial IPX or IP address with a wildcard character to the Network Address Filter. This will filter the workstations outside the parameters you define. You should add addresses here when you need to limit which workstations are imported.

- ▶ Remove — Click the Remove button to remove the highlighted address from the list.

- ▶ Remove All — Click the Remove All button to remove all the addresses in the list.

FIGURE A.4   *The Workstation Filter tab for container objects*

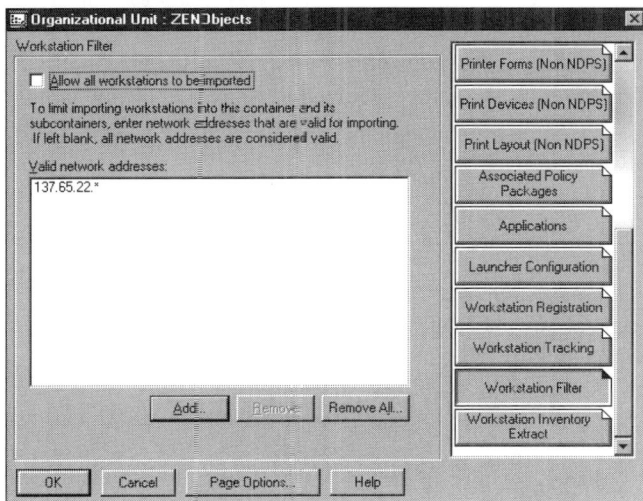

The Add Network Address window for the Workstation Filter Tab for container objects

Add Network Address ☒

Enter a valid IPX or IP network address with an optional wildcard.

Address:

137.65.22.*

Examples:
01020304:* = IPX segment
01020304:010203040506 = IPX address
123.123.123.* = IP subnet
123.123.123.123 = IP address

| OK | Cancel | Help |

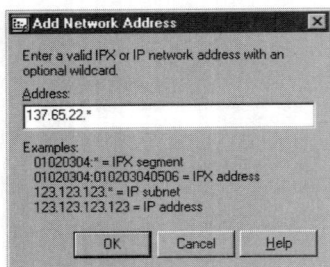

Changes to the User Object

Another major change ZENworks has implemented in NDS is to the user object. The user object has also been part of NDS from the beginning; however, ZENworks has added several properties pages with extended attributes given to it as well. These changes to the user object are very useful in managing policies associated with that container.

To access the new properties pages for a user object, simply right click that user in NWAdmin and select Details. The following property page tabs are available on the right.

Administration of the Associated Policy Packages Page

The first property page we will look at is the Associated Policy Package page. The Associated Policy Package page lists all policy packages associated with the user object. You can use this page to add, view, or modify policy packages associated with the selected user object.

When you click the Associated Policy Package button, a page similar to the one in Figure A.6 is displayed. The following four options are available:

▶ Details — Clicking the Details button enables you to edit the settings for the selected policy package.

- ▶ Add — Clicking the Add button enables you to navigate the NDS tree and add additional policy packages.

- ▶ Remove — Clicking the Remove button removes the selected policy package from the user object.

- ▶ Remove All — Clicking the Remove All button removes all policy packages from the user object.

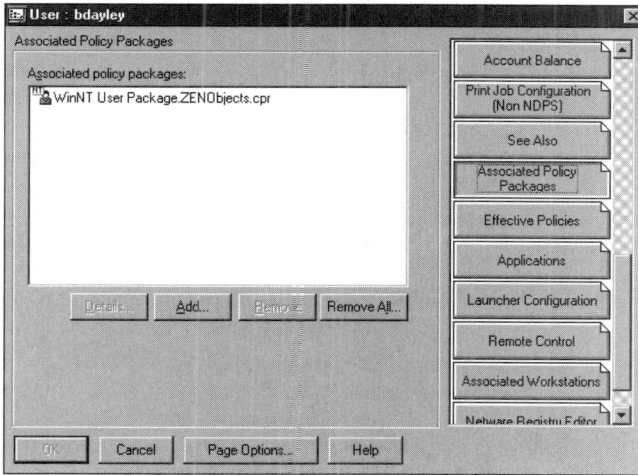

FIGURE A.6 The Associated Policy Packages tab for user objects

Use of the Effective Policies Page

The next property page we will look at is the Effective Policies page. The Effective Policies page enables you to view a list of policies that currently have an effect on this user.

When you click the Effective Policies button, a page similar to the one in Figure A.7 is displayed. From this page, you have the following options:

- ▶ Platform — The platform pull-down menu enables you to select the operating system you wish to use to view the user's effective policies.

- ▶ Policy/Policy Package/Association — This window contains a list of the user policies that affect this user on the platform selected above and the respective Policy Package that contains the policy and the association.

▶ Effective Policies — Clicking the Effective Policies button generates the list of effective polices for this workstation.

▶ Package Details — Clicking the Package Details button displays the details for the policy package containing the policy that is currently highlighted in the Policy/Policy Package list.

▶ Policy Wizard — Clicking the Policy Wizard button launches the Policy Wizard and enables you to create or modify a policy for this user.

FIGURE A.7 *The Effective Policies tab for user objects*

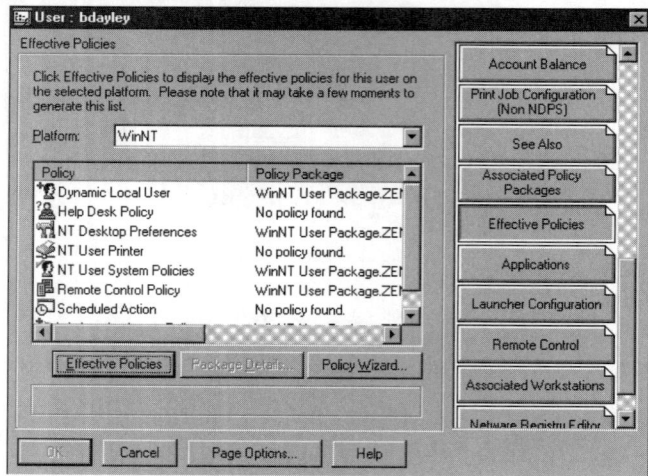

Purpose of the Remote Management Page

The next property page we will look at is the Remote Management page. The Remote Management page enables you to manage remote control functions for the selected user object. When you click the Remote Management button, a page similar to the one in Figure A.8 is displayed.

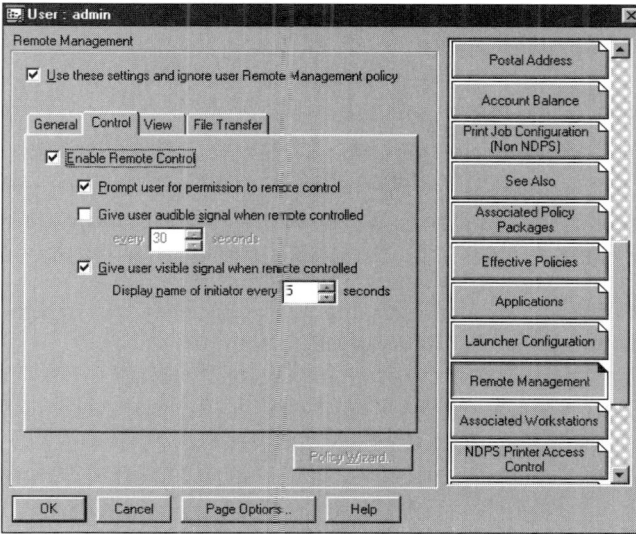

From this page, you have several options from the following tab windows.

General Tab

The following options are available under the General tab:

- Enable Chat — Check this box to enable a real-time messaging tool that allows a console user to communicate with another user at a remotely managed workstation.

- Enable Workstation Diagnostics — Check this box to enable workstation diagnostics, a method of providing real-time information about the Windows 95, Windows 98, or Windows NT workstation that can help users and system administrators diagnose problems.

- Display Remote Operation Agent Icon to Users — Check this box to display an icon on the user's desktop indicating that the Remote Operation agent is loaded on the target workstation. On Windows NT, Windows 95, and Windows 98 computers, the system tray displays the icon. On Windows 3.x workstations, the icon is displayed on the desktop. Users can right-click the icon to display a menu that includes options to terminate the remote control session or to close the Remote Operation agent.

▶ Default Protocol to Use for Remote Control and Remote View — Select which protocol you want to use (IPX or IP) to remote control or remote view workstations.

Control Tab

The following settings are available under the Control tab:

▶ Enable Remote Control — When this box is checked, authorized users can remotely control the workstation associated with this user object.

▶ Prompt User for Permission to Remote Control — Check this box to require the workstation user to grant you permission each time you want to control his or her workstation remotely. If the Enable Remote Control option is checked and this option is not checked, you can remotely control the workstation anytime it is running.

▶ Give User Audible Signal When Remote Controlled Every __ Seconds — Check this box to specify an interval for sounding a tone to alert the user that someone has initiated and is running a remote control session.

▶ Give User Visible Signal when Remote Controlled and Display Name of Initiator Every __ Seconds — When this is checked, a message will appear to alert the user that someone has initiated and is running a remote control session. The message changes at the interval that you set to display the name of the person who initiated the session.

▶ Allow Administrator to Blank the User's Screen During Session — When this is checked, a message will appear to alert the user that someone has initiated and is running a remote control session. The message changes at the interval you set to display the name of the person who initiated the session.

▶ Allow Administrator to Lock the User's Keyboard and Mouse During Session — When this is checked, a message will appear to alert the user that someone has initiated and is running a remote control session. The message changes at the interval you set to display the name of the person who initiated the session.

View Tab

The following settings are available under the View tab:

▶ Enable Remote View — Check this box to authorize users to remotely control the workstation associated with this user.

▶ Prompt User for Permission to Remote View — Check this box to require the workstation user to grant you permission each time you want to control his or her workstation remotely. If the Enable Remote Control option is checked and this option is not checked, you can remotely control the workstation anytime it is running.

▶ Give User Audible Signal when Remote Viewed Every __ Seconds — Check this box to specify an interval for sounding a tone to alert the user that someone has initiated and is running a remote view session.

▶ Give User Visible Signal when Remote Viewed and Display Name of Initiator Every __ Seconds — When this is checked, a message will display to alert the user that someone has initiated and is running a remote view session. The message changes at the interval you set to display the name of the person who initiated the session.

File Transfer Tab

The following settings are available under the File Transfer tab:

▶ Enable File Transfer — Check this box to authorize users to remotely control the workstation associated with this user.

▶ Prompt User for Permission to Transfer Files — Check this box to require the workstation user to grant you permission each time you want to control his or her workstation remotely. If the Enable Remote Control option is checked and this option is not checked, you can remotely control the workstation anytime it is running.

Execute Tab

The following settings are available under the Execute tab:

▶ Enable Remote Execute — Check this box to authorize users to remotely control the workstation associated with this user.

▶ Prompt User for Permission to Remote Execute — Check this box to require the workstation user to grant you permission each time you want to control his or her workstation remotely. If the Enable Remote Control option is checked and this option is not checked, you can remotely control the workstation anytime it is running.

▶ Remote Control button — Click this button to initiate a remote control session and access the Remote Control Console. For more help on using the Remote Control Console, type F1 after initiating a remote control session.

- Policy Wizard button — Click this button to create or modify a Remote Control Policy for this workstation. You can select one policy in the Policy column.

Use of the Associated Workstations Page

The next property page we will look at is the Associated Workstations page. The Workstation Registration page is primarily used to view the workstations associated with this user object.

When you click the Associated Workstations button, a page similar to the one in Figure A.9 is displayed. From this page, the following four options are available:

- Details — Clicking the Details button enables you to edit the settings for the selected workstation object.

- Add — Clicking the Add button enables you to navigate the NDS tree and add workstations to this user object.

- Remove — Clicking the Remove button removes the selected workstation from this user object.

- Remove All — Clicking the Remove All button removes all workstations from the user object.

F I G U R E   A.9   *The Associated Workstations tab for user objects*

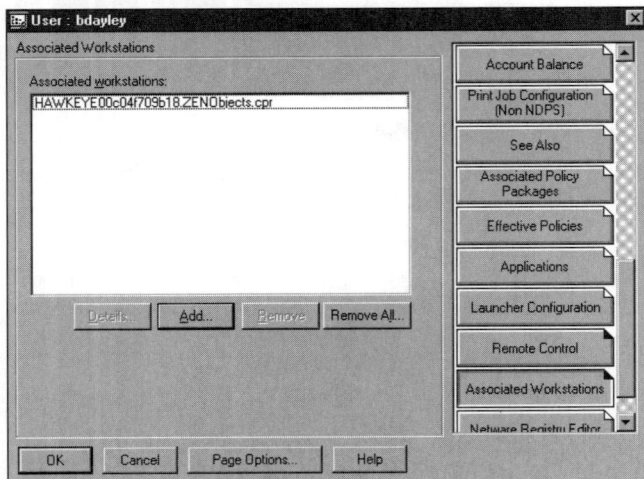

Understanding the New Workstation Object

Now that you understand the changes ZENworks has made to user and container objects, you should be aware of the new objects ZENworks will add to the NDS tree. One of the most important new objects is the workstation object.

Workstation objects enable you to use NWAdmin to manage workstations remotely in an easy and efficient manner. As an administrator, you can perform several workstation management tasks from your own desk, such as distributing applications, scheduling a program to run, and setting client configurations.

To access the properties pages for a workstation object, simply right-click that workstation object in NWAdmin and select Details. The following Property Page tabs will be available on the right.

Identification Page

The first property page we will look at for workstation objects is the Identification page. The Identification page is used to view or modify information about this workstation object.

When you click the Associated Workstations button, a page similar to the one in Figure A.10 is displayed. From this page, the following options are available:

▶ Name — The Name field displays the full context name of the workstation.

▶ Other Name — The Other Name field enables you to specify another name that can identify this workstation.

▶ Owner — The Owner field enables you to browse and select a user, group, or other object that is responsible for this workstation.

▶ Description — The Description box displays information that is required or is helpful in managing this workstation.

▶ Serial Number — The Serial Number field enables you to enter the serial number of the workstation. The serial number can be up to 64 characters long.

▶ Location — The Location field enables you to enter the physical location of the workstation in your office. The location can be up to 128 characters long

F I G U R E A . 1 0 *The Identification tab for workstation objects*

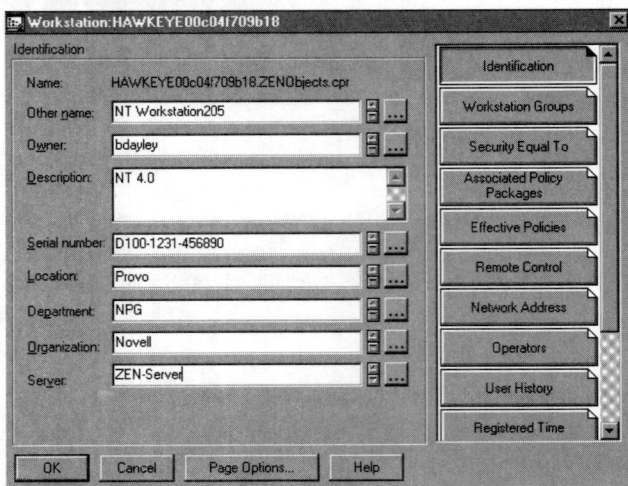

► Department — The Department field enables you to enter the name of the department to which the workstation belongs. The department name can be up to 64 characters long.

► Organization — The Organization field enables you to enter the organization name or company name to which the workstation belongs. The organization can be up to 64 characters long.

► Server — The Server field enables you to browse and select a server to associate this workstation with.

Workstation Groups Page

The next property page we will look at is the Workstation Groups page. The Workstation Groups page keeps a list of all workstation groups with which this workstation object is associated.

When you click the Workstation Groups button, a page is displayed where you have the option to view, add, or remove workstation groups that this workstation object is associated with.

Associated Policy Package Page

The next property page we will look at is the Associated Policy Package page. The Associated Policy Package page lists all policy packages associated with the workstation object. You will be able to use this page to add, view, or modify policy packages associated with the selected workstation object.

When you click the Associated Policy Package button, a page similar to the one in Figure A.11 is displayed. The following four options are available:

▶ Details — Clicking the Details button enables you to edit the settings for the selected policy package.

▶ Add — Clicking the Add button enables you to navigate the NDS tree and add additional policy packages.

▶ Remove — Clicking the Remove button removes the selected policy package from the workstation object.

▶ Remove All — Clicking the Remove All button removes all policy packages from the workstation object.

F I G U R E   A . 1 1   The Associated Policy Package tab for workstation objects

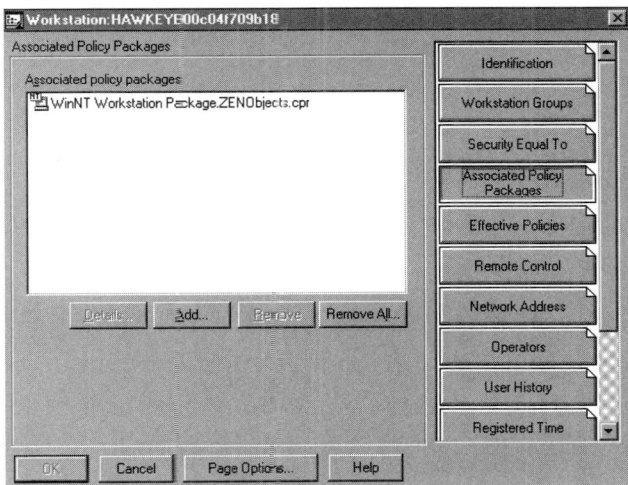

Effective Policies Page

The next property page we will look at is the Effective Policies page. The Effective Policies page enables you to view a list of policies that currently have an effect on this workstation object.

When you click the Effective Policies button, a page similar to the one in Figure A.12 is displayed. From this page, you have the following options:

► Policy/Policy Package/Association — This window contains a list of the workstation policies that affect this workstation and the respective policy package that contains the policy and the association.

► Effective Policies — Clicking the Effective Policies button generates the list of effective polices for this workstation.

► Package Details — Clicking the Package Details button displays the details for the policy package containing the policy that is currently highlighted in the Policy/Policy Package list.

► Policy Wizard — Clicking the Policy Wizard button launches the Policy Wizard and enables you to create or modify a policy for this workstation object.

FIGURE A.12 The Effective Policies tab for workstation objects

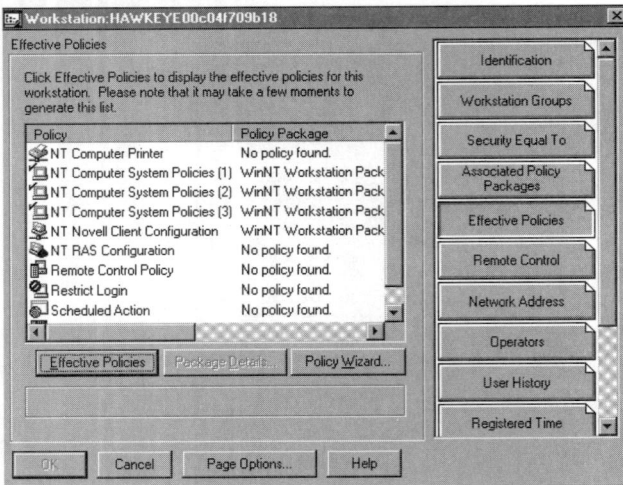

Remote Management Page

The next property page we will look at is the Remote Management page. The Remote Management page enables you to manage remote control functions for this workstation, as well as begin a remote control session and access the Remote Management Console.

When you click the Remote Management button, a page similar to the one in Figure A.13 is displayed.

F I G U R E   A . 1 3   *The Remote Management tab for workstation objects*

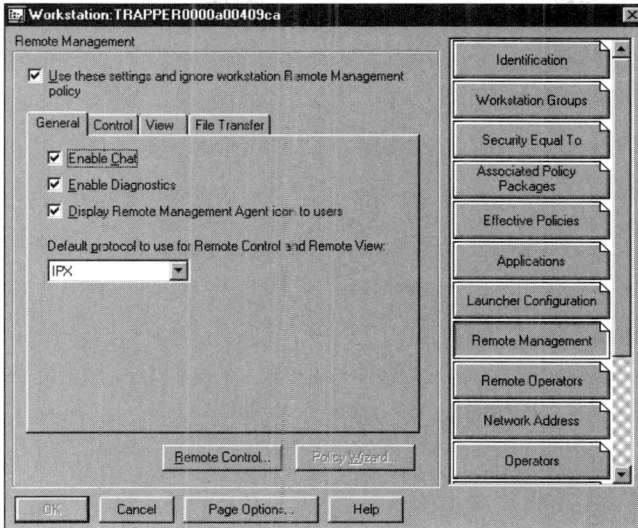

From this page, you have several options from the following tab windows.

General Tab

The following options are available under the General tab:

► Enable Chat — Check this box to enable a real-time messaging tool that allows a console user to communicate with another user at a remotely managed workstation.

► Enable Workstation Diagnostics — Check this box to enable workstation diagnostics, a method of providing real-time information about the Windows 95, Windows 98, or Windows NT workstation that can help users and system administrators diagnose problems.

► Display Remote Operation Agent Icon to Users — Check this box to display an icon on the user's desktop indicating that the Remote Operation agent is loaded on the target workstation. On Windows NT, Windows 95, and Windows 98 computers, the system tray displays the icon. On Windows 3.x workstations, the icon is displayed on the desktop. Users can right-click the icon to display a menu that includes options to terminate the remote control session or to close the Remote Operation agent.

▸ Default Protocol to Use for Remote Control and Remote View — Select which protocol you want to use (IPX or IP) to remote control or remote view workstations.

Control Tab

The following settings are available under the Control tab:

▸ Enable Remote Control — When this box is checked, authorized users can remotely control the workstation associated with this workstation object.

▸ Prompt User for Permission to Remote Control — Check this box to require that the workstation user grant you permission each time you want to control his or her workstation remotely. If the Enable Remote Control option is checked and this option is not checked, you can remotely control the workstation anytime it is running.

▸ Give User Audible Signal when Remote Controlled Every __ Seconds — Check this box to specify an interval for sounding a tone to alert the user that someone has initiated and is running a remote control session.

▸ Give User Visible Signal When Remote Controlled and Display Name of Initiator Every __ Seconds — When this is checked, a message will appear to alert the user that someone has initiated and is running a remote control session. The message changes at the interval you set to display the name of the person who initiated the session.

▸ Allow Administrator to Blank the User's Screen During Session — When this is checked, a message will appear to alert the user that someone has initiated and is running a remote control session. The message changes at the interval you set to display the name of the person who initiated the session.

▸ Allow Administrator to Lock the User's Keyboard and Mouse During Session — When this is checked, a message will appear to alert the user that someone has initiated and is running a remote control session. The message changes at the interval you set to display the name of the person who initiated the session.

View Tab

The following settings are available under the view tab:

▸ Enable Remote View — Check this box to authorize users to remotely control the workstation associated with this user.

- Prompt User for Permission to Remote View — Check this box to require the workstation user to grant you permission each time you want to control his or her workstation remotely. If the Enable Remote Control option is checked and this option is not checked, you can remotely control the workstation anytime it is running.

- Give User Audible Signal When Remote Viewed Every __ Seconds — Check this box to specify an interval for sounding a tone to alert the user that someone has initiated and is running a remote view session.

- Give User Visible Signal When Remote Viewed and Display Name of Initiator Every __ Seconds — When this is checked, a message will appear to alert the user that someone has initiated and is running a remote view session. The message changes at the interval you set to display the name of the person who initiated the session.

File Transfer Tab

The following settings are available under the File Transfer tab:

- Enable File Transfer — Check this box to authorize users to remotely control the workstation associated with this workstation.

- Prompt User for Permission to Transfer Files — Check this box to require the workstation user to grant you permission each time you want to control his or her workstation remotely. If the Enable Remote Control option is checked and this option is not checked, you can remotely control the workstation anytime it is running.

Execute Tab

The following settings are available under the Execute tab:

- Enable Remote Execute — Check this box to authorize users to remotely control the workstation associated with this workstation.

- Prompt User for Permission to Remote Execute — Check this box to require the workstation user to grant you permission each time you want to control his or her workstation remotely. If the Enable Remote Control option is checked and this option is not checked, you can remotely control the workstation anytime it is running.

- Remote Control button — Click this button to initiate a remote control session and access the Remote Control Console. For more help on using the Remote Control Console, type F1 after initiating a remote control session.

▶ Policy Wizard button — Click this button to create or modify a Remote Control Policy for this workstation. You can select one policy in the Policy column.

Network Address Page

The next property page we will look at is the Network Address Page. The Network Address page enables you to view or remove the network addresses associated with this workstation object. Both IP and IPX address are displayed, as shown in Figure A.14.

FIGURE A.14 *The Network Address tab for workstation objects*

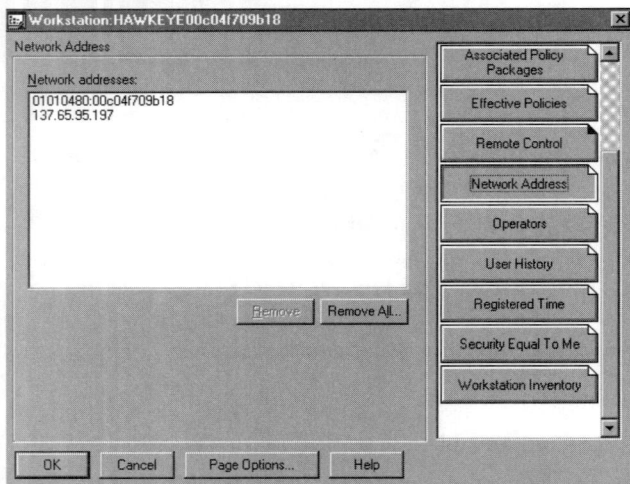

Operators Page

The next property page we will look at is the Operators page. The Operators page enables you to manage the list of users who have rights to modify this workstation.

When you click the Operators button, a page is displayed where you have the option to view, add, or remove operators of this workstation. You should use this option when multiple users use one workstation, or when multiple users need to remote control this workstation.

User History Page

The next property page we will look at is the User History page. The User History page enables you to view the users who have been accessing and registering this workstation.

All fields on this page are updated whenever the workstation registration program is run — for example, when a user logs in to the workstation if the program is set to run in the login script or some other startup program.

When you click the User History button, a page similar to the one in Figure A.15 is displayed. From this page, you have the following options:

▶ User History — This text window displays a list of the users who have registered at this workstation.

▶ Remove — Clicking the Remove button removes the highlighted username from the list.

▶ Remove All — Clicking the Remove All button removes all the usernames from the list.

▶ Last User — This text window displays the username of the last known user to use this workstation.

▶ Last Server — This text window displays the last server accessed from this workstation.

F I G U R E   A . I 5   *The User History tab for workstation objects*

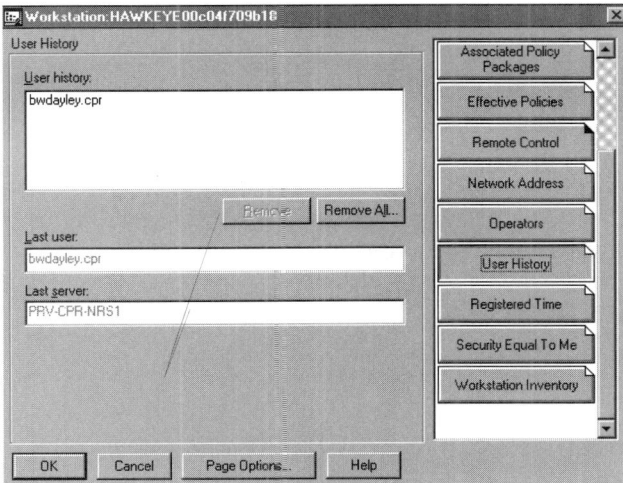

Workstation Inventory Page

The last property page we will look at for workstation objects is the Workstation Inventory page. The workstation inventory page enables you to view information about the inventory of the workstation object if an inventory policy has been associated with the object.

When you click the ZENworks Workstation Inventory button, a page similar to the one in Figure A.16 is displayed. From this page, you can view the following information about the workstation:

- ▶ Computer type
- ▶ Computer model
- ▶ Model number
- ▶ Serial number
- ▶ Asset tag
- ▶ Operating system type
- ▶ OS version
- ▶ Novell client
- ▶ BIOS type
- ▶ Processor
- ▶ Video type
- ▶ NIC type — network adapter
- ▶ Memory size
- ▶ Disk information
- ▶ MAC address
- ▶ Subnet mask
- ▶ IP address

When you click the More Workstation Information button on this property page, a new window appears, similar to the one shown in Figure A.17. From this window, you can view the following information about the workstation:

- ▶ Software:
  - • Drivers
  - • Packages
  - • Operating systems
  - • Scanner
  - • Information

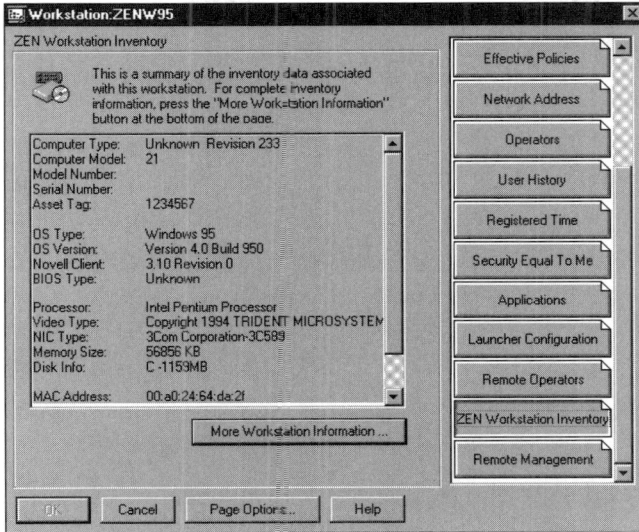

The Workstation Inventory tab for workstation

- ► Hardware:
  - Mouse
  - Keyboard
  - Display
  - Bios
  - Processor
  - Memory
  - Disk
  - Ports
  - Bus
- ► Network:
  - Server connection
  - Adapter
  - IP address
  - DNS configuration
  - IPX address

- ► Configuration files
- ► Environment:
  - • IRQ settings — Int./vector, bus #, bus type, device
  - • I/O port settings — Address, bus #, bus type, device
  - • DMA settings — Channel, port, bus #, bus type, device
  - • Memory settings — Address, bus #, bus type, device
  - • Display settings — Horizontal res., vertical res., colors, and refresh rate
- ► Windows NT services:
  - • Active services — Network, audio, etc.
  - • Active devices — Sound, video, etc.

►

F I G U R E   A . 1 7   *The advanced options for the Workstation Inventory tab*

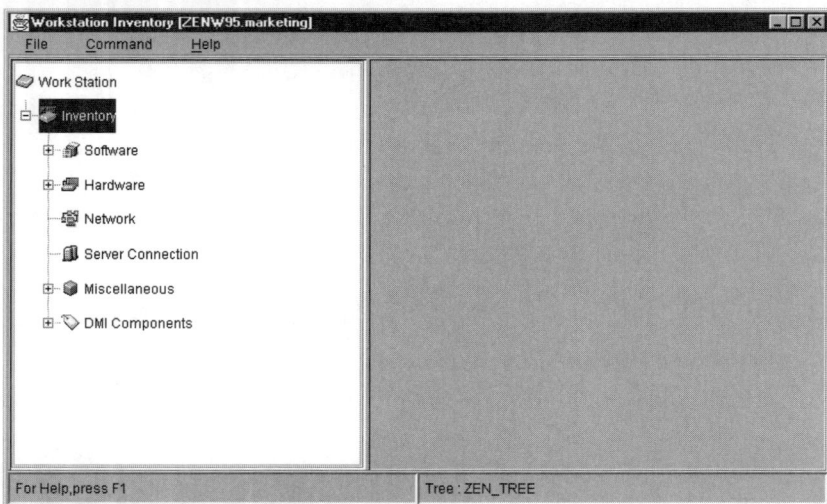

Using snAppShot to Create Application Object Packages

In this appendix, we discuss an example of using the snAppShot utility to create an application object package for distribution to other workstations. This appendix is split into the following two sections:

- ► Using snAppShot to Package Netscape 4.06
- ► Review of the Created Object Template

Using snAppShot to Package Netscape 4.06

In this example, we use the Custom Mode in snAppShot to set specific options for snAppShot, and then use snAppShot to capture the changes made in an application object template package when installing Netscape Communicator on a client workstation. This way, you can use the created template later to distribute Netscape Communicator to several other clients.

You will use the Custom Mode of snAppShot to perform the operations described in the following sections, to create the application object template for Netscape.

Launch snAppShot

The first step in creating an application object template for Netscape Communicator is to launch the snAppShot utility by double-clicking on the Snapshot.exe icon, as shown in Figure B.1.

F I G U R E   B . I   *Folder displaying the snAppShot utility icon*

Choose Custom Mode from Main Menu

The next step is to select which mode you will use to create the application object template for Netscape Communicator. In this example, you will choose the custom mode so you can use some specific preference settings, as shown in Figure B.2.

FIGURE B.2 *snAppShot window for specifying which mode of discovery to use in application object template creation*

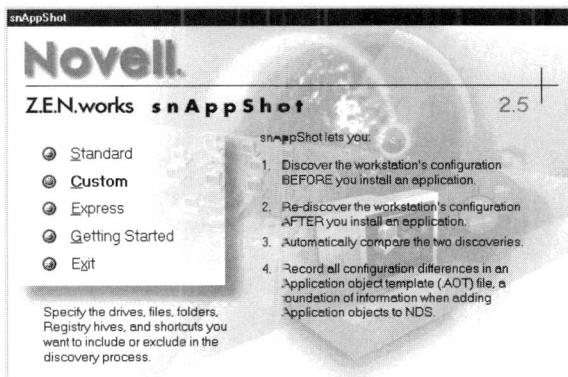

Choose the snAppShot Preferences File

The first window that comes up after you select the custom mode in snAppShot enables you to either choose a previously saved snAppShot preference file, or use the snAppShot default settings.

Because you have not previously created and saved a preference file in a previous custom mode, you will use the default settings.

Name the Application Object and Icon Title

Once you have selected to use the default preference settings in snAppShot, input the name that the application object will have in the DS tree (Netscape Communicator 406) and a title for the icon that represents the application object (Netscape).

Specify the Network Location of the Application Source (.FIL) Files

Once you set the name for the application object and the title for its icon, set the network location to store the application source files (.FIL) for the Netscape object template to the following directory:

```
T:\Snapshot\Netscape Communicator 406
```

Specify the Network Location of the Application Template (.AOT and .AXT) Files

Once you have specified a network location for the .FIL files, set the network location to store the application template (.AOT and .AXT files) for the Netscape object template to the following directory:

```
T:\Snapshot\Netscape Communicator 406\Netscape
Communicator 406.AOT
```

> **NOTE**
> By specifying a network location for these files, you can more easily access them when it comes time to create the Application object and distribute it to users. Notice that you set the network location for both the source files and the application template files to the same directory. This makes for easier handling of the application object package later on.

Specify Which Parts of the Workstation to Include or Exclude

Once you have selected the network location in which to store the application object support files, use the snAppShot screen in Figure B.3 to select the parts of the workstation to include or exclude, as covered in the following sections.

Files and Folders

From the workstation scan customization menu in snAppShot, you can modify which files and folders you wish to include or exclude. However, you do not need to ignore any specific files or folders, so leave the setting at the default shown in Figure B.4.

Specifying which parts of the workstation to include or exclude

Modifying which files and folders will be created in the application object template

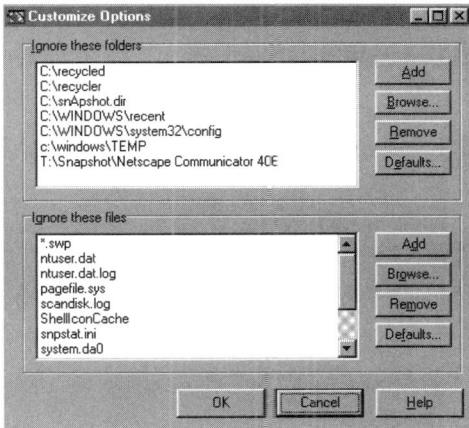

.INI Files

From the workstation scan customization menu in snAppShot, you can modify which .INI files to exclude. However, you do not need to ignore any specific .INI files, so leave the setting at the default.

System Configuration Text Files

From the workstation scan customization menu in snAppShot, we can modify which system configuration text files you wish to include in the scan. You do have the NETWORK.BAT file, which is executed when all workstations are booted setting specific preferences. This file is specific to each workstation, and even though the Netscape install shouldn't affect it, you should add it to the list just to be safe.

Windows Shortcuts

From the workstation scan customization menu in snAppShot, you can modify which Windows shortcuts to exclude. However, you do not need to ignore any specific Windows shortcut files, so leave the setting at the default.

Registry

From the workstation scan customization menu in snAppShot, you can modify which registry hives you wish to include or exclude. However, you do not need to specify any specific registry sections to ignore or exclude, so leave the setting at the default.

Specify the Drives That Will Be Discovered

Once you have specified which parts of the workstation to include or exclude, select which disk drive to scan on the workstation to determine changes. In this case, since you are installing Netscape Communicator to the C drive, you only need to select the C drive for scanning.

Read the Pre-discovery Summary

Now that you have set all the preferences for the first discovery, you are given a summary of the preferences in the snAppShot window. The information displayed includes:

- ▶ Application object name
- ▶ Application icon title
- ▶ Template filename
- ▶ Application files directory
- ▶ Snapshots working drive
- ▶ Scan options
- ▶ Disks to scan
- ▶ Directories to exclude

- ▶ Files to exclude
- ▶ System text files to scan

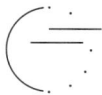

NOTE Notice that the file you selected as a system configuration text file to ignore is listed in the summary: C:\NETWORK.BAT. This is a good example of things to check for before proceeding with the first discovery.

You can click Save Settings to save the snAppShot preferences you have defined thus far to a file. Later, if you use snAppShot to create a template for a Netscape Communicator upgrade, you can use that preference file in the Express mode.

Run the First snAppShot Discovery

The first snAppShot discovery is run when you click Next from the preference summary window. The screen in Figure B.5 shows the status of the discovery and a count of the following items that have been discovered:

- ▶ Folders and files
- ▶ Windows shortcuts
- ▶ .INI files
- ▶ System configuration files
- ▶ Registry entries

FIGURE B.5
The current status and statistics about the first discovery scan currently running

Run the Application's Installation or Upgrade

Once the first snAppShot discovery is completed, a Run Application Install button becomes available.

When you select the Run Application Install button, a file pop-up menu appears, and you can navigate to the application install executable and execute it.

Specify How to Handle the Creation of Files, Folders, .INI File Entries, and Registry Settings

Once the Netscape installation is complete, snAppShot enables you to specify how to handle the creation of entries for the application object. From the screen shown in Figure B.6, you can set the addition criteria for the entries described in the following sections.

FIGURE B.6
Specifying how snAppShot will handle the creation of file, folder, INI file, and registry entries in the application object template

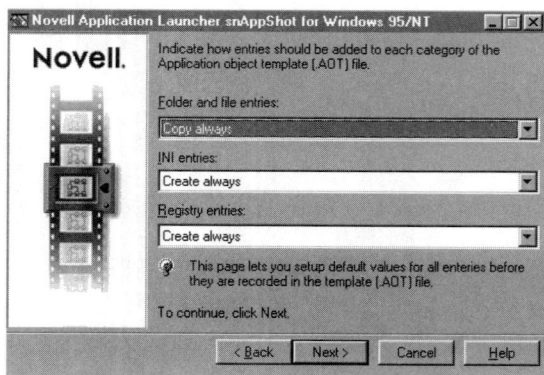

Folder and File Entries

From the application object entry addition window in snAppShot, you can configure whether or not files and folders will be added to the application object by clicking the down arrow under the Folder and files entries option and selecting the Copy if newer version addition criteria shown in Figure B.7.

NOTE
You should use the Copy if newer version option because you do not want to overwrite any files that may have been added by the user in a local workstation-specific installation.

Selecting how snAppShot will create file and folder entries in the application object template

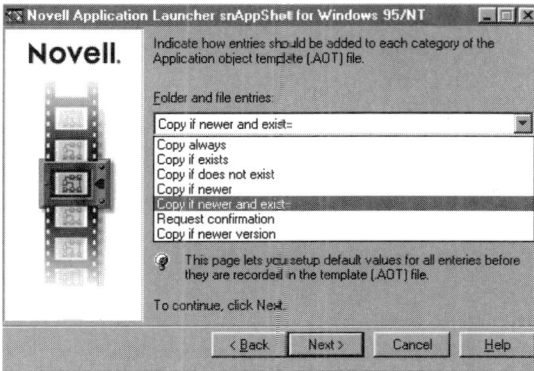

.INI Files

From the application object entry addition window in snAppShot, specify whether or not .INI files will be added to the application object by clicking the down arrow under the .INI files option and selecting the Create if does not exist addition criteria.

NOTE

You should use the Create if does not exist option because you do not want to overwrite any existing .INI files that may have been added by the user in a local workstation-specific application installation.

Registry Entries

From the application object entry addition window in snAppShot, configure whether or not registry entries will be added to the application object by clicking the down arrow under the registry entries option and selecting the Create always addition criteria.

NOTE

You should use the Create always option because you want to overwrite any registry entries that may be pointing to invalid files or directory locations that do not match the current application installation.

Enter the Path to the Application's Executable File

Once you have defined the addition criteria for entries into the application object, specify a path to the application's executable on this workstation. To do so, enter the location (E:\DOWNLOADS) of the Netscape application installation files on this workstation in the text field, as shown in Figure B.8.

▶ . . . . ◀

F I G U R E   B . 8   *Setting the path for the application's executable file*

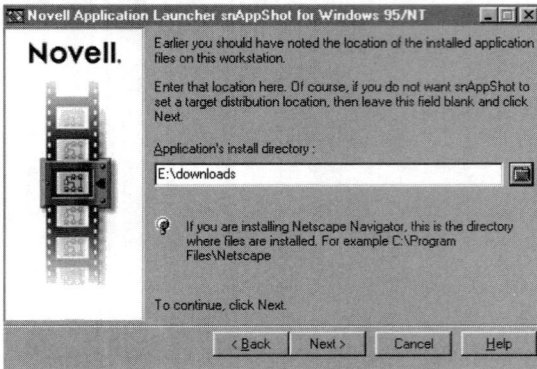

Define Macros for Distribution Automation

Once you have finished setting the path to the applications executable and clicked the Next button, use the screen shown in Figure B.9 to define macros to control the distribution of application objects.

Click the Add button in the macro definition window. You are given the option to specify a variable name and a string that it will be replaced with in the template data.

Run the Second snAppShot Discovery

Once you have finished defining macros to automate application object distribution, click Next; snAppShot runs the second discovery, as shown in Figure B.10. Once again, you can monitor the status of the discovery by noting the count of the following items, as shown in Figure B.10:

- ▶ Folders and files
- ▶ Windows shortcuts
- ▶ .INI files

- ► System configuration files
- ► Registry entries

Adding, editing, and removing macros to be used in the application object template

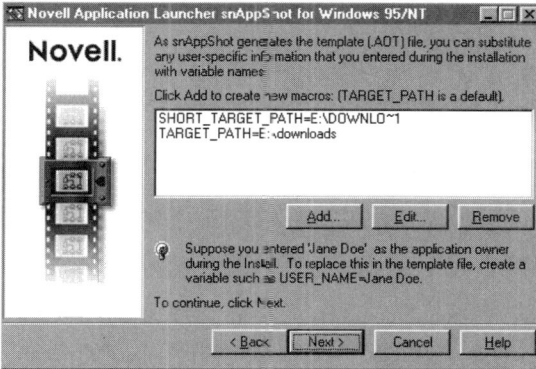

Showing the user the current status and statistics about the second discovery scan while it is running

Once the discovery is finished, snAppShot will begin generating an object template. This is where the actual differences between the two discoveries are discerned and the template files are created.

Read the Completion Summary

When the second snAppShot discovery is completed and the template files are generated, a completion summary of what took place is displayed in the next window. The completion summary contains information about the application template creation, including:

- ▶ The location of the new application object template (.AOT)
- ▶ The location of the new .FIL files
- ▶ The location of the textual version of the application object template (.AOT)
- ▶ Listing of the steps to take to create the application object
- ▶ Statistical totals from the second discovery
- ▶ Statistical totals from entries added to the application object template (.AOT)

Review of the Created Object Template

Once you have reviewed the summary from running snAppShot and clicked Next, the process is complete and the application object template package has been created. You can now go to the network location where the application object template was created, and review the items described in the following sections.

Directory Listing

Figure B.11 shows a directory listing of the files in the application object template directory. These files represent the packaged object ready for distribution. You can see the following files:

- ▶ .AXT file
- ▶ .AOT file
- ▶ FILEDEF.TXT file
- ▶ Various .FIL files

FIGURE B.11 Directory listing of the files located in the Netscape Communicator application object template directory

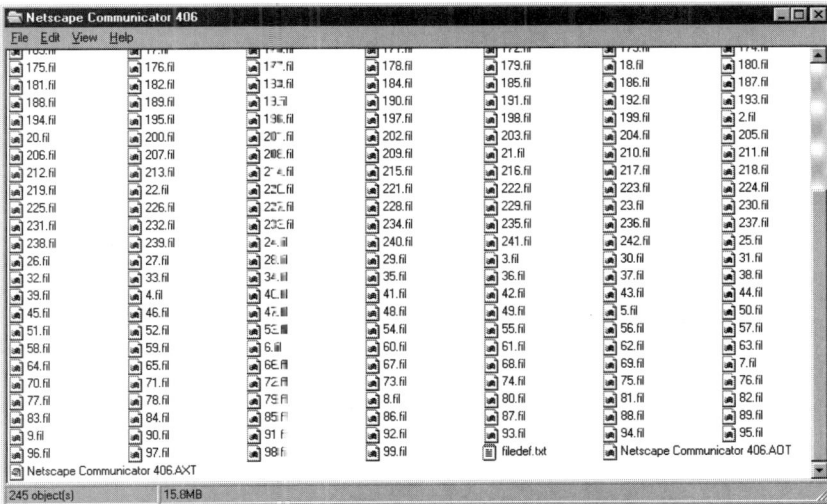

FILEDEF.TXT File

Looking at the FILEDEF.TXT file in Figure B.12, you can see the mappings of .FIL files to the actual Netscape Communicator application files.

FIGURE B.12 FILEDEF.TXT file for the Netscape Communicator application object package

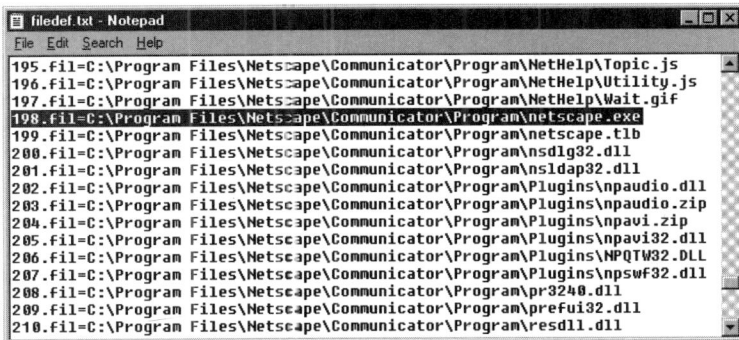

Application Object Template File (Text Version .AXT)

Looking at the text version of the Netscape Communicator object template, shown in Figure B.13, you can see all the changes that snAppShot recorded from the Netscape installation that took place. These changes can be applied to other workstations when the application object is distributed.

Looking at the FILEDEF.TXT file in Figure B.13, you can see the mappings of .FIL files to the actual Netscape Communicator application files.

▶ . . . . ◀

F I G U R E   B.13   *Textual version of the application object template file for the Netscape Communicator application object*

```
Netscape Communicator 406.AXT - WordPad                              _ □ ×
File  Edit  View  Insert  Format  Help

 □ ☞ 🖫  🖨 🖳  🛤   👗 🗈 🛢 ∽  🖳

AXT_FILE 2.5

[Application Date]
Value=36053

[Application Time]
Value=1

[Application Name]
Value=Netscape Communicator 406

[Application Caption]
Value=Netscape

[Application Flags]
Flag=Install Only
Flag=Always Prompt Reboot

[Macro]
Name=SOURCE_PATH
Value=T:\Snapshot\Netscape Communicator 406

[Macro]
Name=SHORT_TARGET_PATH
Value=E:\DOWNLO~1

[Macro]
Name=TARGET PATH

For Help, press F1                                              NUM
```

Index

(continued)

T

U

V

my2cents.idgbooks.com

Register This Book — And Win!

Visit **http://my2cents.idgbooks.com** to register this book and we'll automatically enter you in our fantastic monthly prize giveaway. It's also your opportunity to give us feedback: let us know what you thought of this book and how you would like to see other topics covered.

Discover IDG Books Online!

The IDG Books Online Web site is your online resource for tackling technology — at home and at the office. Frequently updated, the IDG Books Online Web site features exclusive software, insider information, online books, and live events!

10 Productive & Career-Enhancing Things You Can Do at www.idgbooks.com

1. Nab source code for your own programming projects.

2. Download software.

3. Read Web exclusives: special articles and book excerpts by IDG Books Worldwide authors.

4. Take advantage of resources to help you advance your career as a Novell or Microsoft professional.

5. Buy IDG Books Worldwide titles or find a convenient bookstore that carries them.

6. Register your book and win a prize.

7. Chat live online with authors.

8. Sign up for regular e-mail updates about our latest books.

9. Suggest a book you'd like to read or write.

10. Give us your 2¢ about our books and about our Web site.

You say you're not on the Web yet? It's easy to get started with IDG Books' *Discover the Internet*, available at local retailers everywhere.